THE DYNAMICS OF ADMINISTRATIVE REFORM

The Dynamics of Administrative Reform

RICHARD A. CHAPMAN and J.R. GREENAWAY

CROOM HELM LONDON

© 1980 Richard A. Chapman and J.R. Greenaway
Croom Helm Ltd, 2-10 St. John's Road, London SW11

British Library Cataloguing in Publication Data

Chapman, Richard Arnold
    The dynamics of administrative reform.
    1. Civil service – Great Britain – History
    2. Civil service reform – History
    I. Title II. Greenaway, J R
    354'.41'01   JN428
    ISBN 0-85664-107-3

Printed and bound in Great Britain by
REDWOOD BURN LIMITED
Trowbridge & Esher

CONTENTS

The Impetus of Events

The Direction of Administrative Reform

The Civil Service and Society

ACKNOWLEDGEMENTS

We wish gratefully to acknowledge the assistance of the following
people and institutions from whom we have received help in various
ways. The Social Science Research Council awarded us a grant of £575
and this was supplemented by £160 from the University of Durham.
We acknowledge permission to quote copyright material from the
Librarian, British Library of Political and Economic Science in respect
of quotations from the Webbs' Reconstruction Papers; and from the
Trevelyan family in respect of the papers of Sir Charles Trevelyan.
The following people helped us by answering questions: Professor
C.E.B. Cranfield, Mr. J.M. Lee and Dr. E.S. Taylor. Mrs. R. McCarthy
enabled us to have access to the archives of the National Whitley
Council Staff Side. Our special thanks must be expressed to the
following who at short notice read the manuscript in draft and made
helpful comments: Professor A. Dunsire, Mr. George W. Greenaway,
Professor Henry Parris and Dame Enid Russell-Smith. The responsibility
for the final manuscript is, of course, ours alone.

Richard A. Chapman
University of Durham

J.R. Greenaway
University of East Anglia

INTRODUCTION

Administrative reform, as one of the underdeveloped areas of study in public administration, suffers from a variety of constraints and difficulties. First, the term 'administrative reform' has somewhat different meanings in different countries with different political systems. In Britain and other liberal democracies the term generally relates to reform of the administrative system; it is the process of making changes in administrative structures or procedures within the public services because they have become out of line with the expectations of the social and political environment. In other countries, including many in the Third World and the USSR, the term is more frequently applied to attempts to modernise or change society by using the administrative system as an instrument for social and economic transformation. Such differences in the meaning of a term are not uncommon in the social sciences but do not make for easy international co-operation or comparative analysis.

Secondly, even when the subject is studied in the context of a single country like Britain, there is no general agreement on its meaning. The term may be loosely used by non-specialists or by politicians, and perhaps more precisely by academic specialists, although the latter may disagree among themselves over the meaning to be adopted. If the term is to have any significance it seems important to distinguish 'reform' from 'change', 'innovation', 'evolution' and 'development'. 'Change' may imply no more than difference (whilst all reforms imply change not all changes are deliberately introduced); 'innovation' tends to be used where administrative structures or processes have been newly created in the public sector; 'evolution' may refer to the process whereby administrative structures or procedures which were originally simple have become increasingly sophisticated and elaborate; and 'development' may be reserved for changes associated with progress towards a clearly defined goal known in advance. However, such distinctions cannot be watertight. Administrative reform is intimately related to these phenomena; it may overlap or include them. One might attempt in the British context to distinguish different types or levels of reform such as those applying to the whole civil service, those relating to the structures of particular departments or those concerned with management procedures or techniques. Such an undertaking might raise the possibility of quantification and require lavish research funds, but it is doubtful whether any conclusions would appear as more than platitudes or tautologies even if distinctive patterns emerged from the classification. As the studies in this book attempt to show, different aspects of administrative reform react upon each other and merge together.

Thirdly, attempts to give the term any exact meaning with general applicability tend to raise expectations that cannot be fulfilled. For a comprehensive study of administrative reform cannot be made in isolation from the many social and political pressures with which it is interrelated and which have motivated particular changes. To be anything more than a superficial account such a comprehensive work would be on a large scale. It would have to give a full account of the growth and development of the civil service, and to trace the changes in the internal organisation of government departments and their relationships with each other. It would have also to consider the relationship of local to central government, social and political pressures within British society, and the interaction between ideas and practical developments. The concept of 'administrative reform' might well be lost to sight amid this detail.

For reasons of practical necessity we had to limit the scope of our study and the length of our book. The idea for the book arose when we were colleagues in the University of Durham. We originally intended to make a study of the contributions of commissions of inquiry to administrative reform in the civil service since 1850, seeing where ideas for reform came from, tracing how they were implemented and attempting to reach conclusions about the origins and nature of the processes of administrative reform in Britain. However, it soon became apparent that a study of the commissions would be unduly narrow, and there would be a serious risk of distorting the complexity of administrative reform. We therefore modified our plans as our work progressed in favour of a more flexible and wider-ranging analysis of administrative reform. We decided to select a broad theme — the dynamics of the administrative reform process — and to study this in the context of the British civil service from 1850 to 1970. Such a work would span our respective academic interests in British political history and in management in the public services. Moreover, there seemed room for a further study of the British civil service. Most existing work on the subject takes one of three forms. The first comprises essentially historical accounts which either describe the evolution or development of the service as a whole, or analyse in depth particular proposals for reform, or describe in detail, but not necessarily with analysis, the work of particular departments of state. The second are in the nature of sophisticated 'tracts for the times' which may survey aspects of past experience but are mainly concerned with prescribing remedies for contemporary problems. The third are works of either a descriptive or theoretical nature, aimed at students studying for examinations in public administration. Examples could be given of each of these, but as readers of this present book are already likely to be aware of the literature on the subject they are unlikely to have difficulty in thinking of the works we have in mind.

Having determined the general scope of the book we had to decide on particular themes for our attention. Our object, it must be stressed, was not to give a comprehensive account of reform in the British civil service, but rather to select certain themes, episodes or case studies which would illuminate the dynamics of administrative reform. We wished to focus on themes which in retrospect would appear to have been significant reforms. For a number of reasons this presented more of a problem in the later period than in the earlier. Distance helps provide perspective; the scope of government activity and the size of the civil service has increased so much since 1850; and, as with some other aspects of the study of British central government, it is not easy for the 'outsider' to gain access to research material revealing what has been really happening. We are conscious of many areas which might well have repaid examination, but which we have had to exclude. Readers will unfortunately find no adequate discussion of, for example, reforms associated with the employment of women, the introduction and adaptation of various management techniques, or the history of what have become known as 'hiving off' or of 'quangos'. Nor have we been able to treat in a comprehensive or systematic manner such important areas as internal reorganisations within government departments or the relationships of government agencies with each other. Recognising the need to make choices we used two criteria to make our selection: the importance of the topics and the likely accessibility of research materials. The latter problem became an increasingly burdensome constraint in the period after 1939. Students of public administration in Britain should bear in mind that it is possible for 'outsiders' to write far more authoritatively about decision-making in the late-nineteenth and early-twentieth centuries than it is about our own day. The result may be a long way from ideal but we believe it is only through making such attempts as this that advances will be made in understanding the underdeveloped areas of our subject. We hope that what is lost in comprehensiveness is more than compensated for by gain in depth and that readers will not feel we have wasted our time or misused our resources.

Our object is therefore not to offer a comprehensive history of either administrative reform in Britain or of the British civil service; nor is it to offer prescriptive guidance for the improvement of British government; nor is it to write a textbook for a public administration syllabus. Our concern instead has been to write an essay on the pattern of administrative reform in the British civil service which provides new evidence and new interpretation on aspects of administrative reform in Britain as well as a contribution to the more general debate on the nature and processes of reform in public administration. Accordingly the book consists of three historically-oriented chapters each of which examines three separate areas of reform in a thematic manner. The fourth chapter contains a general analysis of the nature of administrative reform in the British civil service throughout our period, 1850-1970.

1

1 THE CIVIL SERVICE AND THE STATE IN VICTORIAN BRITAIN

During the 60 years before the First World War the organisation,
content and style of British central government changed substantially.
These changes took place without there being either any dramatic
constitutional upheaval or political revolution, or, at any rate before
1900, any very striking shift in political leaders' conceptions of the
role of the state in society. In this respect the British experience of
administrative reform in central government is unique. The changes in
administration tended, after the period of the Crimean War, to occur
gradually and undramatically, and are best observed amid the shadowy
confines of Whitehall, rather than in the arc-lights of parliamentary
debate or the public platform. In contrast to British local government,
which was periodically consciously 'reformed' after considerable
debate, there are no real 'key dates' or turning points in the development of central government administration in late-Victorian or
Edwardian Britain. In part this is due to the fact that the civil service
was so fully debated at the beginning of our period with the publication
of the Northcote/Trevelyan Report on the reorganisation of the civil
service. This report with its vision of an efficient, permanent civil
service, free from corruption and patronage, recruited by open
competition, divided into grades and centrally directed, was indeed
remarkably prescient. So much so that it is tempting to write the
administrative development of the late-Victorian state in terms of the
implementation or working out of the Northcote/Trevelyan
'programme'. Certainly, the main features of this development
correspond closely to the ideas of the liberal reformers of the 1850s:
first the clarification of thought concerning distinction between
'politics' and 'administration' along with the growth of ministerial
responsibility to Parliament; secondly the eclipse of patronage as an
instrument of selection and promotion in government offices and its
replacement by a system of competition based upon intellectual merit;
and thirdly the gradual emergence of a fairly uniform pattern of
grading in administration, reflecting different types of work and
centrally administered by the Treasury and the Civil Service
Commissioners. In short the complexly-organised and highly
individualistic 'public establishments' of the early nineteenth century,

15

penetrated with political connections, evolved into a fairly coherently organised 'civil service' which had sunk below the level of party politics.

However, this view has its dangers. The sense of inevitability which it implies obscures the complexity of the process of administrative reform. Moreover it can lead to too great a concentration upon the 1850s and 1860s when there was much open debate upon the principles of reform, at the expense of the last quarter of the century when significant, if unspectacular, changes occurred. Here it must be recognised that the Northcote/Trevelyan vision owed much of its success and subsequent popularity, not only to the administrative benefits but also to the political and social advantages which it brought. For one of the chief objectives of the exponents of the Northcote/Trevelyan plan was the purification of *political* life, in particular the heightening of the tone of Parliament and the conduct of elections, and the furthering of meritocratic as opposed to hereditary values – an ideal which was enthusiastically endorsed by many leading education-ists. Thus the Northcote/Trevelyan ideals – a career open to talent, a separation between 'intellectual' and 'mechanical' work, promotion by merit, and a firm career structure – fitted in very well with the liberal political ideals which dominated the thought of the period 1860-1900, namely the political supremacy of the House of Commons, ministerial responsibility to Parliament, and electoral politics determined by issues rather than vested interest.

In a rather odd way, however, the *theory* of the Northcote/Trevelyan ideal, which so dominated the period after 1870, remained in many respects at odds with the *practice* of the period. For the civil service and the administrative structure of Edwardian Britain was a good deal more complicated and varied than either contemporaries or later (mainly liberal) administrative historians have often supposed. Thus Graham Wallas, the Fabian thinker and a member of the 1912-14 Royal Commission which investigated the civil service, spoke of 'the invention of a competitive Civil Service, when it had once been made and adopted', dropping 'from the region of severe and difficult thought in which it originated' and taking its place 'in our habitual political psychology', so that open competition had 'become a "principle" '.[1] Yet when Wallas was writing, open unlimited competition, though widespread in the more purely 'administrative' categories, was only used for about one-third of the total number of civil service appoint-ments; unlimited competition was considered unsuitable for most professional and technical positions, as well as the bulk of more manual

work.[2] The evidence before the MacDonnell Royal Commission on the
eve of the First World War reveals clearly how many reservations the
permanent heads of departments had about the practical difficulties of
operating a competitive entry scheme. When the state was faced with
new responsibilities, like the running of the new labour exchanges,
open competition was abandoned, much to the disquiet of parliamentarians. Similarly the idea of a division of labour in government offices
proved far more attractive and appealing in the abstract than it was
feasible in practice. The evidence before the three large-scale investigations into the civil service between 1870 and 1914 all showed how it
was virtually impossible to classify or grade the service on uniform
principles, without giving rise to great anomalies. Ironically one of the
major forces assisting the creation of grades was the growing influence
of clerical trade unions or associations, whose rise was viewed with
distaste and alarm by the liberally-inclined administrative elite. Again,
the concept of a unified 'civil service' was at odds with the practice of
central administration. Transfers between departments were very rare
before 1910, Treasury control was limited in scope, and conditions
varied widely from department to department. This variation was often
fiercely defended. As late as 1913, for example, Sir Henry Primrose, an
experienced administrator who was responsible for the minority report
of the MacDonnell Commission, 'objected that there was no such single
thing as the Civil Service, and that this should be recognised before
discussing the proper methods of recruitment which might be found to
vary ...'[3]

Indeed perhaps the most striking feature of Victorian administration
was the comparative autonomy of the various departments of state.
These often had had very venerable and varied origins, and the
development and history of each was 'almost as complex as the history
of the constitution itself'.[4] Apart from the marked difference in tone —
some aristocratic, some businesslike, some slack — each department
had evolved its own procedures and organisation to meet the widely
differing tasks which it had to face. Each tackled the administrative
demands which unprecedented social and economic changes had
brought about by a variety of administrative devices and expedients.
Developments were empirical and *ad hoc*, rather than systematic or
deductive. Generalisation about the nature of Victorian government is
therefore difficult since

> differing traditions and differing patterns of development in
> different departments reflect the impossibility of describing

government growth in the nineteenth century as a single phenomenon or process. Rather, there seem a series of impulses towards
change and new development. From time to time they interact, but
the connections seem coincidental as much as casual.[5]

Another distinguishing feature of British nineteenth-century administration is the relative divorce between central administration and the
work of government in localities. Although a few departments, notably
the Post Office and the Customs and Excise, controlled large field
services, the tendency was for much of the work of government (e.g.
in education, housing and highway maintenance) to be performed
either by local authorities or independent or semi-autonomous agencies
or commissions. This was in contrast to most continental practice. The
effect was to encourage still further variations in administrative practice
and diversity in constitutional arrangements. The British state
possessed a remarkably resilient digestion. Its administrators were not
generally self-conscious gourmets, anxious for experimentation in novel
fields, but were remarkably tolerant of novelty and able to extend their
menu as occasion demanded. New devices — for example the increased
use of delegated legislation at the turn of the century — could be
gradually adopted without much publicity and without any great
discussion about their 'constitutional' propriety. Thus what was in
reality a period of considerable change was also a period strangely
devoid of applicable theorising. H.R.G. Greaves has summed this up
very well.

> There is a certain elusiveness, however, about the nineteenth
> century. That arises partly because it was a period of transition.
> In part the cause is the contrast between ideas and what was
> increasingly proving necessary in practice ..... For the most curious
> fact about this nineteenth-century state is that it never existed.
> Historians may chase it and try to set limits of time and place upon
> it, but they do not succeed. It eludes them between the oligarchic
> administration and interfering paternalism of the eighteenth century,
> on the one hand, and the social service democracy on the other. For
> the former was not dead before the latter had been born.[6]

Reform could not therefore easily flow from any coherently thought-
out programme.
    It is extremely difficult to generalise about the state of central admini-
stration in Britain during the early part of the nineteenth century. The

stereotype which is most commonly held is one of a series of stuffy, idle offices which were inefficient, and where jobbery and patronage reigned supreme. This view owes much to the radical tone of the Northcote/Trevelyan Report. It has a measure of truth. It was a standing joke that civil servants, like the fountains in Trafalgar Square, played from 10-4. We are told that young gentlemen clerks, recruited in a wholly haphazard manner, often used to idle the office hours away by playing illicit games of cricket or squash in remote attics, or by shining mirrors at pretty girls in streets, or even piling the furniture on top of itself inside the offices.[7] At the India House, where it was the custom for clerks to receive a free breakfast, one clerk waxed lyrical in describing the daily routine:

> From ten to eleven, ate a breakfast for seven;
> From eleven to noon, to begin 'twas too soon;
> From twelve to one, asked what's to be done?
> From one to two, found nothing to do;
> From two to three, began to foresee
> That from three to four, would be a damned bore.[8]

This state of affairs even continued into the 1860s. Sir George Kekewich, for example, vividly recalls, with some nostalgia, the lackadaisical conditions of his youth, when he was an 'Examiner' in the Education Department.

> The hour for attendance was eleven o'clock, but it was not often that any of us put in an appearance before half-past eleven or twelve; and we were supposed to leave at five, but most of us usually disappeared long before that hour. Included in the day's attendance was, of course, the necessary period for reading the *Times*, which was provided for us at the public expense, and the hour interval for luncheon, which was generally prolonged, in fact, we attended practically as much or as little as we liked. Some of us (and I amongst them) were often guilty of going to the office late in the afternoon, sometimes after office hours, and putting in one or two hour's work which were necessary; and sometimes, but rarely, a full holiday was taken on French leave without discovery.[9]

The calibre of the clerks was often deplorable. Many examples can be given of incompetent and inefficient employees who had gained their position because they were the sons or nephews of friends of MPs or the aristocracy. Sometimes tests were made of the ability of entrants, but these were usually for form's sake and sometimes farcical. Trollope's Charley Tudor in *The Three Clerks* secured employment in the 'Internal Navigation Office' by an exercise of copying a leading article from a newspaper, misspelling several words and blotting the paper in the process. On seeing this the Secretary sent him home to produce a more accomplished article; but he found on his return next day that he had been already accepted without any further evidence of ability. And this was an account in fiction of the precise manner in which its author, Anthony Trollope, had been admitted to the Post Office.[10] It is no wonder that Sir Charles Trevelyan went so far as to describe the civil service as 'a sort of Foundling Hospital' where the 'high Aristocracy' could deposit the 'waifs and strays of their families. The Dukes of Norfolk, for instance, have provided for their illegitimate children in this manner, generation after generation.'[11] Sometimes whole departments of state were largely staffed by near incompetents or even criminals. This even applied to such a new department as the Registrar General's Office, set up in 1836 and itself the product of reform. When Major Graham was appointed Registrar General he found 'a great number' of those previously appointed to be 'very objectionable on account of their bad character and want of proper qualifications'. Alongside some efficient officers he found an insolvent debtor who had been in prison for fraud, a clerk who subsequently tried to embezzle office money, and an unfortunate invalid whose physical condition was such that he was unable to work in a room with anyone else. The Accountant was dismissed for inefficiency and the Deputy Registrar successfully avoided attending the office for 15 months before his duties were dispensed with.[12]

However, this was only one side of the coin and it is equally possible to discover cases of well-organised offices staffed by hard-working and imaginative public servants. Some excellent appointments were made by patronage, and some departments took the business of examining recruits very seriously indeed: Trollope in *The Three Clerks* carefully portrayed such an office in the shape of the 'Weights and Measures' under the austere regime of 'Sir Gregory Hardlines' (a representation of Sir Charles Trevelyan.) As Sir James Stephen, Permanent Secretary of the Colonial Office, pointed out, the personnel of the public offices could be divided into three classes. The first and most numerous, consisted of worthless and uneducated clerks, mere drones, who owed their positions to the influence exerted by their local MPs or family connections. The second comprised a body of well-educated and diligent clerks of limited potential who were often the backbone of offices; these usually performed routine tasks with little hope of advancement. The third was an elite corps of proven men having the highest intellectual, scholastic, administrative and personal qualities, who were drawn from outside the civil service, from the professions and the business world.[13] These titans played a key role in enabling early Victorian governments to cope with many of the problems posed by industrialisation. Perhaps the oustanding example of this was the initiative taken in the field of public health after the cholera epidemic of 1832 by Edwin Chadwick and others. The creation of the Post Office, the organisation of Poor Law administration, and the trans-formation of the Board of Trade before 1860, all bear witness to the vitality of administration at this time and the enormous potential for the bold innovator.[14] Nevertheless, as Professor MacDonagh has pointed out, the practice had disadvantages. It tended to produce 'war-lording and empire building within the service, and to a grievous extent, exorbitance and excursions into politics ... The very system bred "statesmen in disguise". And its effect upon the ordinary Civil Service was wholly bad. The rank and file felt all the more certainly and irrevocably condemned to their servile status when the plums of office seemed reserved for the world outside.'[15]

Just as the personnel of the service varied enormously, so did the methods of work. Although many offices were lax, in others work was performed efficiently. Sir Edmund Harrison at the Privy Council, for example, insisted on each incoming letter being dealt with on the day of its receipt; and many leading civil servants rejected the rather sensational strictures in the Northcote/Trevelyan Report as a gross calumny upon a largely dedicated group of public servants. The truth was that central government administration in Britain in the early 1850s was extremely varied and erratic, both in structure and in organisation. Various new boards and commissions had been tacked on in an *ad hoc* and unsystematic manner to the older public establish-ments; while the older offices themselves jealously preserved their own traditions, each being virtually a law unto itself regarding conditions of work. Nevertheless, reform was in the air. Since the turn of the century the nation's accounting methods had been overhauled and stricter Treasury financial control imposed. Some of the worst sinecures had been abolished and an end put to the overt selling of paid offices. A superannuation Act had been passed, and moves to replace fees and commissions by graduated salaries were largely implemented. The initiative here came from reforming, radical MPs anxious to cut down the cost of government and to attack excessive Crown patronage. However, as yet reforming efforts had been piecemeal and largely negative in character. It was left to reformers in the 1850s to formulate more extensive principles of reform which were designed to benefit both the administrative and the political health of the nation.

The Principle of the Division of Labour in Government Offices

The idea that work in the departments of state could be divided between 'mechanical' and 'intellectual' tasks was unorthodox in the 1850s, but by the turn of the century it received almost universal endorsement. The implications were far-reaching. The doctrine implied that administration could always be divided into different categories — higher and lower — and that these were best performed by different 'classes' of clerk. Since the work which they would perform was by its nature so different, these classes could have little in common with each other; hence avenues of promotion should be limited. Each class, on the contrary, should be recruited from the appropriate levels of educational attainment in the community. This in turn meant that the horizontal divisions between the different classes in the public service might be seen as more intrinsically important than the vertical divisions between the different government departments. Hence the idea of dividing labour encouraged radical new ideas concerning both recruitment to the public offices, and the structure and relationship of those offices themselves.

The idea of distinguishing routine from intellectually demanding work was not an original one in the 1850s. James Stephen and Henry Taylor, two leading administrators of the 1830s, had recognised the practical benefits which might stem from making such a distinction when they wrote treatises on the art of government; and periodic, although largely short-lived, attempts had been made to divide the work of some departments along these lines, for example the Colonial Office, and the India Office in 1831.[16] Nevertheless, the standard pattern in the 1840s was for departments to be organised on a 'single-tier' basis. New recruits, irrespective of ability, generally began by working on routine tasks, and only slowly climbed their way up the hierarchy to more responsible positions. It was practical rather than theoretical considerations which first led to the prevailing pattern being questioned. Ever since 1830 successive governments had faced fierce demands on the part of radicals for the wholesale reduction of public expenditure on the 'civil establishments'. Administrative reform was conceived in terms of financial reform consisting of a sharp cut-back of overpaid sinecures.

The government offices were to be pruned and freed from the aristocratic incubus in the interests of a liberal society.[17] However, during
the 1840s several public servants began to question the limited outlook
of parliamentary radical forces and their supporters. In 1848, for
example, Edward Romilly, Chairman of the Board of Audit, circulated
a paper criticising the way in which the civil service was being made a
scapegoat. Reforms were needed, particularly regarding the selection
and promotion of officers, but efficiency was not to be equated with
reduction. 'The truth is that we are beginning at the wrong end. Our
establishments should be first made efficient, then they may be
reduced, or rather, they will reduce themselves.'[18] Although support
for these views was far from negligible, little action would have resulted
had it not been for the zeal and energy of Sir Charles Trevelyan, who
was appointed Assistant (i.e. Permanent) Secretary to the Treasury at
the age of 32 in 1840.

In character Charles Trevelyan was the very reverse of the conventional picture of a mandarin. Energetic, incisive and intensely self-confident
he was also impulsive, tactless and insensitive to the difficulties of
others. Life for him was a battleground where the forces of enlightened,
altruistic moral progress were to triumph over the dead weight of
obscurantism and self interest. Born in 1807 into a well-established,
evangelical West Country family, he went in 1826 to work in the East
India Company's service. Then in 1834 he married the sister of T.B.
(later Lord) Macaulay, who, under the India Act, had recently been
appointed to the Supreme Council of India. At the age of 21, he had
caused a sensation by bringing about the dismissal of his superior
officer for bribery. Back in England in his new post he rapidly set about
turning the Treasury into a highly efficient machine. Trevelyan's
correspondence in 1848 shows that he had long nursed an ambition to
reorganise the civil service in Britain. 'There was never a subject which
promised so largely to reward the pains bestowed upon it', he lectured
the Prime Minister, Lord John Russell, 'for there cannot be a doubt
that the practical Executive Administn. has, as a general rule, been very
much neglected in this country.'[19] In 1848 he found a forum for
expressing his views in evidence before a parliamentary select
committee on public expenditure. Trevelyan urged the committee to
consider the question of efficiency in its broadest sense rather than
the narrow issue of economies. He believed a drastic improvement in
morale and efficiency could be brought about by dividing work into
routine and intellectual categories.[20] Such a division, he declared to
Russell, would provide a means of rewarding ability and encouraging

talent among the junior civil servants.[21]

The select committee did not care for Trevelyan's ideas, but this was hardly a setback since events over the next five years allowed him ample opportunity to develop them. In 1848 there began a whole series of *ad hoc* committees of inquiry into various departments as a response to the demand for economy. It was important that representatives of the Treasury should be invited to join any such investigations. The investigations were not at first at all systematic. They were occasioned by particular requests for additional staffing or an increase in salaries. But Trevelyan from the start seems to have envisaged some more general overhaul. In September 1848, for example, he urged Sir George Cornewall Lewis, MP, Under Secretary for the Home Office, to adopt his draft plan for a somewhat drastic reorganisation of that office on the grounds not only that such a 'permanent arrangement' was necessary to put the Office on a 'satisfactory footing' but also that this general overhaul would 'be a great help to us in dealing with other Offices which want a thorough revision as much as the Home Office'.[22]

By February 1852 when Russell's Whig government was succeeded by the Tory ministry of Lord Derby, the Home Office, the Treasury itself, the Foreign Office, the Colonial Office, the Irish Offices and the War Office had all come under review, with Trevelyan or one of his associates as a member of the investigation. In every case Trevelyan tended to favour some 'decided change of system'. The new principles propounded were: promotion on grounds of merit, division between intellectual and mechanical work and the employment of temporary 'copyists' to perform much of the routine work. The report into the Colonial Office, which was accepted by Earl Grey, the Colonial Secretary, marked a decisive point, furnishing, Trevelyan wrote, 'the first model for the constitution of a Public Office on the principle of making a proper distinction between intellectual and mechanical labour'.[23] However, Trevelyan did not have everything his own way. The permanent heads of the Home Office and the Foreign Office totally rejected his views and even refused to allow the reports on their offices to be published.[24] Benjamin Hawes of the War Office wrote a counter-report of his own, an action rather pompously described by Trevelyan as a 'flagrant breach of trust & dereliction of duty'; and even at the Treasury Sir Charles Wood, the Chancellor, declined to implement fully Trevelyan's ideas for a division of labour, although this did not stop Trevelyan over the next five years from comprehensively restructuring the department.[25]

Following a series of scandals in the Customs in mid-1852 politicians in both parties were sympathetic to the cause of reform. In December 1852 Trevelyan was fortunate in the person of the new Chancellor, the ex-Peelite W.E. Gladstone, an indefatigable reformer beginning to make his mark upon the political scene. Gladstone decided to continue the series of departmental investigations and was responsible for bringing Sir Stafford Northcote into the picture. Northcote came from a genteel but rather impoverished West Country family, and had recently given up a promising career as a civil servant in the Board of Trade for personal and domestic reasons. Gladstone eagerly accepted Northcote's suggestion that he might be able to assist at the next investigation into the Board of Trade and thereafter he assisted Trevelyan on a regular basis.[26] Northcote, apart from his sterling capacity for work, played a useful part in cementing the alliance between the civil service reformers and educational reformers, which was to develop later in 1853. The report into the Board of Trade, a 'masterpiece' (Trevelyan), was completed by 20 March 1853. It endorsed the principle of a permanent division of labour and the creation of distinct classes of clerks to be recruited separately; both classes of clerks would have to prove themselves fit for appointment by passing an examination.[27]

By the end of March 1853 therefore a series of investigations had been held into a variety of civil service departments. Some of these had pointed to the desirability of a more general analysis of certain matters which affected the service as a whole. The investigators into the Irish Offices, for example, felt difficulty in recommending any general scale of salaries and regretted 'that some general classification of public offices has not been made, which ... would ... remove many difficulties which now present themselves'.[28] Similarly Northcote, Trevelyan and James Booth, in the Board of Trade Report, 'cannot avoid expressing our opinion, that the whole subject of the examination of candidates for public employment is well worthy of consideration, and that it would be of great advantage if a proper system were devised, and a Central Board of properly qualified examiners appointed ...'[29] Gladstone accordingly decided in April to round off the various departmental investigations with a more general report:

> for the purpose of considering applications for increase of salary, abolishing or consolidating redundant offices, supplying additional assistance where it is required, getting rid of obsolete processes, and introducing more simple and compendious modes of transacting business, establishing a proper distinction between intellectual and mechanical labour, and generally, so revising and readjusting the

public establishments as to place them on the footing best calculated for the efficient discharge of their important functions, according to the actual circumstances of the present time.

Here were far more precise terms of reference than those which had been given to the earlier *ad hoc* committees upon which Trevelyan had served. It was

highly necessary that the conditions which are common to all the public offices, such as the preliminary testimonials of character and bodily health to be required from candidates for public employment, the examination into their intellectual attainments, and the regulation of the promotions, should be carefully considered, so as to attain every practicable security for the public that none but qualified persons will be appointed, and that they will afterwards have every practicable inducement to the active discharge of their duties.[30]

These instructions were laid out in an official Treasury Minute dated 12 April 1853.

The detailed investigations for which Trevelyan had been primarily responsible confirmed him in his opinion that the principle of the 'division of labour is the key to the improvement of many Public Offices. Without it they cannot be efficiently or economically conducted.' Such a division 'must be carried out with a careful attention to the circumstances of each department', but without any such structuring it was impossible to secure the cheapest and most suitable clerks appropriate for each category of work.[31] Under the existing system talented young men of a liberal education were often ground down with years of drudgery on routine tasks until they were fit for nothing. The absence of any promotion by merit exacerbated the situation. In most professional occupations

the able and the energetic rise to the top; the dull and inefficient remain at the bottom. In the public establishments, on the contrary, the general rule is that all rise together ... The feeling of security which this state of things necessarily engenders tends to encourage indolence, and thereby to depress the character of the Service.[32]

As Trevelyan and Northcote proceeded with their work they became increasingly convinced that the whole problem of efficient organisation was aggravated by the low calibre of the recruits for the service and the harmful effects of the system of patronage. As a result in their final general report — as we shall examine later in this chapter — they came to recommend a thoroughgoing alteration in the pattern of recruitment by substituting open competitive examinations for patronage. These far-reaching and far-sighted proposals stemmed from the original concern with the division of labour and were presented as an integral plan for wholesale reform, but the immediate effect was to distract attention from the question of the internal organisation of departments. Critics of the idea of academic literary examinations tended to ignore the fact that Trevelyan and Northcote suggested a variety of tests appropriate for different departments and different levels of work.

Part of the hostility was due to the differing views of the role of the civil servant. The conception in the Northcote/Trevelyan Report that the government of the country needed an 'efficient body of permanent officers, occupying a position duly subordinate to that of the Ministers ... yet possessing sufficient independence, character, ability, and experience to be able to advise, assist, and, to some extent, influence, those who are from time to time set over them' was in many respects far in advance of its time.[33] When the Northcote/Trevelyan Report was circulated among leading officials and public figures much criticism centred upon what was seen as an unrealistic conception of the duties of the public servant. To put leading scholars into government offices would be like putting racehorses to the plough. 'You stand in need, not of statesmen in disguise, but of intelligent, steady, methodical men of business,' declared Sir James Stephen, 'why invite an athlete into a theatre, where no combat, and no applause, and no reward, awaits him?' Even at the highest level of administration, claimed H.V. Addington of the Foreign Office, 'a good Departmental Clerk is, in fact, mainly an aggregation of cumulative daily experience and tradition, combined with that readiness of mind and pen which practice gives, and which enables a man to come to the assistance of his superiors at the right moment, and in the right manner'. The 'drudgery of the desk' was the necessary foundation upon which the efficiency of each individual government office must be built.[34]

There was therefore strong resistance to the implementation of this part of the Northcote/Trevelyan proposals. Departmental permanent heads at this time were not to be dictated to as to how their offices were organised and many argued cogently that any division of labour would be totally misconceived. In the Foreign Office, for example, routine copying might be a highly confidential and responsible task. The War Office and the Admiralty both required flexibility in order to cope in times of crisis when temporary labour rather than a large staff of permanent 'mechanical' clerks would be adequate. In the Home Office the work was specialist, and officers offered invaluable advice on specific issues; but this function 'did not correspond to Northcote and Trevelyan's idea of intellectual labour. It was rather a specialist professional knowledge derived from long experience'.[35] Promotion by seniority rather than the recruitment of highly qualified intellectuals made sense here. Moreover, even where departmental heads approved of the idea it became difficult to maintain without more centralised and systematic recruitment procedures than then existed. Time never stood still, and it was always difficult to take on new work without upsetting the balance. Most of the offices reformed by Trevelyan along the new 'model' lines before 1853 soon lapsed into their former state. A vicious circle operated: pressure of work led to the more capable 'supplementary' clerks being employed on high-grade work, better qualified men then tended to be employed as 'supplementaries', and more 'intellectual' work was pushed their way. By March 1859 only seven of the 32 supplementary clerks of the Board of Trade, for example, were employed on 'mechanical' work;[36] and a Treasury Committee appointed by Gladstone in 1860 concluded that the supplementary establishments had 'in almost every instance, already changed their character'. This Committee, which included Stafford Northcote, recommended the merging of the supplementary and the established classes and the creation of a central copying service under the control of the Civil Service Commissioners – the latter being a resurrection of a proposal of 1852.[37] This report stood little chance of adoption, since departments were hostile to any proposal which would centralise employment in the service and which would in effect deprive them of the control and appointment of junior staff. Opinion in the Treasury was also divided. It was pointed out that many 'routine' tasks nevertheless required a certain amount of experience which could only be gained by service within a department. Furthermore, despite Northcote's desire for some 'more decided advance' in civil service organisation, the question of the division of labour had been treated in isolation from that of recruitment. Any effective division of labour would have involved a radical measure of reform whereby two distinct classes or grades were created for the service as a whole. Such a far-reaching reform would have required the initiative of a far more thorough investigation or some substantial political impetus. Failing this it was in every way more convenient for the Treasury and the departments to continue to make *ad hoc* arrangements concerning the pay and prospects of civil servants, regardless of the long-term confusion which was thus created. Lacking the institutional apparatus to create a system of grades or classes, the best the Treasury could hope to achieve in the late 1850s and 1860s was to preach the virtues of the principle of the division of labour, but to leave the responsibility for enforcing the division to the departmental heads themselves.

In 1869, by contrast, Robert Lowe, the Chancellor of the Exchequer, together with Ralph Lingen, the Permanent Secretary to the Treasury, determined to bring some order into the chaos of grading and classification. This was to be tackled as part of the important reforms in recruitment which Lowe and Gladstone were eager to press ahead with, but it was also presented to the Cabinet as an important economy measure. Under an Order in Council of 1870 two separate schemes of examination were to be introduced. Scheme I was to attract the best class of university graduates, who would form an elite 'Grade I' to perform intellectually demanding work; scheme II was to be used to recruit a Grade II from school leavers. Different departments were to have different ratios of Grade I to Grade II appointments in accordance with the nature of their work. Below this, lower quality work such as copying was, where possible, to be performed by temporary civil service writers, who were to be paid on piece-work rates and to have no claim to permanent employment or pensions. In this way the Order in Council recognised and endorsed Trevelyan's principle of division of labour into two basic grades. Its importance lay in the fact that it marked 'the first recognition of the government, as distinct from the Treasury, of the principle of division of labour and of a pattern of establishment for the Civil Service as a whole'. Whatever the difficulties of application, 'it was now generally accepted that the work could and should be divided' between intellectual and mechanical tasks.[38] But if the principle of a division of labour was increasingly coming to be accepted, the implementation of that principle remained fraught with difficulty as the experience of the next few years was to show.

In 1874, when the Conservatives returned to power, Sir Stafford Northcote became Chancellor of the Exchequer. Northcote's career is an interesting example of the ease with which public figures could at this period move from the permanent to the political service of the Crown and from one political party to another. Now for the third time in 20 years he found himself confronted with the problems of the civil service. When he took office he found that 'great dissatisfaction' prevailed in the public offices. Mindful perhaps of his not altogether happy experiences in the past and chary of getting the ministry directly involved in a difficult and unpopular question, he hit upon the expedient of an outside inquiry on the somewhat specious grounds that they had 'not time to take the question up at the Treasury without some assistance'. Accordingly he begged Sir Lyon Playfair, who had been Postmaster General in the outgoing Liberal Government, to under-take 'a piece of important public service' by presiding over 'a small committee' to investigate the general organisation of the civil service.[39] Playfair, who had wide knowledge and practical experience of scientific matters, education and public administration both in Britain and on the Continent, was well-placed to conduct such an inquiry. The Commission over which he agreed to preside was an essentially Whitehall body, comprising senior civil servants and one 'cultivated mind untrammelled by any official prejudices', Lord Claud Hamilton.[40] It worked very rapidly, concentrating its investigations on a few departments, but also taking evidence from representatives of the commercial world about their employment arrangements as well as from a few representative rank-and-file officials. Within six months the Commission had produced its reports.[41]

The 'great dissatisfaction' which alarmed Northcote was quite simply the result of the confusion of grading and salary scales both within and across the various departments of state. As R.G. Hamilton, the Secretary to the Commission, later recalled, 'Discontent and agitation were rife. The Treasury scarcely knew when vacancies arose in the different offices, at what rates of pay the new men should be appointed, and, as a way out of the difficulty, writers were frequently engaged temporarily to fill vacancies' at inadequate rates of pay.[42] The position of the temporary, unestablished 'writers', of whom some 1,600 were registered with the Civil Service Commission, was particularly unsatisfactory. The rationale behind the employment of temporary clerical labour was clear enough: such a device would enable departments to cope with sudden influxes of work without contributing a permanent charge on the public purse. But the situation had got out of hand. Many of the writers were employed on what was effectively a permanent basis, and what is more tended to be given responsible work. In some instances long serving 'temporary' staff seem to have acted as the mainspring or prop of the whole department. It was claimed that one such stalwart in the Education Department, as a result of two decades of experience, knew 'the whole geography and business of the department. He could find any document in the office that might be required at a minute's notice.'[43] In other cases the work the writers performed was said to be 'precisely identical with that which is being discharged by many clerks whose salaries rise up to £300 a year'.[44] Many heads of department, moreover, bore witness to the excellent quality of the writers.[45] The position of such writers, performing permanent work but without security of pension rights, was unenviable. But the position was aggravated in the Customs and Admiralty where as a result of Lowe's reorganisation schemes of 1870-1 the departmental classes of writers had actually undergone a considerable loss of income as well as status upon assimilation to the general Treasury scheme.

The difficulty of the writers was part of the much broader question of grading and classifying the service as a whole. Experience had shown that the distinction under the Order in Council of 1870 between entry schemes I and II (for higher and lower classes of clerks), so neat and logical on paper, was in practice fraught with difficulty and complication. Some departments, like the War Office, had not adopted the system at all. Here all applicants took the same examinations, and a class of 'supplementary clerks' had simply been created out of those who had not been lucky enough to obtain a superior class appointment. Other departments had been wholly classified under scheme II, on the grounds that the work was such that there was no real need for a superior class of clerks. But these departments had felt their position to be somewhat inferior and had striven where possible to obtain appointments under scheme I in order to elevate their tone and status. In Lowe's view this state of affairs was the result of the weakness of the Treasury. There were too many grade I appointments in the Service and this was the price the Treasury had had to pay to buy the departments' acquiescence in the system for reorganisation and open competition which had been laid down in the Order in Council of 1870.[46] The result was a generally haphazard distribution of graded posts that bore little relationship to the work undertaken. Even where attempts had been made to introduce a division of labour, much of the evidence given before the Commission showed how quickly they had broken down. In extreme instances writers, grade II and grade I clerks were employed on identical work. In every department there seemed to be grave anomalies. Overall the Commission judged that there were too many writers and grade I clerks. This meant that the writers were discontented because of their temporary position and the grade II clerks because of promotion blockages.

The Playfair Commission believed that the question of the division of labour, although 'beset with difficulties' was nevertheless 'the key of the position'. In the 20 years since the Northcote/Trevelyan Report opinion among senior officials had clearly changed. The idea of a division was no longer viewed askance. The commissioners found two schools of thought on the question. The first was held by the more conservative officials who maintained that, although it might be possible to hive off purely mechanical copying work as the province of a temporary class of writers, it was unnecessary, impractical and positively dangerous to try to separate the work of the permanent clerks. Sir Louis Mallet, Under-Secretary in the India Office, for example, objected strongly to the system which decided once and for all a man's future destiny at the age of 20. He favoured ministers choosing the men in their own departments: the present system encouraged 'a sort of dead level of men of a uniform although perhaps of a high average general capacity without any great variety'. The government service, however, required a variety of talents and abilities. It was a grave error to introduce too many gifted young men who would in most departments have little to do except superintend a mass of routine work.[47] Such views received strong support understandably from the representatives of many of the junior supplementary clerks who believed that they were capable of performing effectively the highest quality work; these, however, pressed for some uniform salary scale. The second school of thought was upheld by those who adhered to the Northcote/Trevelyan conception. They believed that in most offices some sort of division was essential, and the weakness of the existing 1870 scheme was that some departments had recruited wholly under the division II regulations. Moreover, it was important that 'gentlemen' should occupy all positions of responsibility where they would come into contact with persons outside the service of high status and standing.

The Playfair commissioners recognised the enormous difficulties of dividing labour systematically since work varied so much from one department to another. However, they concluded that unless 'some division of labour and of pay can be effected, it is impossible to establish either any general system for testing efficiency, or any system of pay or promotion which will stimulate and reward efficiency, or remove grounds for discontent'. They recommended a drastic reduction in the number of writers and the division of the clerks into higher and lower divisions. However, they also suggested certain measures to cater for departmental individuality: duty pay, opportunities for promotion and a revised pattern of competitive recruitment.[48] Their Report received a stormy reception from the writers, and Stafford Northcote's own welcome was somewhat guarded. He cautioned against 'precipitate action' and was anxious not to offend the susceptibilities of the permanent departmental chiefs, who themselves later gave the Report a somewhat cool reception.[49] However, in February 1876 an Order in Council embodied some of the Playfair proposals. It formally established a 'Lower Division' of the Service. No department henceforth was to be 'permanently increased or regulated afresh, without providing for the introduction of a system whereby such of its duties as are of a suitable character shall be performed by members of the Lower Division'. No vacancies were to be filled or new appointments made above the rank of the new Lower Division 'until the Commissioners of the Treasury have been satisfied that the duties in question could not adequately be performed by clerks of the Lower Division'. Below this men and boy copyists were to be employed on routine work on piece-work rates.[50] So far as it went this was in line with the Playfair Report, but the Order said nothing about any 'Higher Division', and instead of there being a general assimilation of all existing personnel into a new system (as happened after 1920) the new Playfair Lower Division was rather unsatisfactorily imposed on existing arrangements.

When the civil service was next investigated by the Ridley Commission in the late 1880s little had been done formally to create a new class of Higher Division clerks. Sir Reginald Welby, Permanent Secretary to the Treasury in 1888, told the Ridley Commissioners that they would

> find hardly any of the Whitehall offices have had the upper part of the Playfair scheme applied to them ... it has been a matter of very great consideration as to whether it is desirable to apply that part of the Playfair scheme universally. So far as I see there has been no determination come to by the Government upon that point.

The Treasury itself recruited its own higher clerks by open competition or by transfer from other offices, but Welby was careful to stress these clerks 'belong to the Treasury alone, and are not interchangeable'. They had their own scales of salary which were above the Playfair maximum. The Treasury thus sought to preserve its own elite standard and acquire the best 'Balliol first class men' and the cream of other departments. Lord Basing voiced a suspicion that the Treasury had never approved of the Playfair scheme to which he received the evasive reply that 'I think I should rather say that the question of the universal application of the upper division of the Playfair scheme has not been considered by the

Treasury for the whole service as yet'. This was 'a very important question, and the Government will have to take it into consideration'.[51] Even more striking was the failure to implement effectively the Playfair Commission's recommendations concerning the future of the writers or copyists. Economic considerations prevented the Government from discharging any considerable number, and the Treasury failed to find any satisfactory criteria for judging which writers should be incorporated into the Lower Division. Agitation from the writers continued, and as a result a departmental committee of the Treasury investigated the situation in 1886. This estimated that of the 1,279 copyists still in existence – the Playfair Report had envisaged the number being cut to about 100 – some 40 per cent were engaged on work that was of more than a routine nature.[52] Even after this no serious attempt was made to rationalise the situation and the Ridley Commission found in 1888 that many 'temporary' writers were still performing work identical to that performed by some lower division clerks, and, in some extreme cases, by the old established superior clerks.[53]

     The history of the civil service during the three decades after 1870 illustrates how difficult it was to implement the principle of a division of labour, and how far the reality of departmental structure fell short of the ideal. Nevertheless the theory of the division came to be universally acclaimed by senior administrators. The Ridley Royal Commission in 1888 found that the principle had received 'the sanction of almost every experienced administrator from whom we received evidence', and its successor, the MacDonnell Commission, concluded that 'with the lapse of time the principle has become not less, but, if possible, more cogent'.[54] How is one to account for this gulf between theory and practice? The answer lies in the widely differing forces and impulses which helped to promote the principle; indeed the whole question illustrates very well the complexity of the process of administrative reform. The principle had originally been formulated not as a result of abstract speculation but as a result of concrete investigations into the deficiencies of government offices. It was propounded by Trevelyan and others as a cure for specific abuses or shortcomings: the uneconomic employment of staff and the demoralisation of talented young clerks. The goal was efficiency. The movement for a division of labour then came to be assisted by powerful forces from within government, in particular the need for economy, and the determination of the Treasury to encourage a more systematic use of resources in departments. But as far as the administrative benefits were concerned, a law of diminishing returns clearly applied. Economic savings, for example, were easily effected once a *basic* distinction had been made between different categories of work, but thereafter it was often actually more economic to fudge the distinctions by employing cheaper categories of staff on as much work as possible. Time and time again short-term benefits were secured at the expense of the long-term integrity of the principle. Similarly with office efficiency, when the principle was *broadly* applied the benefits were instantaneous and obvious. It made no sense whatsoever to confuse the work of — to take two extremes — a writer copying letters and a senior Treasury official assisting the Chancellor to prepare a budget; but if the principle was refined too far it led to complications and confusions, since not all work could be easily categorised and conditions varied from one department to another. Further administrative benefits would only have been secured from the principle if it had been accompanied by a panopoly of additional administrative devices such as systematic promotion procedures, centralised Treasury direction and uniform salary and conditions of work.

The impetus from within the bureaucracy for the principle therefore had its limits, but here broader political and social developments came into play. For the principle of the division of labour which had indirectly given rise to the concepts of recruitment by open competition and of a unified 'civil service' was itself in turn assisted by their success. Liberal reformers linked open competition and the division of labour as integral parts of a single programme of reform which had ideological and political as well as administrative objectives. This viewpoint was reinforced by the social changes in the second half of the nineteenth century, particularly educational changes. For these were years when education not only expanded but became far more heavily structured. It is no accident that the ideal of a three-fold division of labour into routine, clerical and higher administrative corresponded with the three main strata of educational attainment: elementary, good secondary and university. The MacDonnell Commissioners on the eve of the First World War, for example, were particularly concerned to emphasise and strengthen these links. They believed that 'the State as Employer and Examiner should co-operate more closely than it has apparently done hitherto with the State as Educator' and recommended that the Treasury and Civil Service Commission should consult regularly with the Board of Education in framing their recruitment examinations.[55] To administrators of the 1850s this would surely have seemed like putting the cart before the horse: the civil service instead of first determining its requirements and recruiting accordingly, was being asked to shape its recruitment procedures according to the educational divisions within society. That this did not in 1914 appear an absurd suggestion was because educational divisions reflected social divisions in a way that had not been the case 50 years before. One of the chief original objections to written examinations was that they provided no guarantee of the social or moral character of candidates. It was important to have 'gentlemen' manning the highest offices of the public service so that they would not be at a disadvantage when dealing with MPs, magistrates and other gentry with whom they would be brought into contact. However, with the growth of a clearly-defined ladder of education for the English higher classes – through the new public schools, and Oxford and Cambridge – the problem disappeared. Robert Lowe in 1874, for example, in justifying competitive examinations spoke of 'that sort of free-masonry which exists between people who have had a certain grade of education' which the civil service needed. By 1900 education was largely a guarantee of social status. Thus the classification of labour in the civil service came to reflect the classification of British society itself; and the division of labour might be justified in principle even where it was difficult to apply in practice.

The Northcote/Trevelyan Report and the Principle of Recruitment by Open Competition

Before the 1850s recruitment to the civil service was controlled by a system of patronage, though 'system' is perhaps hardly the correct word to describe a process which was essentially complex and unsystematic. The political head of an office exercised his patronage by filling vacancies in such a way as to benefit those to whom he had some obligation: his family, his dependants, his friends, his tenants, his constituents, his servants, or past or potential political supporters. By the early nineteenth century much of this patronage had become highly organised, broadly on party lines, and much of it was concentrated. The patronage system was a complicated network, whose threads penetrated into distant corners and played an important part in binding together the political and social fabrics. Since patronage was such an integral part of the social system, its nature necessarily evolved as society itself changed.

As far as the administration of central government was concerned the operation of patronage brought both strengths and weaknesses.[56] One of its inherent strengths lay in its flexibility. At a time when

government departments varied considerably both in the work
performed and in organisation, some such flexibility was not merely
useful but essential. Patronage ensured that each post was treated
individually and so provided the opportunity of fitting the right man to
the right job. At its best the process meant that the heads of a
department could exercise a close control over its personnel and the
conduct of its business. Patronage, in theory, also offered some kind of
a guarantee of the moral character and ability of new recruits: the sons
or cousins of trusted friends, loyal supporters or able servants were
more likely to prove satisfactory than perfect strangers. Moreover, at a
time when no national examination system existed and when the
educational structure of the country itself was ill-formed it was hard to
conceive of any other method of recruiting to the public services.
Personal recommendation was the accepted way of filling all posts in all
areas of life. The weakness of patronage stemmed from the necessarily
erratic way in which it was distributed and the consequent ease with
which it degenerated into jobbery and nepotism. Administrative
requirements or interests were all too readily sacrificed to political,
social or familial needs, with the result that the civil service tended, in
Charles Trevelyan's words, to become a 'secure asylum' in which the
'dregs of all other professions' might find refuge.[57] Patronage, which
extended to promotion as well as to recruitment, tended to ignore the
claims of ability and stifled initiative. Politicians usually took care in
filling the most senior public offices since these were too important to
give to incompetents, but few patrons or permanent departmental
heads were prepared to pay the price in terms of effort and
unpopularity to ensure that junior posts were properly filled. However,
since juniors in time became seniors, this only stored up trouble for
their successors who in their turn might be forced to look outside the
service when filling key posts; thus was established a vicious circle of
demoralisation. Finally by the 1840s patrons themselves were
beginning to find the system as much a nuisance as a benefit. An
influential patron's postbag might bulge with requests which he was
unable to grant, and after the extension of the franchise in 1832 the
supply of patronage 'fell so far short of the demand that, for every
friend gained by the award of a post, the patron had to reckon one or
more enemies made by the refusal of their requests'.[58] By the time of
the Northcote/Trevelyan investigations the essentially personalised
system of patronage of the eighteenth century had already evolved
into something else. Political factors, such as the growth of the
electorate and of political parties, were already altering the nature of

patronage. The parliamentary climate was growing hostile to jobbery, and, as Henry Parris has pointed out, political leaders had begun to recognise that 'the best way of securing the good-will of Members as a whole was to choose men on their merits'.[59] In a few departments sporadic attempts had already been made to improve the calibre of recruits to the civil service and to impose a probationary period. It was clear that the time was ripe for some more concentrated effort at reforming procedures; what was by no means so obvious was whether a completely new system should be instituted.

When Charles Trevelyan began his investigations into government departments in 1848, his primary concern was, as we have seen, to improve the internal organisation and administration of the various offices. The principles of a division of labour and of promotion by merit were the basis of the reforms which he and Stafford Northcote advocated. However, from an early stage Trevelyan showed disquiet at the calibre of recruits.[60] In August 1849 he sent Lord John Russell, the then Prime Minister, a paper proposing checks upon the selection of new clerks, and he was already clearly turning over in his ever-fertile mind the idea of reforming the process of patronage itself. However, at this stage he believed 'the main question of *how the qualifications of Persons so nominated are to be tested*' should be treated separately since it 'might be prejudiced by being united with a proposal to rest in the Govt. the whole patronage of Public Offices'.[61] By 1853, however, the question of civil service reform became linked with reforms in other fields where reformers were busy promoting the idea of competitive examinations.

The idea of testing merit by means of written examinations, although common in ancient China, was comparatively novel in England. It gained favour as part of the efforts made around the turn of the century to raise the intellectual and moral standards of the English universities from the slough of lethargy, corruption and nepotism in which they had wallowed in the eighteenth century. At Oxford many of the professors had ceased to lecture, and degrees were awarded in a most perfunctory manner. In 1770, for example, John Scott (later Lord Eldon) was asked by his oral examiners two questions to test his knowledge of Hebrew and History: 'What is the Hebrew for the place of a skull? ' and 'Who founded University College? ' His replies, 'Golgotha' and 'King Alfred', were sufficient to satisfy them.[62] Over the next 50 years procedures at both Oxford and Cambridge were tightened up, and it became commonplace to include written tests which duly developed into systematic schemes of university examinations. In 1852 a Royal

Commission on Oxford University reported that 'the Examinations have become the chief instrument not only for testing the proficiency of the students, but also for stimulating and directing the Studies of the place'.[63] Many in academic and literary circles were so impressed at the effects of the new procedures that they concluded that examinations were the best means of testing not merely academic skills but also general character. The classic statement of this point of view is to be found in an eloquent speech of Macaulay in the House of Commons in 1833 on the future government of India; Macaulay argued in favour of recruiting Indian civil servants by means of open examinations.

> It is said, I know, that examinations in Latin, in Greek and in mathematics are no tests of what men will prove to be in life. I am perfectly aware, that they are not infallible tests; but that they are tests I confidently maintain. Look at every walk of life — at this House — at the other House — at the Bar — at the Bench — at the Church — and see whether it be not true, that those who attain high distinction in the world are generally men who were distinguished in their academic career.

The subject-matter of the examinations did not have to be relevant to the future work of the recruits.

> Whatever be the languages — whatever be the sciences, which it is, in any age or country, the fashion to teach, those who become the greatest proficients in those languages, and those sciences will generally be the flower of the youth — the most acute — the most industrious — the most ambitious of honourable distinctions. If the Ptolemaic system were taught at Cambridge, instead of the Newtonian, the senior wrangler would nevertheless be in general a superior man to the wooden spoon. If, instead of learning Greek, we learned the Cherokee, the man who understood the Cherokee best, who made the most correct and melodious Cherokee verses — who comprehended most accurately the effect of the Cherokee particles — would generally be a superior man to him who was destitute of these accomplishments. If astrology were taught at our Universities, the young man who cast nativities best would generally turn out a superior man. If alchemy were taught, the young man who showed most activity in the pursuit of the philosopher's stone, would generally turn out a superior man.[64]

In the summer of 1853 the three movements for the reform of the government of India, of the universities and the British civil service converged in a remarkable manner. Before 1858 British control over India was exercised through the East India Company, which employed for its extensive administration a large body of elite administrators, recruited and trained in Britain. The Company's directors had early perceived the necessity for some kind of training for their young recruits before launching them on their varied and responsible careers. Early in the century a college had been set up at Haileybury which provided a two-year course in useful academic subjects and training in the administration of the Company. New recruits were chosen by nomination of the directors, but there had been strong moves at various times to open up the entry on the basis of academic competition. By 1853 the Company's charter came up for renewal, and it was clear that the British Government would soon have to assume a far more direct control over the government of India. The Whig ministers were worried at the prospect of the Company's patronage passing directly into the hands of the Crown and thus becoming the plaything of party and factional struggles, so a bill was introduced which opened up Hailey-bury College to entrance by competitive examination. Trevelyan's brother-in-law, Lord Macaulay, was the foremost protagonist of this idea and he undoubtedly influenced Trevelyan in favour of the competitive principle.

At this very moment the question of the reform of the University of Oxford also became important. The Royal Commission in 1852 had revealed a state of affairs which shocked many, including Gladstone, who represented the university in Parliament.[65] But moves for further reform were afoot, headed by Benjamin Jowett, a tutor of Balliol, who at the age of 36 already exercised a powerful influence within the university. Jowett's idea was to reform the university, while preserving its distinctive character. Fellowships should be opened up, more scholarships offered, and general academic teaching standards improved. In July 1853 Trevelyan, Northcote and Lingen arranged to visit Oxford to consult with Dr Vaughan, Headmaster of Harrow, and Jowett about their current investigation into the Committee of the Council for Education (one of the departmental investigations). During the visit conversation turned to the question of the Government's proposals for the reorganisation of the Indian Civil Service. Jowett argued strongly that Oxford graduates, as well as the leavers from Haileybury College, should have a chance of the Indian appointments. This new opening for graduates 'would provide us what we have always wanted, a stimulus reaching far beyond the Fellowship, for those not intending to take [Holy] Orders'. 'The inducement thus offered to us would open up a new field of knowledge: it would give us another root striking into a new soil of society.' Trevelyan was impressed by these arguments and over the next few months Jowett, Trevelyan, Gladstone, Vaughan and other leading educationists managed to persuade Macaulay and the Whig ministers to modify their proposals for the Indian reform, so that the universities secured a virtual monopoly in providing applicants.[66] Jowett and his allies in the educational world saw no reason why their proposals for the reform of the Indian Service could not equally well be applied to the British government departments and thus regenerate the universities, which, instead of being ivory towers, would in the future become pioneering centres for reform.

During the summer of 1853 Trevelyan – and perhaps still more Northcote – under the influence of Jowett and the other education reformers had come increasingly to see the virtues of *academic* competition. Even so the main initiative in this area seems to have come from Gladstone, by now Chancellor of the Exchequer. Trevelyan back in 1848 had clearly seen the advantage of some graduates entering the civil service, but he had not considered the question in relation to academic success alone, being keen to 'take young men who have some experience and success in life; for I conceive that no test of fitness for public service is equal to that of a person having succeeded in some line of life'.[67] Trevelyan evidently wrote the first draft of the Report in late October or early November;[68] but it is clear from the correspondence of Gladstone that the final version of the Report as circulated in January 1854 differed in important respects from the draft which Trevelyan had drawn up in November. For on 3 December 1853 Gladstone wrote to Northcote thanking him for 'your and Sir C. Trevelyan's able paper on the organisation of the permanent Civil Service'. From this letter it appears that Trevelyan and Northcote in their draft had not recommended a complete abolition of patronage and recruitment by open competition, but were prepared to retain a considerable power of patronage in the hands of the Treasury. 'You recommend in p. 12 that the clerkships in the higher offices should be disposed of by selection among the successful candidates and that this selection should rest with the First Lord of the Treasury, who would give due weight to the recommendation of his colleagues and also *of his Parliamentary supporters.*' In addition, the Treasury was to continue to appoint to its subordinate departments, like the Customs and the Inland Revenue, without any prior competition. Such a scheme, Gladstone objected, smacked of departmental privilege. 'It will I am afraid be viewed as a device for the aggrandisement of the functionaries of the Treasury at the expense, it may be said by the plunder of other departments.' Gladstone favoured an altogether bolder approach.

> You may be right in saying that too much ought not to be *tried* at once. It may be well to put into execution piecemeal a plan in which the first operations on a limited scale will so greatly help & guide what remains to be done. But let us get the principle sanctioned in its full breadth ... our first object is the establishment of a very broad principle: and I am convinced that this is one of the cases in which a large and bold design is more practicable, as well as more just, than one of narrower limits.[69]

By early January, Northcote and Trevelyan had modified their draft in accordance with Gladstone's suggestions, Trevelyan conceding after 'further consideration' that almost all clerks should be recruited on the basis of open competition.[70]

In its final form the Northcote/Trevelyan Report was a terse and somewhat polemical production only 20 pages long. The public service, which was indispensable to the efficient running of the country, had become a refuge for 'the unambitious, and the indolent or incapable'. The twin evils were absence of promotion by merit and poor recruitment procedures. The Report recommended selection of future civil servants by open competitive examination; the separation of mechanical from intellectual work wherever possible; promotion by merit; and more transfer of personnel between the departments of state. Candidates should compete in a literary examination, although this should be supplemented by 'careful previous enquiry into the age, health and moral fitness of the candidates'. The examinations should be centrally organised and administered by a new central board of examiners but would vary in substance according to the requirements of different departments and different grades of work. After entry there should be a probationary period, and full and systematic records should be kept of each clerk's service and performance over the years. With this information promotion could be based upon merit rather than favouritism.[71]

The Report was received very badly when it was published in February 1854. Macaulay spoke of 'open-mouthed' criticism at Brooks, the fashionable London club, and Northcote was soon complaining to his wife about the 'terrible storm in the Civil Service about our plan'.[72] Apart from *The Times* and *The Globe*, press reaction too was very cool. Politicians and administrators alike resented the tone of the Report, and considered its criticisms of the quality of civil servants to be exaggerated and unfair. They mostly rejected the view that academic skills would be the best test of administrative ability, and they considered the idea of a unified professional civil service to be totally unrealistic. The intensity of feeling on the subject encouraged the Government to seek the widest possible reaction to the scheme from administrators and leading public figures, and throughout 1854 comments were solicited, which were published the following year and in due course presented to Parliament. From these comments it appears that most senior civil servants were aware of the need for reforms in recruitment procedures, but shrank from the completely novel plan which Gladstone, Jowett, Northcote and Trevelyan were urging. They most favoured instead some 'intermediate plan', some scheme for examinations which would test the fitness of nominees.[73]

Gladstone's colleagues in the Government were equally unenthusiastic. The Home Secretary, Palmerston, did not conceal his dislike, and inspired a hostile series of articles in the *Morning Post*. Lord John Russell thought the scheme quite unsuitable for Britain — whatever the case for India — it would substitute 'talent & cramming for character', destroy all *esprit de corps*, and create a class of ambitious and discontented professional 'bureaucrats'. He was even more alarmed at the broader political implications of the end of patronage.

> In future the Board of Examiners will be in place of the Queen. Our institutions will become as harshly republican as possible, & the new spirit of the public offices will not be loyalty, but republicanism. I cannot say how seriously I feel all this, nor how averse I am to take part in such a change.

Not even a 22-page letter from Gladstone could shake his feelings on this point.[74] Even the Peelite reformer, Sir James Graham, First Lord of the Admiralty, had grave doubts; he disliked the idea of a central board of examiners and shared Russell's fear of the broader political consequences.[75] Nevertheless at a Cabinet meeting on 26 January the Cabinet decided to draw up a short Act of Parliament authorising the formation of an examination board, the operation of which would be governed by a subsequent Order in Council. Meanwhile Gladstone was to draw up a memorandum explaining the proposals to the Queen, who was known to have grave misgivings about 'opening up' the Service.[76] After the unfavourable reactions when the Report was published, however, matters took on a new complexion. The Report was not debated in the Commons, but received critical attention in the Lords in March, and by May even Gladstone was forced to admit that the Government saw no prospect of legislation in the current session.[77] Trevelyan continued to work hard at preparing successive drafts of an Order in Council, but these fell far short of the original plan. Although the Aberdeen Ministry approved a watered-down version of a plan for limited competition in January 1855, little concrete progress was made, and when the Coalition fell in February, and Gladstone was replaced as Chancellor of the Exchequer by Sir George Cornewall Lewis, an opponent of open competition, it must have seemed as if the idea had been relegated to the limbo of lost reforming causes.

Two factors, however, ensured that all was not lost. In the first place, the continued circulation of the Report among the heads of department months after its publication meant that the issues raised by Northcote and Trevelyan remained alive and subject to debate within the administration. Few heads of department claimed that all was perfect however much they might object to the Northcote/Trevelyan plan. Secondly, the public concern at the mismanagement and incompetence shown by the military and civil administration in the course of the Crimean War over the next year soon came to be expressed in terms of the demand for further instalments of reform – both political and administrative. There was an eruption of spontaneous public agitation, which the Radicals at Westminster turned to account. Early in 1855, a select committee was appointed, against the wishes of the Government, to 'inquire into the conduct of our army before Sebastopol, and into the conduct of those departments of the Government whose duty it has been to minister to the wants of the army'. Throughout the spring and summer, public meetings continued to be called, and by the 5 May the Administrative Reform Association had been founded. The leaders of this Association aimed at an apocalyptic programme of reform or political regeneration, which would once and for all sweep away 'aristocratic privilege' and open the doors of power to the dynamic and progressive middle classes. This movement, which appeared dangerous to Conservatives, and many parliamentary Radicals as well as to the Government, was championed at Westminster by several ambitious MPs, like Henry Layard and William Lindsay, and in the press by many literary figures, of whom Charles Dickens was the most influential.[78] Layard moved a resolution in Parliament which attributed the recent disasters to 'the manner in which merit and efficiency have been sacrificed, in public appointments, to party and family influences, and to a blind adherence to routine'. Thus the issue of the state of the civil service was brought to the fore of the political agitation against the Ministry. Palmerston and his ministers therefore became alarmed at the way in which public agitation threatened to be reflected in political difficulties at Westminster. They astutely delayed the debate on Layard's motion, and, as matters turned out, much of the heat was taken out of the situation by the Conservatives' decision to put forward a reasonable amendment, to which all but the most extreme reformers might subscribe.[79]

The Administrative Reform Association in no way favoured the Northcote/Trevelyan plan for competitive entry by academic examination. Academic qualifications, its leaders believed, were irrelevant, and the plan would perpetuate the aristocratic stranglehold of appointments. The decision by the Government to reform recruitment procedures for the civil service thus in no way represented a capitulation to popular agitation. On the contrary, the timing of the measure was dictated not so much by the force of outside pressure as by the logistics of the parliamentary situation.[80]

The Order in Council fell far short of the Northcote/Trevelyan proposals. It represented a triumph for the views of the new Chancellor, Cornewall Lewis, and all those permanent heads of departments who had voiced their preference for either a 'fixed test' for nominees, or for some form of limited competition. The political heads of departments were to retain control over all appointments in their departments. They could choose whether to fill vacancies by simple nomination, by limited competition, or by open competition. However, a Civil Service Commission of three members was established, from which all nominees who were appointed were to obtain a certificate of fitness. The Commissioners had the duty of ensuring that all those appointed were within the age limits prescribed by the department, were healthy and of suitable character, and possessed the 'requisite knowledge' to carry out their duties. In future, all examination and testing of candidates was to be undertaken, not by the departments which nominated candidates, but by the Commissioners; the content of any examination being agreed by consultation between the department concerned and the Commission. Northcote, who now sat in Parliament, made no secret of his disappointment. Any such system of partial competition would do nothing to rid the service of the 'great bane of patronage' and ensure proper promotion. 'Unless they altered the whole code and *morale* of the service, they would do nothing.'[81] Trevelyan, on the other hand, was far more sanguine. He was impressed by the 'intelligent, liberal interest' which the Commons had taken in the subject. 'It seemed to me as if that for which I had been labouring for so many years in obscurity and discouragement was all at once realised.' The debate, he assured Gladstone, seemed to have 'already established *our* principle'.[82] Trevelyan recognised that the time-span for reform would be long-term. He saw the appointment of the Civil Service Commission as a most encouraging sign, since here was an agency within the civil service itself which might press the case for reform. Here was created a 'new spring' inside the existing official machinery. 'Some time must elapse and some cases of experience as they arise must be gained before such a matter can be *thought out* to its just conclusion.'[83]

The subsequent history of the Civil Service Commission largely justifies Trevelyan's assessment. The Commission's influence was achieved first through its annual reports, which publicised the shortcomings of the existing system; secondly by its constant interaction with the departments who made use of its services; and thirdly by the support of the Treasury. Trevelyan noted with approval how, after only a year's work, the Commission 'without making any organic changes in our institutions' had nonetheless 'turned a stream through them which will purify & invigorate them all'.[84] Much of the Commission's initial success was due to the tactful manner in which it dealt with departments. Every attempt was made to match the examinations of nominees with the particular requirements — the Commissioners deeming it 'expedient to adopt not only in substance but with almost literal exactness, the suggestions furnished by the authorities of the several departments'.[85] But departments themselves soon discovered that it paid to let the Commission itself undertake the chore of devising the tests, and to be guided by the expertise of the Commissioners. The War Office, in 1855, for example, readily accepted their view that an examination in book-keeping was not a suitable, or necessary, subject for its work, and that some subject should be substituted 'which may be a better test of natural intelligence and educational attainment'.[86] The Treasury, for its part, greatly assisted the Commission by always supporting its recommendations, and by enforcing a requirement of a Superannuation Act of 1859, which laid down that all new recruits should have a certificate of fitness from the Commission in order to qualify for pension rights.

The Commissioners did not openly campaign for the universal introduction of open competition, but it was clear that this was the tenor of
their thinking. From the first they argued the merits of greater
uniformity and a 'greater simplicity of standard' of examinations and
procedures, and pointed out that candidates recruited under
competition possessed 'considerably higher attainments' than those
who came in under simple nomination.[87] Otherwise, the Commission's
annual reports spoke for themselves. The first in 1855, for example,
revealed that 309 out of 1,078 nominees had been rejected on the
grounds of gross deficiencies of knowledge, arithmetic and spelling.
This stark fact alone destroyed the argument that personal patronage
guaranteed the calibre of nominations for the public service.[88]
Successive reports constantly reminded MPs and others outside the civil
service interested in reform of the continued low standard of those
nominated; and this, allied with unease at the workings of patronage,
and the concern of departmental heads for efficiency, prompted the
Commons in 1860 to set up a committee of inquiry 'with a view to
ascertaining whether greater facility may not be afforded for the
admission of properly qualified persons'. This was done despite the
opposition of the Prime Minister and other ministers.[89] The
Committee, chaired by Lord Stanley and including Northcote, took
evidence from the Civil Service Commissioners and from several
permanent heads of departments. Most of the latter confessed that
many of their earlier fears of competition had been groundless, but
emphasised the degree to which genuine competition was more
apparent than real, owing to the large number of totally unqualified
nominees. The Committee, in a somewhat cautious and verbose report,
while desiring the 'ultimate success of the competitive method' were
'anxious to avoid such precipitancy in its adoption as might possibly
lead to a temporary reaction of public feeling'. It recommended some
form of preliminary test of fitness for nominees and, wherever possible,
the grouping of similar vacancies in a single competition. The exact
procedures should be 'left to the discretion of the Civil Service
Commissioners, and of the Executive'.[90] This was hardly calculated to
ensure any radical change. The Treasury and its subordinates adopted
the device of preliminary examinations in a minute of 1861, but this
example was only followed by a few other departments, and the Civil
Service Commission still complained in 1868 of the lack of any really
adequate competition.[91]

By the end of the 1860s therefore the procedures for the recruitment
of civil servants had been to some extent systematised, and minimal

tests of fitness established. But conditions still varied erratically from one department to another; in no sense was there any 'new system' of open competition for the Service as a whole. The establishment of the Civil Service Commission had, however, served an educative function and provided a useful catalyst for further instalments of piecemeal reform. The indications were that changes would evolve gradually as a result of the changing views within the bureaucracy. Any 'new system' of open competition or radical reform seemed to require some sort of politically-inspired initiative from above.

This initiative came in June 1870, when an Order in Council introduced a system of open competitive entry for most government departments — a move which had far more radical repercussions than the modest changes of 1855. It was, in fact, the very meagreness of the changes since 1855 that stimulated further reform. Of the 9,826 certificates of fitness issued between 1855 and 1868, no less than 7,033 (over 70 per cent) went to men appointed without any competition; 2,763 went to those appointed after *limited* competition; and a mere 28 to the victors in a completely open competition.[92] The system, far from being, as was popularly supposed, 'limited competition', was really 'limited nomination'. Neither Gladstone, by then Prime Minister, nor his Chancellor of the Exchequer, Robert Lowe, were prepared to tolerate this situation. Both were wholehearted devotees of the Northcote/Trevelyan ideals, and saw the abolition of patronage as part of a more general political regeneration.

In June 1869, under pressure from these two, the Liberal Cabinet discussed the idea of opening up the service more fully, and it was agreed to set up a Cabinet Committee of seven to consider competitive examinations, and the question of the division of labour. Despite the opposition of two of its members, Clarendon and John Bright, the Committee proposed to apply open competition to all superior and supplementary clerkships. But the Cabinet as a whole was unhappy. Bruce, the Home Secretary, and Fortescue, Chief Secretary for Ireland, joined Bright and Clarendon in opposing the plan.[93] By autumn an impasse seemed to have been reached, and Lowe wrote to Gladstone in despair, stressing that 'something must be decided', as it was impossible to 'keep matters in this discreditable state of abeyance'. He suggested some form of compromise, which would increase the number of candidates competing for each appointment, but which would fall short of a purely open system. Five or ten men might compete for each vacancy: or alternatively, some of the first-class posts could be thrown open, while the majority continued to be filled on a basis of limited

competition.[94] Gladstone, however, favoured an altogether more
ingenious plan. He suggested that posts should be thrown open
completely in those departments where the minister himself favoured
open competition. In other departments, the *status quo* might prevail.
In this way, not only would the immediate political difficulties be
surmounted, but also the path would be opened for the long-term
triumph of the Northcote/Trevelyan ideal. The obstructive heads of
department would not hold office for eternity, and in time, their
departments would come to conform with the prevailing practice. Lowe
quickly appreciated the advantages of this idea. He recognised that 'to
force the plan on unwilling Heads of Departments when there are so
many ready to adopt it would be a waste of time and temper'.[95] Open
competition could be applied straight away to all the major departments, with the exception of the Foreign Office, the Home Office, the
Colonial Office, and the Irish Office. The Cabinet agreed to this scheme
on 7 December 1869. Lowe and Lingen, the Permanent Secretary of
the Treasury, then drafted an Order in Council, which was approved by
the Cabinet in May 1870, and promulgated in June. Under this Order,
all clerks to be employed in the civil service were — with certain
exceptions — to be examined by the Civil Service Commissioners and
to receive a certificate of fitness before entering their employment. In
addition to this, a completely competitive system of examination was
to be introduced, except in departments where the Minister opposed
the idea. Examinations were to be held according to regulations framed
by the Civil Service Commission, and to be approved by the Treasury.
In the event, only the Home Office and the Foreign Office successfully
resisted the pressure from the Treasury to adopt open competition on
the grounds that the peculiarly confidential and sensitive character of
their work required them to take special precautions when recruiting
clerks.

In contrast to 1854-5, reform was introduced without attracting much
interest or excitement outside immediate governing circles. Debate in
Parliament, and in journals and the press, was muted and low key.[96]
There were no great scandals to debate, and no provocative investigation or report to spark off reactions. Above all, in the public mind, the
battle for the *principle* of competition as against patronage had already
been won. The Civil Service Commission was already in existence, and
its work and influence had already served to establish the ideas, both
of competition, and of some kind of central surveillance of recruitment.
Thus the change in 1870 appeared as the logical extension of a principle
already established.

The replacement of recruitment through patronage by open competition offers a good illustration of the different levels at which administrative reform took place at this period, and of the different perspectives from which it can be judged. For from one point of view the change can be seen as naturally evolving from within the administration. The implementation of the reform was gradual and determined as much by administrative convenience as by anything. Before 1854 the existing pattern of patronage was already changing and there was a widespread feeling in favour of tightening up methods of recruitment. Tests of fitness of one kind or another had already been introduced in some offices, although very erratically and sporadically. The reform of 1855, according to this view, can be interpreted, not as any radical change of system but as the working out of a trend already in being. The 1855 Order in Council setting up the Civil Service Commission greatly systematised and consolidated a tendency already in being. Between 1855 and 1870 this consolidation went further, and the Civil Service Commission itself did much to accustom administrators to the working of examinations and to the principle of the 'open door'. 'Nomination' evolved first into 'limited nomination' then 'limited competition' and finally 'open competition'. For even after 1870, reform did not necessarily imply any radical alteration in policy. There were still special provisions for recruiting by nomination if recruits possessing particular skills were needed. Even at the Treasury eight years elapsed before the first vacancy was filled by open competition in 1878, both Gladstone and Disraeli having filled earlier vacancies by transfer from other departments. Even then, as Henry Roseveare has pointed out, the result looks contrived, as the successful candidate was Stephen Spring-Rice, grandson of a former Whig Chancellor of the Exchequer who possessed an impeccable educational and social background[97] and it took many years before the first generation recruited by open competition reached the senior positions.

According to a second perspective the change from patronage to open competition appears in the light of a gradual adjustment to changing social, political and educational conditions outside the civil service. Patronage was in general declining throughout society as the electorate expanded and as social and geographical mobility increased. The very considerable increase in the scale of commercial undertakings – e.g. railway companies, insurance, banking and retailing – transformed the conditions and character of clerical work, especially at the junior levels. More impersonal and systematic recruitment procedures became appropriate, in these circumstances. Above all the considerable changes in educational organisation between 1850 and 1900 provided an indispensable background for the administrative changes we have been describing. Examinations came to be regarded no longer as sinister Chinese devices but as a natural means of testing the ability of young people. And opinion generally became far more sympathetic to Macaulay's view that success at examinations generally speaking betokened the presence not only of brains but of other qualities, such as determination, self-discipline, common sense and powers of discrimination.

A third perspective would emphasise far more the political dimensions of the question. Open competition was championed by self-conscious reformers whose horizons extended far beyond the civil service, to the worlds of education and Parliament. Their aims were the purging of corruption from society and the encouragement of a meritocracy at the expense of vested interests. The ideal of open competition had a great attraction for moderate liberal reformers. Gladstone in particular welcomed the scheme as much for its political as for its administrative advantages. The purification of the administration would consolidate the social fabric of the nation, the interests of the aristocracy and the 'great middle class' of professional people would become one. He saw the reform as taking its place in a broad historical development. Government by prerogative had given way to patronage, and bribery to influence: 'I cannot think that the process is to end here'. He cherished the hope that 'in pursuit not of visionary notions, but of a great practical and economic improvement, we may safely give yet one more new and striking sign of rational confidence in the intelligence and character of the people'.[98]

By the 1870s such liberal interpretations had come increasingly to dominate political thinking. The idea of competition was more and more valued as a means of abolishing corruption, and it was further helped by the concept of a 'politically neutral' civil service below the level of party politics. By the time of the Playfair and Ridley Commissions the climate had changed so much that criticism of open competition in administrative terms was scarcely possible because of the political advantages. The Playfair Commissioners actually suggested some modification in the 1870 scheme for administrative reasons. They suggested that the Civil Service Commissioners should draw up a list of successful grade I candidates which would amount to slightly more than the number of vacancies expected during the forthcoming six monthly period. This list would show the marks obtained by each candidate in different subjects. The heads of departments might then choose from the list those candidates which they considered to be most qualified, reserving the right to make 'any inquiries [they] might think fit concerning the character and antecedents of the candidates on the list'. The candidates for their part would then have the right of refusing an offer of a place in the hope of a better offer at a later time. 'There would thus be considerable freedom of selection on the part of the Office, and of refusal on the part of the candidate.' The lower division should continue to be recruited on a more straightforward competitive principle. The Commissioners realised that such a plan listed in some respects a 'partial return to the system of patronage', but believed the dangers not to be great, and outweighed by the administrative benefits of fitting the right man to the right job.[99] However this part of the Playfair recommendations proved unpopular and controversial, and Stafford Northcote was clearly uneasy at altering the system because of the political pressures involved.[100] Candidates who achieved the highest number of marks in the competition continued to have the pick of the vacant places.

By the turn of the century the Northcote/Trevelyan principle of selecting recruits for the various levels of work by means of competitive examinations based upon the educational standards of the time had won almost universal approval. The highest grade posts were to go to those who excelled in the highest academic skills. The principle however was by no means as 'democratic' as it seemed at first sight. The MacDonnell Commission on the eve of the First World War found that the syllabus for the higher examinations greatly favoured candidates from Oxford and Cambridge (particularly classical scholars). Men from the newer universities and those studying more modern subjects were gravely disadvantaged (a situation which has continued to give grounds for complaint up to the present day). Gladstone, Trevelyan and Macaulay's ambition to rejuvenate the aristocracy of breeding with an aristocracy of talent had succeeded beyond all expectations; indeed the principle of rewarding talent in academic fields had been approached in a manner more dogmatic than they had wished.

Radical and liberal critics in Parliament before 1914, however, were not greatly concerned with these points, and concentrated their attention on trying to get the remaining bastions of patronage in the foreign and diplomatic services 'opened up'. Yet at the very time that the principle of open competition seemed to have reached a triumphant vindication, there were clear indications that it was no longer offering a wholly satisfactory answer to the needs of the service. Between 1900 and 1914, in particular, the work of government was becoming more complicated. This led to an increase in the employment of 'professional' civil servants, lawyers, doctors, scientists, engineers and the like, who already possessed their own professional qualifications. There were signs that the direct recruitment of specialists might become more of a feature. In 1911 the Board of Trade, faced with the need to provide at short notice well-qualified staff to administer the new labour exchanges and the National Insurance Acts, had taken the unusual step of filling administrative posts directly by press advertisement, a procedure which aroused much disquiet in parliamentary circles. However, the battle for competition as opposed to patronage was by now clearly won. Radicals, however, were far less concerned about the real nature of that competition than they had been about securing its introduction.

The Consolidation of Civil Service Structure, 1870-1914

By 1870 the chief features of a 'constitutional bureaucracy' had emerged in Britain: ministerial responsibility and a permanent, anonymous civil service.[101] But until this date statesmen and leading administrators were reluctant to talk of the 'civil service'; they used instead such terms as the 'public offices' or the 'public establishments'. During the next 50 years, however, this was altered and, although the civil service remained far from an integrated structure, the change in terminology reflected a change in the perception of central administration in Britain. What was happening here was less the imposition of a particular reform than the working out of a complex pattern of administrative change, to which many interlocking factors contributed. Chief of these were the effects of the various attempts to introduce the division of labour and common open competition; the growth of staff associations; and the growing complexity of senior administrative work.

The Northcote/Trevelyan Report offered a remarkably far-sighted vision of the future civil service, but one which was greatly at odds with contemporary reality. It envisaged a high degree of centralised direction not merely in matters of recruitment and the division of labour but in such areas as promotion and office organisation; it was full of such original ideas as the creation of a pool of temporary clerical labour. The excessively departmental organisation of the civil service, the Report maintained, served 'to cramp the energies of the whole body, to encourage the growth of narrow views and departmental prejudices, to limit the acquisition of experience, and to repress and almost to extinguish the spirit of emulation and competition'.[102]

All these ideas were far too radical to secure much support in 1854, and one of the chief criticisms which senior administrators levied at the Report was its indiscriminate treatment of the diverse government offices.[103] However, over the next two decades the slow movement in favour of a more systematic division of labour and of competitive recruitment ensured that some measure of uniformity in organisation spread throughout the service. The Order in Council of 1870 marked a significant step in this direction, giving the Treasury additional responsibilities. The effect of systematising examination procedures and grades was further to accentuate anomalies across the departmental structures. The Playfair Commission in 1875, when reviewing the operation of the 1870 reforms, drew attention to the anomalous situation which could result from common examinations.

> Two Clerks, who have passed the same examination, may pass into different offices. The more fortunate Clerk may find himself in an office of high pay and quick promotion, while the other may be in one where pay is low and promotion is in stagnation. At the end of a given number of years, without superior merit on one side or demerit on the other, the two Clerks, who started with equal claims, would find that whilst one had advanced with rapid strides the progress of the other had been stopped.[104]

When discontent over salaries was added to confusion over grading and prospects, the result was a growth of combinations or associations of staff within the civil service. Commodity prices fluctuated considerably in the 1870s and this caused considerable discontent which was directed as much against the anomalies as the level of pay. Rates varied erratically from one department to another, and different men performing identical work often received widely different salaries. The Playfair Commission attempted to meet the situation by recommending a more systematic division of labour and suggested that the Treasury should assist the different departments in introducing the change; a 'small Committee or Council composed of Heads of Departments' might be created to assist the Treasury 'and thus bring the experience of one office to bear on another, and assist in introducing such an amount of uniformity as is practicable and desirable'.[105] The recommendations of the Playfair Commission, as we have seen, were only very partially implemented, and this further exacerbated the undercurrent of discontent among copyists and junior clerks in many departments. At a time when the parliamentary franchise was very limited and when civil servants often formed an important part of the electorate — particularly in ports or naval dockland areas — the new associations found parliamentary lobbying and canvassing to be a most effective means of promoting their causes. Many of the older heads of departments viewed these developments with the gravest concern, but were often astute enough to see that it was a direct consequence of the more systematic grading and recruitment procedures. As Sir Thomas Farrer, former Permanent Secretary of the Board of Trade, gloomily reflected in 1887 when the departments selected their own men, the clerks 'did not act together in the same way; they were not fused. Now they form one body, who can act altogether, and who bring pressure to bear upon members of Parliament and act as a sort of trades union.'[106] Sir Reginald Welby, Permanent Secretary of the Treasury, agreed that the growth of 'trade union' activity was a direct consequence of the development of common grading. There were 'some 3,000 Lower Division clerks belonging to one body under the same terms of association and forming an association. These men act practically like one man, and bring all their political influence to bear ... We have seen some very formidable meetings, from a Government point of view, held in consequence.' This he believed constituted a 'very great danger'.[107] What was happening was a cumulative spiral of development: grading or classification of clerks fostered the growth of organised associations which in turn pressed for more uniformity in pay and conditions.

The 30 years after the Playfair Commission saw a gradual consolidation of civil service structure without the process being in any way centrally directed or political initiatives taken. In contrast to the 1920s there was neither the institutional apparatus nor the political will to impose any policy on this question. Nor was a great deal of interest taken in the administration of central government among political commentators or informed public opinion. In the absence of any great external stimuli important mechanisms for reform were the investigations of royal commissions and the operation of Treasury *ad hoc* investigatory bodies. Between 1875 and 1914 the civil service was investigated by two royal commissions: the Ridley Commission of 1886-8 and the MacDonnell Commission of 1912-14. In contrast to the earlier Trevelyan and Playfair investigations these were large, rather cumbersome, bodies representative of the various interests involved in the question. Neither body was in any sense imaginative or original in its approach. Both stuck closely to their rather narrow terms of reference, and neither was very concerned to relate the organisation and structures of administration to the changing functions of government at the time. Both inquiries saw their role, to use the somewhat pompous words of MacDonnell, less as

> attempting a reconstruction of the Service upon a new and different plan, but rather in promoting the conservation and the fuller application of those principles of organisation which, laid down by the earliest reformers, accepted and developed by their successors, have been justified by the test of experience.[108]

Nevertheless the somewhat negative and unexciting character of the Commissions' work itself played a role in consolidating civil service structure.

The Ridley Commission, chaired by a future Conservative Home Secretary, Sir Matthew White Ridley, was appointed in 1886 largely in response to parliamentary pressure in favour of economy and in particular to the zealous activities of that *enfant terrible* of the Conservative Party, Lord Randolph Churchill, who, as Chancellor of the Exchequer, was at this time at the height of his meteoric political career. He had what almost amounted to an obsession about what he considered to be the waste and inefficiency of the two greatest spending departments, the Admiralty and the War Office.[109] The Commission in origin therefore was conceived as a political weapon in the complex game of power politics in which Randolph Churchill was engaged with his Conservative colleagues. However, by 1887 Churchill had fallen from office and had found a far more potent instrument to pursue his vendetta, a parliamentary select committee, chaired by himself, which investigated the War Office and the Admiralty. Some of the findings of this body were sensational. One branch of the War Office, for example, was estimated to cost £5,000 in supervising an expenditure of £250 *per annum*.[110] All this rather vitiated the immediate purpose of the Ridley Commission which got itself bogged down in a fruitless and lengthy attempt to survey various departments in depth before clarifying its views on the civil service as a whole or the workings of Treasury control.

The Ridley Commission endorsed the principle of a division of labour common to the service as a whole, but was clear that the interests of economy should prevail over systematic organisation for its own sake. The commissioners in general favoured the idea of transfers between departments, but in a somewhat defeatist manner also recognised the 'difficulties' which these entailed given that 'within certain limits efficiency and economy alike demand the separate organisation of each department'. But they made few concrete suggestions trusting that 'the difficulty which at present exists in carrying out such transfers will be greatly lessened when the regulations are made more uniform through- out the Service, and the prospects and advantages of the various offices are more generally equalised'. In order to strengthen overall control they recommended the appointment of a 'Permanent Consultative Committee' of four comprising representatives of the Treasury, the Civil Service Commission and the great Revenue departments. This body should consider all establishment questions and in time 'would be of great value in suggesting reforms, in facilitating transfers, and, not least, in bringing about harmonious action between the Treasury and the other departments'.[111]

The Ridley Commission's proposals did not lead to any sudden changes. Orders in Council in 1890 broadly speaking adopted the Commission's recommendations concerning the Lower Division which now became known as the Second Division. Hours of work and salary scales were standardised and general rules laid down for holidays and sick leave.[112] But this was only after considerable agitation among the clerks which spilled over into the press and parliament. *The Times*, for example, published no less than 15 letters and two leading articles on the subject during the first two months of 1890. The Treasury was at the centre of the storm and according to *The Times* the criticism marked the 'opening of the sluices of bitterness long dammed up and gradually accumulating'.[113] Despite the new scales of 1890 and some removal of anomalies the Second Division clerks continued restive, complaining particularly strongly against the lack of promotion to the higher divisions. By 1894 a powerful lobby of 65 MPs were prepared to table motions in the House of Commons on the question.[114] As far as the Higher Division was concerned far less was achieved. No Order in Council applied to this division and it continued to consist less of a unified class or grade than a medley of officers who had come into the service by various means: patronage, Lowe's open competition, and the Playfair scheme. The hours of labour remained unstandardised until 1910 and no attempt was made to introduce standard scales of pay. Clerks in the Foreign Office, the Home Office, the Colonial Office and the India Office — those ancient aristocrats of Whitehall — continued to enjoy salaries far above those of their less fortunate colleagues in the Local Government Board, the Board of Trade and the War Office.[115] The result of this inaction was that the upper echelons of the service remained essentially fragmented until the reorganisation of 1919. One reason was undoubtedly the reluctance of certain senior officials of the Treasury during this period to undertake such innovations.[116]

The MacDonnell Commission was appointed in 1912, in response partly to political pressures from MPs anxious to destroy the last bastions of patronage and partly to continued discontent among the rank and file of civil servants. Its appointment really marked the establishment of a convention that the civil service should be investigated by an outside body once every generation. It spent a great deal of time considering the question of recruitment and grading as well as topical issues such as the employment of women and the use of 'mechanical aids' in government offices. It paid particular attention to the relationship of the civil service to the educational system of the country. It was undoubtedly the most thorough and systematic inquiry into the civil service before 1914, even though it lacked imagination and incisiveness. As it reported on the eve of the First World War its actual recommendations for an overhaul of the recruitment system and a thorough reorganisation of the grades of the service were put into cold storage and soon overtaken by events, although they formed the basis of subsequent proposals.[117]

The Ridley and MacDonnell Commissions played an important, if unspectacular, part in consolidating the pattern of administrative change set in motion in the reforms of the early 1870s. In their concern to impose a measure of order and uniformity they encouraged the idea, if not always the reality, of a single unified 'civil service'. Their weakness, as in the case of Playfair, lay in the sphere of implementation. Both the Playfair scheme and the Ridley proposals for grading of labour suffered badly from half-hearted application. The Playfair, Ridley and MacDonnell Reports all recognised the need for some kind of strengthening of central administrative direction, but the various suggestions for setting up co-ordinating committees representative of the departmental heads came to nothing, leading Treasury officials being among the chief opponents.[118] The large-scale investigations after 1870 were perhaps more significant in what they averted than in what they achieved. They prevented undue departmentalism. They discouraged the growth of specialist methods of recruitment or wildly idiosynchratic methods of administration. They provided a safety valve for the airing of grievances outside the arena of party controversy and prevented party considerations imposing themselves into administration. None of these were inevitable developments.

However, as the Ridley Commissioners found to their cost, formal rather grandiose bodies were quite unsuited to overhauling particular departments. Here the most fruitful form of procedures was the very small informal *ad hoc* committee of inquiry comprising representatives of the Treasury and the department concerned. It was from such informal *ad hoc* bodies that the Northcote/Trevelyan investigation had sprung and the use of these periodic reviews has been termed 'the Treasury's outstanding administrative innovation' of the period.[119] Large departments, like the Board of Trade and the Local Government Board, were regularly overhauled after these investigations. Here was a very flexible way of manipulating and adjusting the needs of departments. Nevertheless the general pattern of departmental reorganisation was often undertaken at random and not always for the purest motives: one witness before the Ridley Commission went so far as to declare that a desire for promotion was really at the bottom of most of the departmental reorganisations he had known.[120] The essentially erratic nature of late Victorian administrative control prevented any systematic review of government work.

Yet during the 30 years before 1914 very substantial changes took place in both the tempo of work and the style of administration within government departments. These changes reflected a shift in the nature of government itself, as departments had to come to terms with increasingly complex problems. Certainly by the standards of post-1914, to say nothing of post-1945, the amount of work and the degree of organisation was modest. But the overall qualitative change and effect of a transformation from a situation of 'routine administration' to 'policy administration' was immense. It marked the transformation from what has been termed the 'regulatory state' to one that was increasingly 'interventionist'.[121] Such issues as the development of technical education, the introduction of national insurance schemes, the promotion of health and safety and the administration of vast new colonial areas posed problems of a highly technical and complex nature. The long-run implications for the management and organisation of government departments were far-reaching. Henceforth a department was destined to resemble less 'a small family party' than a 'large insurance office, or, in times of stress, a central railway station on a bank holiday'.[122] It was important that the department as a whole worked smoothly as a unit. Gone were the days when titans such as Palmerston, Gladstone, and Salisbury could lord it over their departments supervising every detail of business.[123] Henceforth the Minister, like the rest, was to have a carefully orchestrated part to play, with opportunity for only occasional solo flourishes. Sir William Harcourt, Liberal Chancellor of the Exchequer in the early 1890s, was an early victim of the new pattern when he would on occasions furtively enter

> our room when untenanted, select a file at random and carry it off
> as a dog conveys a bone. He might then, if he had nothing else to do
> (or indeed equally if he had other work which ought to be done),
> with his own hand write and dispatch privily a letter which undid
> weeks of patient spade work by his prudent assistants.[124]

Henceforth such shortcircuiting was to be used sparingly, for carefully calculated ends.

This change in tempo in government is best illustrated by a few examples. W.A. Baillie Hamilton, for example, when joining the Colonial Office in the 1860s found himself 'in a sleepy and humdrum office, where important work was no doubt done, but simply because it had got to be done; where there seemed no enthusiasm, no *esprit de corps*, and no encouragement for individual exertion'.[125] The tone of the office began to change in the 1880s but was completely transformed under the regime of Joseph Chamberlain, 1895-1903. From this point the work became more demanding, the officials more lively, and its business the reverse of routine.[126] The Board of Education was similarly transformed, although the initiative here came from its permanent officials. When Robert Morant became its permanent head he 'found the office dominated by the "dry administrative aspect of the Education Acts" '. After the 1902 Act the whole picture was transformed. The old geographically-centred structure of the department was replaced by sectors dealing with different types of education, and regular conferences were held at which the inspectors in the field were encouraged to bring forward ideas for improvements.[127] The Local Government Board on the other hand, although increasingly burdened with new responsibilities and deluged with work, became something of a Cinderella, characterised by a demoralised staff, poor political leadership and procedural conservatism. Policy initiatives on social questions rarely emerged from its labyrinthine depths. But even here after 1910 a turnover of personnel in the senior secretariat stimulated positive thinking on questions of public health.[128]

The Foreign Office, by contrast, remained until the early years of the twentieth century 'a small self-contained establishment ... a stronghold of the aristocracy and everything was done to preserve its class character and clannish structure'.[129] Lord Salisbury, who dominated it during much of the 1890s, held particularly conservative views about the duties of officials.[130] However, what one survivor recalled as the 'robot era' soon vanished in the early years of the century. The growing complexity of foreign affairs led necessarily to devolution of authority, and this coincided with the advent of a group of ambitious and intelligent clerks who were keen to play a positive role in policy-formation.[131] It was largely due to their influence that the office developed its strong anti-German bias after 1900.[132] Quite as conservative was the Home Office. It was one of the last to admit clerks by open competitive examination, and the last to adopt new devices such as typewriters or carbon copies. As late as the 1880s 'almost every paper had been handled personally by the Permanent Secretary and very often by the Home Secretary himself'.[133] But already there were signs of change. Sir William Harcourt, Home Secretary in 1883, declared that the work-load of the Office had increased fivefold in 20 years.[134] What remained of the old leisurely routine was fast disappearing by 1914. By that date the Office had become responsible for workmen's compensation, the Shop Acts, probationary care of children, aeronautical regulations and reduction of liquor licences in addition to its traditional responsibilities. But perhaps the most spectacular developments occurred in some of the subordinate financial departments. In the late 1880s Sir Algernon West and Sir Charles DuCane, permanent heads of the Inland Revenue and the Customs, considered that their departments, being largely concerned with routine administration, had no need of graduate Higher Division clerks recruited by open competition.[135] Thirty years later their successors were singing a quite different tune.[136]

These changes in the tempo and character of government work necessarily had far-reaching implications for the organisation and management of government. Yet in retrospect perhaps the most surprising feature of these years was the persistent failure of those in office to survey systematically either the tasks which government was undertaking or the machinery by which they might best be carried out. The consolidation of the period had little effect upon the overall functioning of government. The relationship of departments to each other was particularly confusing. The Board of Agriculture and Fisheries illustrates very well the deficiencies of British central government on the eve of the First World War. There was in fact no central 'Board' but, in the words of S. Oliver, its Permanent Secretary, a 'fragmentary and diffuse organisation ... gravitating like the shreds of a shattered planet, around the personality of the President and his two satellites, the Permanent Secretary and the Parliamentary Secretary'. The department was in effect 'an aggregation of the ghosts of extinct bodies of commissioners and sections detached at intervals from other public Departments discharging services more or less subsidiary to Agriculture (with Fisheries crammed into the bundle), but not exhibiting any central intention or understanding in relation to the National Art of Agriculture'. Its work was badly organised, its functions were unduly limited in scope, the calibre of its staff was weak and it lacked any proper buildings.[137]

Between 1870 and 1914 there was no longer the same lively debate about the nature of 'government' as opposed to 'politics' that had characterised the middle years of the century. The 'constitutional' issues of the later period concerned issues such as Irish Home Rule, the role of the House of Lords, the nature of the electoral system and the possibility of referendums. Other key political issues centred around the social problems, where attention was concentrated on the possibility of legislative reform through Parliament. By the turn of the century the 'constitutional' position of the administration by contrast appeared reassuringly stable. Most of the important government business was conducted in departments of state headed by ministers responsible to Parliament. Autonomous commissions or boards, previously so powerful, now played a strictly subordinate role.[138] The power of the Crown had sharply diminished, and monarchs were no longer able to use patronage as a means of advancing their political influence.

Overall this meant that administrative reform no longer tended to be seen as an aspect of broader political or social reform, in the way that Trevelyan and Gladstone had seen their proposals as helping to rejuvenate the educational and political systems of their day. The administration of central government thus came to be seen as in some sense 'neutral' in respect of the key political issues, an attitude which tied in well with the increasing public self-effacement of the permanent heads of departments after 1850. Nevertheless after 1900 new schools of thought were making themselves heard, critics who believed that administrative factors had a potentially powerful role to play in furthering economic and social progress. The Fabian thinkers constituted the most systematic of these schools of thought. They believed that only when government was ordered and conducted in a rational and efficient manner would key issues emerge and future progress be assured. As it was, in George Bernard Shaw's words, a huge bureaucracy had 'grown up almost unnoticed, haphazard, without system, overlapping in all directions, every department performing functions proper to other departments and leaving to other departments functions proper to itself'.[139] Before 1914 such thinkers had only an indirect influence upon governments, but when the emergencies and pressures of the First World War strained to bursting point the structure of central administration, an opportunity arose for a general reappraisal of the system of government.

Notes

1. Graham Wallas, *Human Nature in Politics* (Constable, London, 1948 edn.), p. 268.
2. *54th Report of Civil Service Commissioners, 1909*, App. I, p. 2, *P.P.*, 1910 [Cd. 5277] , XIII; *55th Report, 1910*, App. I, p. 2, *P.P.*, 1911 [Cd. 5751] , XIII.
3. Minutes of MacDonnell Commission, 1 May 1913, PRO/T100/1.
4. K.B. Smellie, *A Hundred Years of English Government*, 2nd edn. (Duckworth, London, 1950), p. 56.
5. Gillian Sutherland (ed.), *Studies in the Growth of Nineteenth-Century Government* (Routledge and Kegan Paul, London, 1972), p. 6.
6. H.R.G. Greaves, *The Civil Service in the Changing State* (Harrap, London, 1947), pp. 8-9.
7. Sir Algernon West, *Contemporary Portraits: Men of my Day in Public Life* (Unwin, London, 1920); Sir Robert Anderson, 'The Lighter Side of My Official Life', *Blackwoods Magazine*, vol. 186 (Nov. 1909), pp. 608-9; Sir E. Hertslet, *Recollections of the Old Foreign Office* (Murray, London, 1901), p. 25; H. Preston-Thomas, *Work and Play of a Government Inspector* (Blackwood, Edinburgh & London, 1909), p. 11; Maurice Wright, *Treasury Control of the Civil Service, 1854-1874* (OUP, London, 1969), pp. xxxi-xxxv.
8. Quoted D.M. Young, *The Colonial Office in the Early Nineteenth Century* (Longmans, London, 1961), p. 27.
9. Sir George Kekewich, *The Education Department and After* (Constable, London, 1920), p. 16.
10. Anthony Trollope, *The Three Clerks* (World's Classics edn., London, 1959), pp. 12-15; Anthony Trollope, *An Autobiography* (2 vols., Blackwood, Edinburgh & London, 1883), vol. 1, p. 47.
11. Trevelyan to Delane, 6 February 1854, Gladstone Papers, Add. MSS. 44333, fo.138.
12. Major Graham, pp. 212-13, *Select Committee on Civil Service Appointments, P.P.*, 1860, IX.
13. *Papers on the Re-organisation of the Civil Service*, pp. 71-73, *P.P.*, 1854-5 (1870), XX (hereafter cited as *Papers on Re-organisation*); cf. Henry Parris, *Constitutional Bureaucracy, The Development of British Central Administration since the Eighteenth Century* (Allen & Unwin, London, 1969), ch. V, pp. 134-59.
14. S.E. Finer, *The Life and Times of Sir Edwin Chadwick* (Methuen, London, 1952); R.W. Prouty, *The Transformation of the Board of Trade, 1830-1855* (Heinemann; London, 1957).
15. O. MacDonagh, *Early Victorian Government* (Weidenfeld and Nicolson, London, 1977), pp. 200-1.
16. Young, *Colonial Office*, p. 253.
17. Edward Hughes, 'Civil Service Reform 1853-55', *Public Administration*, vol. 32 (1954), pp. 24-5; Jenifer Hart, 'The Genesis of the Northcote-Trevelyan Report', in Sutherland, *Studies in Growth*, pp. 68-78.

18. *Papers on Re-organisation*, pp. 273-4.
19. Quoted Jenifer Hart, 'Sir Charles Trevelyan at the Treasury', *English Historical Review*, vol. 75 (1960), p. 106.
20. *Select Committee on Miscellaneous Expenditure, 1848*, evidence qs. 1090-1399, 1561-1790, *P.P.*, 1847-8 (543), XVIII.
21. Trevelyan to Russell, 13 August 1849, Trevelyan Papers, CET 18.
22. Trevelyan to Lewis, 18 September 1848, Trevelyan Papers, CET 52.
23. Trevelyan to Gladstone, 15 September 1853, Trevelyan Papers, CET 18.
24. Trevelyan to Lewis, 3, 18 and 20 September 1848, Trevelyan Papers, CET 52; Ray Jones, *The Nineteenth Century Foreign Office, An Administrative History* (Weidenfeld & Nicolson, London, 1971), pp. 23-40.
25. Hart, 'Trevelyan at the Treasury', p. 105; E. Hughes, 'Sir Charles Trevelyan and Civil Service Reform, 1853-55', *English Historical Review*, vol. 64 (1949), p. 59; H. Roseveare, *The Treasury: The Evolution of a British Institution* (Allen Lane, London, 1969), pp. 166-8.
26. Northcote to Gladstone, 18 December 1852, Gladstone Papers, Add. MSS. 44216, fo. 192.
27. *Reports of the Committees of Inquiry into Public Offices and Papers connected therewith*, pp. 129-59, *P.P.*, 1854 [1715], XXVII.
28. Ibid., p. 73.
29. Ibid., p. 141.
30. *Copy of Treasury Minute appointing Committee for Inquiring into the Public Establishments*, 12 April 1853, *P.P.*, 1854-5 (439), XXX, p. 375.
31. Paper by Sir C.E. Trevelyan, 28 February 1854, *Papers on Re-organisation*, pp. 425-6.
32. *Report on the Organisation of the Permanent Civil Service*, 23 November 1853, p. 5, *P.P.*, 1854 [1713], XXVII (hereafter cited as *Northcote/Trevelyan Report*).
33. Ibid., p. 3.
34. *Papers on Re-organisation*, pp. 299, 351, 109-12.
35. A.P. Donajgrodzki, 'New Roles for Old: The Northcote/Trevelyan Report and the Clerks of the Home Office 1822-48', in Sutherland, *Studies in Growth*, pp. 91 and 97.
36. For a full account see Wright, *Treasury Control*, pp. 116-37.
37. *Report to the Treasury to consider the Employment of Supplemental and Temporary Clerks in the Civil Service*, 1 June 1860, *P.P.*, 1865 (294), IX.
38. Wright, *Treasury Control*, pp. 137-43.
39. Northcote to Playfair, 31 March 1874, Lyon Playfair Papers 503.
40. A.C. Taylor, 'The Civil Service', *Fraser's Magazine*, vol. 11 (new series) (1875), p. 722.
41. *Reports of the Civil Service Inquiry Commission* (Playfair Reports), *P.P.*, 1875 [C. 1113, C. 1226], XXIII.
42. Memorandum by Sir R.G. Hamilton (former secretary to Playfair Commission), p. 422, *P.P.*, 1887 [C. 5226], XIX.
43. Playfair *Evidence*, q. 339. *P.P.*, 1875 [C. 1113], XXIII.
44. *Evidence of the Select Committee on Civil Service Writers*, pp. 36-39 (Accountant General of the Navy), *P.P.*, 1873 (370), XI.
45. E.g. The War Office, the Local Government Board, Playfair, Evidence, qs. 91, 5646 *P.P.*, 1875 [C. 1113], XXIII.
46. Playfair *Evidence* q. 3134, *P.P.*, 1875 [C. 1113], XXIII.
47. Ibid., qs. 4238-77.
48. Playfair *First Report*, *P.P.*, 1875 [C. 1113], XXIII.
49. Northcote to Playfair, 8 March 1875, Playfair Papers 946; *Replies from Public Departments ... Respecting the First Report of the Civil Service Commission, 1874*, P.R.O./T1/7503/18283/1875.

50. Ridley *Evidence*, pp. 571-2, *P.P.*, 1888 [C. 5545], XXVII.

51. Ibid., qs. 10438-51.

52. *Report to Consider Civil Service Copyists*, 23 December 1886, *P.P.*, 1887 (82), LXVI.

53. Ridley *Second Report, P.P.*, 1888 [C. 5545], XXVII.

54. Ibid., p. x; MacDonnell, *Fourth Report*, p. 28, *P.P.*, 1914 [Cd. 7339], XVI

55. Ibid., p. 30.

56. The question is fully discussed in Parris, *Constitutional Bureaucracy*, pp. 50-79.

57. Charles Trevelyan, *Memorandum on the Examination and Probation of Candidates for Public Employment. Papers on Emoluments in the Public Service* (London, 1856), p. 89.

58. Parris, *Constitutional Bureaucracy*, p. 71.

59. Ibid., p. 73.

60. Treasury Minute by Trevelyan, 13 February 1849, PRO/T 64/403.

61. Trevelyan to Russell, 7 August 1849, Trevelyan Papers, CET 18.

62. H. Twiss, *The Public and Private life of Lord Chancellor Eldon* (3 vols., Murray, London, 1844), vol. 2, p. 57.

63. *Report of Commissioners Appointed to Inquire the State, Discipline Studies and Revenues of the University and Colleges of Oxford, P.P.*, 1852 [1482], XXII.

64. 19 H.L. Deb., 3s., cols. 525-26 (10 July, 1833).

65. J. Morley, *Life of William Ewart Gladstone* (3 vols., Macmillan, London, 1903), vol. 1, pp. 498-509.

66. See R.J. Moore, 'The Abolition of Patronage in the Indian Civil Service and the Closing of Haileybury College', *Historical Journal*, vol. 7 (1964), p. 550.

67. Trevelyan, p. 177, *Select Committee on Miscellaneous Expenditure, P.P.*, 1847-48, XVIII.

68. Trevelyan to R.M. Bromley, 18 November 1853, Trevelyan Papers, CET 18.

69. Gladstone to Northcote, 3 December 1853, Iddesleigh Papers, Add. MSS. 50014, fos., 76-8, quoted Hart, 'Genesis of the Northcote-Trevelyan Report', pp. 74-7.

70. Trevelyan to Rev. E.O. Trevelyan, 10 January 1854, Trevelyan to Northcote 28 January 1854, Trevelyan Papers, CET 18.

71. *Northcote/Trevelyan Report*, pp. 3-23.

72. G.O. Trevelyan, *Life and Letters of Lord Macaulay* (2 vols., Longmans, London, 1876), vol. 2, p. 375.

73. *Papers on Re-organisation*.

74. Letters between Russell and Gladstone, 20 January 1854, Gladstone Papers, Add. MSS. 44291, fos., 91-119.

75. Sir James Graham to Gladstone, 4 and 11 January 1854, ibid., 44163, fos., 111-14, 117-19.

76. Trevelyan to Gladstone, 20 and 27 January 1854, ibid., 44333, fos., 103, 121.

77. *Memorandum on Civil Service Admissions Prepared for Her Majesty*, ibid., 44743, fo. 132.

78. 131 H.C. Deb., 3s., cols. 640-64 (13 March 1854); 132, H.C. Deb., 3s., cols. 1305-67 (5 May 1854).

79. Olive Anderson, 'The Janus Face of Mid-Nineteenth Century Radicalism: The Administrative Reform Association of 1855', *Victorian Studies*, vol. 8 (1965), p. 235.

80. Olive Anderson, 'The Administrative Reform Association, 1855-57', in Patricia Hollis (ed.), *Pressure from Without in Early Victorian England* (Arnold, London, 1974), pp. 266-7. For the House of Commons debate see 138 H.C. Deb., 3s., cols. 2040-2133, 2154-2225, (15 and 18 June 1855).

81. Ibid., col. 2090.

82. Trevelyan to Gladstone, 19 June and 14 July 1855, Gladstone Papers, Add. MSS. 44334, fos. 206-8.

83. Trevelyan to Romilly, 27 December 1855, Trevelyan Papers, CET 18.

84. Trevelyan to Lowe, 19 December 1855, Trevelyan Papers, CET 18.

85. *First Report of C.S.C.*, p. xxvii, *P.P.*, 1856 [C. 2038], XXII.

86. Ibid., pp. 136-8.

87. Ibid., p. xxvii.

88. Ibid., p. xvi.

89. 156 H.C. Deb., 3s., cols. 1193-1203 (16 February 1860).

90. *Select Committee on Civil Service Appointments, P.P.*, 1860 (440), IX.

91. *Thirteenth Report of C.S.C.*, p. 8, *P.P.*, 1867-68, XXII.

92. Wright, *Treasury Control*, pp. 74-5.

93. Ibid., p. 80.

94. Lowe to Gladstone, 10 November 1869, Gladstone Papers, Add. MSS. 44301, fos. 104-05.

95. Lowe to Gladstone, 22 November 1869, ibid., fos. 106-07.

96. Wright, *Treasury Control*, pp. 76-80.

97. Roseveare, *Treasury*, pp. 177-8.

98. Gladstone to Lord Russell, 20 January 1854, Gladstone Papers, Add. MSS. 44291, fos. 93-103, quoted in J.B. Conacher, *The Aberdeen Coalition* (CUP, Cambridge, 1968), p. 322; Trevelyan to Delane, 2 February 1854, Gladstone Papers, Add. MSS. 44333, fo. 138.

99. Playfair, *First Report*, pp. 10-13, *P.P.*, 1875 [C. 1113], XXIII.

100. Northcote to Playfair, 27 January 1875, quoted in Playfair Report; also Northcote to Playfair, 2 March 1875, Playfair Papers/946.

101. Parris, *Constitutional Bureaucracy, passim*.

102. *Report on the Organization of the Permanent Civil Service*, p. 8, *P.P.*, 1854, XXVII.

103. *Papers on Re-organization*.

104. Playfair, *First Report*, pp. 8-9, *P.P.*, 1875 [C. 1113], XXIII.

105. Ibid., pp. 22-3.

106. Ridley, *Evidence*, q. 19990, *P.P.*, 1888 [C. 5545], XXVII.

107. Ibid., qs. 10742-48.

108. MacDonnell, *Fourth Report*, p. 4, *P.P.*, 1914 [Cd. 7339], XVI.

109. Sir Winston Churchill, *Lord Randolph Churchill* (2 vols., Macmillan, London, 1906), vol. 2, pp. 184-7, 236-9; Treasury Minute relative to the appointment of a Royal Commission of Inquiry into the Establishments of the Different Offices of State, September 1886, PRO/CSS 2/3/173.

110. Churchill, *Randolph Churchill*, vol. 2, p. 320.

111. Ridley, *Second Report*, p. xii, *P.P.*, 1888 [C. 5545], XXVII.

112. Orders in Council of 21 March and 15 August 1890; *Return for Copy of a Paper showing the Manner in which the Recommendations of the Royal Commission with respect to the Civil Service have been dealt with, P.P.*, 1893-94 (183), LXXI.

113. *The Times*, 30 January 1890, p. 9; R.M. Macleod, *Treasury Control and Social Administration. A Study of Establishment Growth at the Local Government Board, 1871-1905* (Bell, London, 1968), pp. 27-28.

114. 22 H.C. Deb., 4s., cols. 919-41 (29 March 1894); *The Times*, 22 February 1894, p. 10; *Copy of Correspondence between the Treasury and Certain Members of the House in relation to Grievance of Clerks of the Second Division of the Civil Service*, (12 February 1895), *P.P.*, 1895 (40), LXXIX.

115. D.A. Thomas, 'Anomalies of the Civil Service', *Fortnightly Review*, vol. 73 (1903), pp. 874-86.

116. Ridley *Evidence*, Welby, qs. 10790-3, *P.P.*, 1888 [C. 5545], XXVII.

117. MacDonnell, *Fourth Report, P.P.*, 1914 [Cd. 7339], XVI.

118. E.g. Welby, P.R.O./T 250/9.

119. Wright, *Treasury Control*, p. 349.

120. W.H. White, Assistant Director of Contracts at the Admiralty, Ridley *Evidence*, qs. 8026-28, 8051-54, *P.P.*, 1887 [C. 5226], XIX; cf. also Sir H.E. Maxwell, qs. 14576-78, *P.P.*, 1888 [C. 5545], XXVII.

121. G.K. Fry, *Statesman in Disguise, The Changing Role of the Administrative Class of the British Home Civil Service, 1853-1966* (Macmillan, London, 1969), pp. 13-33.

122. J.D. Gregory, *On the Edge of Diplomacy ... Rambles and Reflections, 1902-28* (Hutchinson, London, 1929), p. 274.

123. Smellie, *Hundred Years*, p. 76; Parris, *Constitutional Bureaucracy*, pp. 106-10; Young, *Colonial Office*, p. 1.

124. Sir L. Guillemard, in A.G. Gardiner, *The Life of Sir William Harcourt* (2 vols., Constable, London, 1923), vol. 2, p. 212.

125. W.A. Baillie Hamilton, 'Forty-Four Years at the Colonial Office', *Nineteenth Century*, vol. 65 (1909), p. 603; cf. J.W. Cell, *British Colonial Administration in the Mid Nineteenth Century* (Yale University Press, New Haven, 1970).

126. Hamilton, 'Forty-Four Years', pp. 606-8.

127. Minute of examination of Robert Morant, 21 December 1917, Passfield Reconstruction Papers, B, fos. 70-1.

128. Macleod, *Treasury Control*, pp. 48-51.

129. Z. Steiner, *The Foreign Office and Foreign Policy, 1898-1914* (CUP, Cambridge, 1969), p. 16.

130. Lady Gwendolin Cecil, *Life of Robert, Marquis of Salisbury* (4 vols., Hodder & Stoughton, London, 1921-32), vol. 3, p. 205.

131. Gregory, *Edge of Diplomacy*, p. 18.

132. Steiner, *Foreign Office*, pp. 70-92, 152-4.

133. Sir H. Scott, *Your Obedient Servant* (Deutsch, London, 1959), p. 27; Sir L. Guillemard, *Trivial Fond Records* (Methuen, London, 1937), pp. 12-17.

134. Marquis of Crewe, *Lord Rosebery* (2 vols., Murray, London, 1931), vol. 1, p. 170.

135. Ridley, *2nd Report*, p. xi, *P.P.*, 1888 [C. 5545], XXVII.

136. Guillemard, Chairman of the Board of Customs and Excise in 1912 thought 'it fair to say that a department like mine nowadays exercises powers which are often judicial and which sometimes get very near to being legislative', Guillemard, q. 14099, *P.P.*, 1912-13 [Cd. 6535], XV; Sir Robert Chalmers, former Chairman of the Inland Revenue, really did not know how he 'could possibly have got through 1909' without the help of the First Division in his office. 'I found them invaluable in the hour of need', Chalmers, q. 1311, *P.P.*, 1912-13 [Cd. 6210], XV.

137. S. Oliver, 'Criticism of the Department of Agriculture and Fisheries', n.d. but c. March 1917, Passfield Reconstruction Papers, A, fos., 407-25.

138. Bernard Schaffer, *The Administrative Factor, Papers in Organization, Politics and Development* (Cass, London, 1973), pp. 3-26.

139. Memo by G.B. Shaw, February 1918, Passfield Reconstruction papers, B, fos., 59-60. For similar views see Beatrice Webb, Notes to 'Conspectus of Existing Government Departments', ibid., A, fos., 389-93.

2

2
THE FIRST WORLD WAR AND
THE INTER-WAR YEARS

The First World War revealed the inherent flexibility and versatility of British central administration. Under the pressure of the emergency conventional practices were where necessary abandoned or greatly modified, and new expedients adopted. At the centre a small War Cabinet evolved out of the pre-war Committee of Imperial Defence, and a Cabinet secretariat grew up to service it and help co-ordinate the war efforts. These developments, which were to have lasting significance, were unplanned and the result of pragmatic and piecemeal adjustment to changing circumstances.[1] In government departments themselves civil servants tackled a whole variety of unforeseen tasks with initiative, improvising new machinery and methods of business as they went along. Even more striking was the wholesale creation of entirely new government bodies. Ten new ministries were formed to oversee such crucial questions as food supplies, munitions, and shipping, along with over 160 new boards and commissions which were not directly responsible to Parliament.[2] Not only did the work and number of government bodies change, so did their style and methods of work. In some measure this was due to the influx of outsiders into the government machine, and the close connections which were often forged between particular departments and the corresponding interests in the outside world: industrialists, shipowners, the food industry, brewers, trade unions and the universities, to name but a few. All this ferment within government and the pressing problems posed by the reconstruction which would follow the war stimulated a great debate concerning the proper purposes of government and the 'machinery' which might best achieve those purposes. The debate on the relationship of 'efficiency' in administrative organisation to the broader goals of government, which subsequently loomed so large in the vocabulary of British reformers, dates from this period.

However, this debate which was so energetically carried on in the war years, was only indirectly related to the major developments within the British civil service over the next ten or fifteen years. This consisted of the drawing together of the disparate elements of the service. Several factors assisted this process. For example, the labour problems and economic stability of these years encouraged the growth of trade unionism among the rank and file of the service; meanwhile at a higher level the war encouraged transfers from one department to another and broke down departmental barriers. All this highlighted the problem of the co-ordination or control of the administration which had already given cause for concern before 1914. At the end of the war the existing position of the Treasury came under sustained attack both from within higher governmental circles and from the staff associations. For a time it seemed likely that some new controlling agency might be set up. Yet ironically the decade after the war saw the creation of a far more systematic mechanism of control which emanated from the Treasury itself. A remarkable feature of the process, however, was the degree to which such integration was inspired by those working the administration itself and the relative lack of any direction or initiative from the political environment. From the inter-war years can be said to date a gulf between 'insiders' and 'outsiders' which has been so marked a feature of British central administration since 1945. Under the regime of Sir Warren Fisher, Permanent Secretary to the Treasury during the inter-war period, the civil service kept itself aloof from some of the most significant contemporary developments in the study of public administration. Fisher and his associates were more concerned with building up the *esprit de corps* of the service than with applying administrative or political theories to the running of government.

The very cautious attitude of Whitehall to outside interest is clearly revealed in the reaction of the Treasury to the proposal for a 'Whitehall series' of books which aimed to give an account to 'the general reader or the student of administrative methods' of the history and workings of the major departments of state.[3] The editor of the series, which was published by Putnams, was Sir James Marchant, a nonconformist minister, who had a wide range of interests as a writer and was a tireless social worker. Why Marchant should have taken an initiative in the matter is not altogether clear, but he evidently had close connections in Whitehall and in 1924 approached several heads of departments with a view to securing contributions to the series. Warren Fisher, after being consulted by the permanent heads, adopted a distinctly cool attitude. He believed purely historical accounts would 'make dull and unpalatable reading unless the author touched on matters of controversy, and in such cases it might well be desirable for any Civil Servant invited to contribute to the series to refuse to do so'. It should be clearly understood that the authors of the books 'must limit themselves to plain unvarnished narrative'.[4] The volumes of the Whitehall series, which began to appear in 1925, were in fact written by retired civil servants.

Subsequent official interest in the volumes appears to have been confined to financial matters: in particular a concern lest Stationery Office receipts might be reduced as a consequence of the publication of a series of descriptive books.[5]

The Machinery of Central Government

The administrative improvisations which were made in the First World War focused attention upon the broader question of the organisation of government departments as a whole, and the distribution of functions within them. Here the Haldane Committee on the Machinery of Government was of particular significance. For this body marked the first attempt since the Benthamites of the early nineteenth century to analyse British central government in terms of a systematic administrative theory. The Report of this Committee has had a major impact upon subsequent administrative thinking. In particular it helped to mould the climate of opinion in which administrative matters were discussed: the very term 'machinery of government' for example was first popularised by the Committee. Thus even though the immediate recommendations of the Committee may not have been implemented, the indirect effect of its work was far-reaching. The history of the Committee illustrates very well a complicated interaction of theory and practice which is often a characteristic of administrative reform. The theoretical analysis of the Haldane Committee was not the result of *a priori* speculation on the part of its members; it stemmed from consideration of practical problems of government; and the theory which was formulated itself moulded in some respects the future practice of administration.

The Haldane Committee owed its origin to the administrative confusions of the First World War. By 1916 it was clear that many of the improvisations which had been made, while good at solving short-term difficulties, were likely in the long run to lead to long-term frustrations. Considerable overlapping and confusion of responsibilities had occurred, and matters were made worse by the fact that because of the war, the wings of Parliament and the Treasury — the two most effective political and financial checks upon government — had been clipped. The result, in Beatrice Webb's words, was that the 'swollen world of Whitehall' was 'seething' with 'conflicting elements warring against each other'.[6]

It soon became clear to many perceptive observers that some serious thought would have to be given to the problems of post-war 'reconstruction', and that some more systematic and permanent arrangements would have to be made to tackle the problems posed by the return of peace. These were certainly challenging. First there would be the short-term upheavals caused by demobilisation and the run-down of the arms factories; then the longer-term problems of trade and labour relations. Government intervention was clearly necessary in these areas, and many ideas were put forward for new partnerships of one kind or another between government, industry and labour.[7] On 18 March 1916 Asquith, the Prime Minister, therefore set up a Reconstruction Committee of 13 ministers to advise on future peacetime problems and to 'co-ordinate the work which has already been done by the depart-ments in this direction'.[8] This Committee soon set up a large number of sub-committees to deal with a whole host of problems, ranging from forestry policy to the employment of women, from agriculture to the conservation of coal. The Reconstruction Committee lacked both force and cohesion. Other departments had set up enquiries of their own and the situation was fast becoming confusing. E.S. Montagu, Financial Secretary to the Treasury, pointed out in June the anomalous situation. He pressed for the Committee to 'be regarded as the parent Committee of all committees considering after-war policy'. In this context he believed the post-war organisation of government would have to be carefully considered.[9] Changes only occurred, however, with the fall of Asquith's government and its replacement by Lloyd George's ministry in December 1916. The temptation to take an initiative in this area was irresistible to the new premier, with his unusual blend of visionary idealism and cynical political manipulation. Montagu had lost Cabinet office with the change of government, but he was moving closer politically towards Lloyd George, who asked him to act under him as vice-chairman of a new committee. Beatrice Webb gives in her diaries an amusing account of the selection of the members of this committee. Montagu suggested a committee of three Cabinet ministers along with himself.

> But this was too much for the Prime Minister. 'This is a mere shadow of Asquith', he remarked to the young men of his secretariat. 'Bring me a list of persons with ideas': such a list being hastily furnished, he spent a spare ten minutes in considering it. He struck out some of the names — H.G. Wells and G.B.S. for instance, and added some others — among them Jack Hills and Seebohm Rowntree. Then he proceeded to pick out fourteen. He came to the Webbs and pondered: 'Yes, we will have one of the Webbs ... Mrs. Webb, I think ... Webb will be angry, Mrs. Webb won't'. Then, apparently

without consulting Montagu or Vaughan Nash, he ordered a letter
to be written to each of the selected ones inviting them, in the name
of the War Cabinet, to serve on the new Reconstruction
Committee.[10]

The new Committee was launched with panache by the Prime Minister
on 16 March 1917. Comprising 'men and women of wide experience'
its task was to 'survey the whole field of government'. It had 'power to
assist in painting a new picture of Britain ... The nation now was in a
molten condition; it was malleable now ...'[11] Montagu had high
expectations. The new Committee should 'gather all the separate
recommendations [of the existing sub-committees] into one flexible
and co-ordinated policy'.[12] Four 'panels' were set up to survey various
areas of government: housing and health, industrial and commercial
policy, and education.[13] But from the start there were difficulties.
Tensions arose between Montagu and the permanent secretaries on the
one side and some of the Committee members on the other. Beatrice
Webb, for example, described Montagu as a 'great disappointment',
and 'dead failure' as acting-chairman. 'He is a large-limbed, heavy-
featured Jew — moody in temper, with little power of language and
apparently without capacity for work ...' Vaughan Nash, the chief
official, she found 'woolly-headed, easily frightened off any decisive
step and, like most weak men in responsible positions, suspicious and
secretive'. Nor did the other officials shape up to the Fabian ideal:
'dreamy cultivated amateurs, preachers of ideals rather than practical
administrators' who 'seem to spend a very short working day talking
together over cigarettes or tea — or listening to committees talking'.
Her colleagues also she found deficient in crucial qualities: 'The
majority ... do not intend to work: they are not representative of
varied interests nor do they make a homogeneous body of coun-
sellors'.[14] The difficulties, however, were as much structural as
personal. During the very first month Montagu and Vaughan Nash
realised that their terms of reference were inadequate, since to be a
success they badly needed co-ordinating powers.[15] The problem was
in fact very similar to that facing later governments of the 1960s and
1970s: how to incorporate a 'think tank' of outsiders with creative
ideas into the departmental world of Whitehall and how to co-ordinate
without financial or other powers. Beatrice Webb from the start rightly
predicted that the Committee would face either 'open revolt' or 'silent
obstruction' and 'be marooned in one way or another by an enraged
Whitehall'.[16] All the 'panels' found their way blocked by the 'litter of

sub-committees' left behind by the previous Reconstruction
Committee. The employment panel never considered three-quarters of
those in its area, while the education panel fell foul of the Board of
Education when it ventured upon a criticism of the Education Bill. The
plight of the industry panel as described by Beatrice Webb was particularly unenviable:

> This Panel found its way blocked by the existence of the powerful
> Sub-Committee on Commercial and Industrial Policy under Lord
> Balfour of Burleigh, and another on Coal Conservation under Lord
> Haldane. These were in communication with a whole litter of
> Committees, appointed by the Board of Trade, and continually
> increasing in number, dealing with separate industries and subjects.
> Lord Balfour of Burleigh's Sub-Committee was itself in direct
> communication with the War Cabinet; and we were given to under-
> stand that the Reconstruction Committee was not to hold itself
> responsible for its conclusions. We got, after some time, four reports
> of this Sub-Committee. We never formally discussed these important
> Reports in the Reconstruction Committee, nor formally considered
> them in the Panel. But, informally, among ourselves, we nearly all
> objected to their general tenor and specific recommendations ...
> Moreover, the various recommendations of the Reports of these
> separate Committees were inconsistent one with the other, and we
> were in doubt whether the governmental machinery to carry out
> this policy of discrimination was to be a Government Department
> or 'boards' composed of some of the interests concerned ...

The lack of co-ordination she found particularly depressing.

> It may almost be said that the machine had grit in it from the start.
> Each panel sought to get to work in its own way, taking up such
> subjects as most interested particular members, without guidance
> or co-ordination from the committee as a whole, or its officers; and
> without having at their disposal the necessary material or any
> adequate staff, either to investigate new questions, or to co-ordinate
> the investigations that were going on.

The various sub-committees had been appointed, it seemed, quite
haphazardly, and their recommendations were often quite incompatible
with each other. For existing departments the Reconstruction
Committee was a mere nuisance — 'another hurdle'. The lessons were

clear. 'The relation to Government Departments needs the closest
attention.'[17]

In July 1917 Lloyd George created a separate Ministry of Reconstruction, astutely using the opportunity to gain political advantage by
shifting Dr Christopher Addison from the Ministry of Munitions where
he had not been a success. Addison pressed for a seat in the War
Cabinet to strengthen his position and to avoid being 'blocked by
departmentalism', but this was denied.[18] The new Ministry could
never in these circumstances fulfil the high position which Montagu,
and perhaps at one time Lloyd George, had envisaged. It became little
more than a ministry which settled immediate problems of the post-war
period such as demobilisation. By October 1918 Addison was complaining bitterly of the cavalier treatment to which many of his
carefully worked-out proposals were subjected and the 'disregard and
lack of support' which he was receiving from the Prime Minister.[19]
A year later the Ministry was no more.

The 'Reconstruction' question however led directly to the creation of
the Haldane Committee on the 'Machinery of Government'. The
experience had confirmed Beatrice Webb in her conviction that the
laissez faire state was in process of being transformed into a new order,
where the 'conscious, deliberate organisation of society' would be at a
premium. Government and administration in this context were vitally
important. They should be organised on a proper scientific basis.
Systematic analysis should be made both of the problems of government and the means to tackle them.[20] In the case of reconstruction,
for example, once the main guidelines had been laid down, a flexible
series of subordinate investigations should have been set up. But these
should have reported 'week by week' to the centre. 'All the material
should be kept at the Central Office and made accessible to all those
responsible for the other investigations.' A special information officer
should have been appointed to liaise with outside bodies, and a
continual review made of the work 'so that all parts of the work may
proceed together, and work up to a complete scheme of reconstruction'.[21] Edwin Montagu's thoughts on the question of administrative
machinery also became clearer, and were pointing in the same
direction. During the spring of 1917 he had been gradually making a
break with his old Asquithean colleagues, and was angling for high
office under Lloyd George, either the Treasury or the India Office. But
he also urged, perhaps not entirely altruistically, the need for a
Minister of Reconstruction who would be able to 'map out the ground
between and call Conferences of the Government Departments'.[22] This

was important since all economic plans would fail if 'the central
administrative machine is lacking in organisation'. In a long memorandum dated 30 April 1917 he argued the case for a systematic review
of government. For a long time the haphazard and unsystematic growth
of government departments had 'resulted in tremendous overlap, and
at the same time fearful expanses of No-Man's Land'. The whole framework of central government needed an overhaul. He believed recruitment would have to be more varied, transfers from departments more
systematised and remuneration reviewed. Any such review should also
examine the role of the Cabinet. There should be no return to the large
pre-war cabinets with their 'protracted discussion' but neither would
the existing war-time system with its streamlined War Cabinet and lack
of departmental co-ordination prove satisfactory. He suggested a more
organised system comprising an inner cabinet of the Prime Minister,
Chancellor of the Exchequer and five Secretaries of State to cover the
areas of foreign affairs, war, commerce and industry, internal affairs,
and transport and communication. All the specific departments, like
agriculture, education and the Post Office, could be grouped under one
or other of these overlords.[23]

Here was seed which clearly fell on fertile soil. Beatrice Webb learnt
from Montagu that there were 'storms brewing in Downing Street' over
reconstruction. 'The Prime Minister intervenes suddenly when matters
become critical, peremptorily reorganises some department or starts a
new one in a few hours, and then leaves the new organisation to find its
own level in a hostile world of old-established offices.'[24] By June 1917
a special sub-committee was set up under the chairmanship of Lord
Haldane 'to enquire into the responsibilities of the various Departments
of the central executive Government, and to advise in what manner the
exercise and distribution by the Government of its functions should be
improved'.[25] The other members were three politicians: Montagu
himself (Liberal), Sir Alan Sykes (Unionist), J.H. Thomas (Labour);
two leading civil servants: Sir George Murray and Sir Robert Morant;
and Beatrice Webb. None of the politicians played any great part in the
investigation, Montagu having meanwhile been given the India Office.
This left an effective membership of four rather striking and unusual
people. The most conventional public servant was Sir George Murray,
formerly Permanent Secretary to the Treasury, described by Violet
Markham as 'wise, cynical, humorous, a realist without illusions' and
by Beatrice Webb as an engaging 'simple-minded reactionary' who
nevertheless was often receptive to 'a lot of new ideas' which he found
'damned interesting'.[26] Sir Robert Morant was a forceful public servant

with pronounced ideas on the desirability of social reform, reminiscent
perhaps of the dynamic figures of an earlier age like Edwin Chadwick or
Charles Trevelyan. He had been largely responsible for the 1902-3
Education Acts. Beatrice Webb described him at this time as a 'strange
mortal, not altogether sane', of 'somewhat tortuous ways' who had
'done more to improve English administration than any other man'.[27]
Beatrice Webb herself had not only been long active in various movements for social and political reform, but also possessed through her
historical studies an unrivalled knowledge of administrative practice and
the theories behind it. The chairman, Lord Haldane, was a lawyer by
training and had been a Liberal Cabinet minister between 1905 and
1915. He possessed the rare distinction of combining a fine grasp of
philosophy and intellectual theories with the proven abilities of a
successful administrator. Indeed he regarded the search for the rational
principles which he believed underlay all forms of experience as an
essential preliminary for success in politics and administration. His
highest praise for a colleague was that he looked for a clear principle
before advising action; and his own invaluable reforms of British
military organisation before 1912 — based on the principle of the
'General Staff' — were a model of his ideas. Unlike the majority of his
contemporaries Haldane also believed passionately in the importance
of research in the physical and the social sciences, and the possibility
of applying its fruits to government. He had already played an
important part in helping to foster technical education in Britain and
in developing provincial university colleges in England.[28] After the
outbreak of war, however, he had become the subject of an unfair and
vindictive campaign of vilification in the press because of his pre-war
German contacts. The prospect of the new work whetted his appetite;
it was, he wrote to his sister, 'the best Committee I ever had. The Govt.
may or may not carry out the plan but I think we shall produce a lead
in a new direction.'[29] Here indeed was a powerful quartet; but it was
strangely ill-balanced. All four were in their different ways somewhat
'patrician' in the sense that they stood aloof from the hurly burly of
politics, viewing its practitioners with disdain or even contempt.[30] On
the other side of the coin politicians viewed the Committee with
distaste. Bonar Law, the Conservative leader, for example, protested
strongly at Haldane's appointment and complained that the composition '*as a whole* is jolly bad'.[31]

   The Committee was, therefore, given the circumstances in which it
was operating, strangely ethereal in character and academic in tone. 'It is
pleasant sport', noted Beatrice Webb, 'we sit twice a week over tea and

muffins in Haldane's comfortable dining room discussing the theory
and practice of government'.[32] The Committee called for papers from
leading officials who were then examined, and its members themselves
prepared memoranda on the various facets of their work, Beatrice Webb
being particularly active in this respect. The first area of concern for
the Committee was the distribution of functions and work among
various departments. Beatrice Webb drew up a 'Conspectus' outlining
the existing complex organisation to which she added some lengthy
'notes'. Administration, she argued, should be on the basis of a
coherent principle. Departments should be organised around either the
class of people to be served — e.g. a ministry for children which should
look after every aspect of children's needs — or of services performed
— e.g. a ministry to cover all aspects of education.[33] At present there
was great confusion. The other Committee members found Beatrice
Webb's arguments compelling, and in their report called for a redistri-
bution of government work according to the nature of the service
rendered to the community as a whole. This would make government
at once more streamlined and accountable.[34] Here the Committee was
in effect endorsing the earlier idea of Montagu.

Such a reorganisation of government, the Committee believed, would
only bear fruit if there was a far greater degree of co-ordination within
the administration. Many of the civil servants they interviewed drew
attention to the inadequacies of the existing state of affairs. Sir
Edmund Phipps of the Board of Education, for example, complained
of the inadequate knowledge which the Treasury had of staffing
matters. An Establishments Branch there would have made matters
run much more smoothly at the start of the war. Some sort of study of
management questions was badly needed: 'there are no books on this
subject and at present the knowledge lies with the few Staff Clerks who
have discovered it for themselves'. Sir John Anderson agreed.
'Machinery is required for securing the dissemination and general
adoption of the best ideas on administration in the Civil Service
departments.' He recommended the creation of a special representative
Civil Service Standing Committee. Morant also was particularly critical
of the Treasury.[35] The Committee therefore recommended the
creation of a post of establishments officer in every department and a
special Establishment Branch within the Treasury itself, and urged
co-operation between them all.

Along with this desire for greater central administrative direction, the
Committee stressed the need for more sustained research in government. At an early stage Beatrice Webb had called for 'some continuous

organ of thought, initiative and criticism' within departments. In the
post-war period she believed the population would rely on the state
more and more heavily for the 'performance of one service after
another'; in these circumstances administrative practices would be
vitally important: 'We have put too little thought into the construction
of Government Departments and we have hardly become aware of
certain typical diseases which affect the Bureaucrat.'[36] Lord Haldane
enthusiastically agreed. Research in his view would be needed not
merely to secure technical progress but also to ensure effective
policy-making in the broadest sense.[37] The final Report of the
Committee therefore called for the 'systematic application of thought,
as a preliminary to the settlement of policy and its subsequent
administration'. In the past 'the business of executive Government
generally has been seriously embarrassed from the incomplete
application to it' of such provision. Individual departments should
make definite provision for research and higher officials should have
more time to devote to this portion of their duties. In addition a
separate department for broader research and inquiry should be set up,
along the lines of the Committee of the Privy Council for Scientific
and Industrial Research which had been set up in 1915. 'A Cabinet with
such knowledge at its disposal', the Committee believed, 'would be in a
position to devolve with greater freedom and confidence than is at
present the case, the duties of administration, and even of
legislation'.[38]

The reference here to the Cabinet was not incidental. The Committee
regarded the Cabinet as 'the mainspring of all the mechanism of
Government', and devoted the first section of their Report to
considering its proper organisation. Political and administrative reform
could not be separated. 'Efficiency' was not conceived of in micro-
scopic terms relating to the internal arrangements of departments but
was interpreted in relation to the work of government on the grand
scale. The Committee recommended that the Cabinet should be small
in number, preferably ten or twelve ministers, should meet frequently,
and 'should be supplied in the most convenient form with all the
information and material necessary to enable it to arrive at expeditious
decisions'. Junior ministers whose work was likely to be affected by its
decisions should be consulted personally, and 'it should have a systematic method of securing that its decisions are effectually carried out by
the several departments concerned'.[39] Now as a general principle all
these statements were unobjectionable, but the Committee, despite
some prompting by Montagu,[40] failed to spell out the precise manner

in which its recommendations should work. Should the proposed
streamlined Cabinet be a collection of non-departmental overlords, or
the heads of the most important ministries, or should there be some
kind of a two-tier system? What kind of Cabinet Secretariat or Cabinet
Office should be created? Should there be a Prime Minister's Department, and what should the relationship of the premier be to his
colleagues? All these were points upon which the Committee took a
great deal of evidence from leading officials and politicians who were,
as Hans Daalder has shown, themselves considerably divided. The
Committee 'were clearer about what they disliked in the pre-war
Cabinet than about what they wished to see substituted for it' and its
Report 'therefore left matters very much in the air for those who
should wish to apply its precepts'.[41] All this ties in with what was
perhaps the fundamental weakness of the Committee's approach: its
neglect of purely 'political' factors, 'the volatile and disorderly
elements in the picture – the play of political power, the strife of
parties, the ebb and flow of consent'.[42] Nothing at all was said about
perhaps the Cabinet's most important peacetime functions: the
maintenance of the government's ascendancy in the House of
Commons, the arena of the party political battle. The Committee's
decision at its second meeting not to consider 'matters which raised
the question of changes in the system of Ministerial responsibility or
other questions commonly known as political questions' made little
sense, given that they had chosen to interpret 'administrative reform'
in such a broad and general political context.[43]

   In the turbulent political circumstances of the years after 1918 it is
hardly surprising that the Haldane Committee had little immediate
impact. Its Report was received fairly favourably by most of the
national press,[44] but, as it was published shortly after the 'coupon
election' of 1918, most people's minds reverted to more pressing
matters. There is no evidence that it was ever debated by Lloyd
George's cabinet. Many of Lloyd George's administrative innovations
were fiercely attacked after 1918, and the existence of the Cabinet
Secretariat itself seemed for a while precarious. There was little scope
for the more radical suggestions of the Committee. The size of the
Cabinet reverted to the pre-war pattern.[45] Nor was any systematic
attempt made to rationalise the division of work among departments.
Some of the new ministries were dissolved – e.g. Information,
Reconstruction, Munitions, Shipping and Food – whereas others –
Transport and Pensions – survived. The creation of the Ministry of
Health was something for which many reformers had long worked and

ante-dated the Report, but even this hardly conformed to Beatrice Webb's vision since it was also given responsibility for housing and effectively for the structure and finance of local government as well. In 1920 the Treasury examined the possibility of re-allocating the functions of the Home Office, the Ministry of Health, the Board of Trade and the Ministry of Labour, but decided that the *status quo* should remain for reasons of practical expediency.[46] This reflected the considerable scepticism which many leading civil servants had clearly felt about the possibility of a division of functions in their evidence to the Committee.[47] Nothing came of the Committee's recommendation in favour of a Ministry of Justice, a pet scheme of Lord Haldane himself. More striking perhaps than this was the failure of the Committee to foresee the very considerable growth in non-ministerial organisations in the post-war period especially in connection with nationalised industries. The Committee clearly envisaged control over services such as electricity or the railways to take the form of direct ministerial supervision along the lines of the Post Office. This Bernard Schaffer has described as a 'breathtaking misjudgement'.[48] Similarly with regard to research, the Committee's recommendations bore little direct fruit. A Committee of Civil Research was set up in 1925, 'charged with the duty of giving connected forethought from the central standpoint to the development of economic, scientific and statistical research in relation to civil policy and administration'.[49] This was succeeded in 1930 by the Economic Advisory Council, composed of outsiders (from industry, the trade unions and the universities), ministers, and a small staff of economists. Neither body was a success since neither was sufficiently integrated with the policy-making process. The Council was altogether too unwieldy and ill-defined a body. 'A combination of the theory of practical men and the policy of academic men produced pontifical obscurity.'[50] Otherwise there were substantial developments in the areas of medical and agricultural research, but these owed little to the direct promptings of the Haldane Report.[51]

How then should the Haldane Committee be assessed in the context of administrative reform during the inter-war years? How are we to explain the high regard in which it has been held by subsequent generations in contrast to the cavalier manner in which many of its specific proposals were treated? One helpful perspective is to review the Report not merely in the context of what followed but of what had preceded it. For the general tenor of the Report appealed to the majority of high-grade administrators, the new breed of university-trained men — the fruits of the Northcote/Trevelyan vision — who had entered the civil service in the 1880s and 1890s and who had only reached the high positions by the First World War. Central co-ordination of the civil service with opportunities for transfers, a recognised role for research, scope for initiative in policy-making and a positive attitude to the concept of strong 'ministries' of state, had all been clearly pointed to during the previous 30 years. Moreover the Haldane Committee's report really confirmed in theoretical terms what shrewd political administrators had learned from the traumatic experiences of the war. If it did not inspire, it helped set the tone for a great deal of later mid-twentieth-century thinking on British central administration. First it viewed 'Whitehall' as a coherent set of government departments rather than a mere grouping of government 'offices', a view which was heartily endorsed by Warren Fisher. Secondly, it stressed the future importance of inter-departmental relations and of the Cabinet as a co-ordinating mechanism of policy-making. The Cabinet henceforth was not to be regarded merely as a meeting of leading ministers, but had to be seen as part of a complex process of government.

The criterion by which the Haldane Committee should be judged is not so much the extent to which its 'programme' was 'implemented' as the degree to which it contributed towards the creation of a consensus of opinion in favour of reform. In this respect the Haldane Report's analysis of the functions of government departments struck a responsive chord in later generations, even though the practical application of the Haldane principle was fraught with difficulty. The very term 'machinery of government' came in time to dominate administrators' thinking about the organisation of government. Indeed after 1950 it became almost commonplace to believe that there was a 'correct' machinery of administration which would in some sense itself ensure successful political or economic policies: an attitude which ignored the fact that decisions about the machinery of government often emerged from decisions about goals. Both Beatrice Webb and Haldane were well aware of the dangers of this attitude.

In another area the Haldane Report was responsible for shaping the general ethos of British administrative attitudes in the subsequent 20 years. The Report certainly played a part in the evolution of a distinctively British approach to public administration, which in contrast to contemporary American writing, placed more emphasis upon the fusion of politics and administration, and the close relationship of administration to both science and ethics. 'Efficiency' was thus interpreted in a broad sense, in qualitative as well as quantitative terms, with ethical and political goals, and there developed an appreciation of organisations as living phenomena as well as mechanical entities.[52]

However, in many respects Haldane's vision of a continuous and fertile interchange between the practitioners and theorists of administration was frustrated. In October 1918 a group of senior civil servants established a 'Society of Civil Servants' and this body, with the support of Haldane, Morant and others sponsored a series of lectures on administration. Between 1921 and 1923 this body was responsible for founding the Institute of Public Administration with Haldane as its President.[53] Haldane saw this body as a catalyst for the continual interaction of administrative theory and practice to the benefit of both. He believed that the new institute should 'fashion ... a school of thought which may permeate the whole Civil Service and enable people to lift themselves to a higher level and thereby gain more influence and potency in the community'.[54] Such a vision, for its realisation, would have required a degree of co-operation from Whitehall circles which in the event was not forthcoming. In order to understand the gulf which developed between Whitehall and the outside world it is necessary to examine pressures from within the bureaucracy, first the growing influence of trade unions and staff associations, and secondly the changing role of the Treasury after 1919.

The Creation of Whitley Councils and the Development of Labour Relations in the Civil Service

Relations between employer and employed were institutionalised in a pioneering fashion in the British civil service at the end of the First World War. The development of the Whitley system was significant enough to attract the attention of one of the father-figures of the academic study of public administration, L.D. White, Professor of Public Administration at Chicago University and author of one of the first textbooks of public administration, who made a study of it as early as 1933.[55] Since then the Whitley Council system has been the subject of regular enquiries from other countries and may be judged an original British contribution to public administration. In Britain itself the creation of these councils introduced a wholly new element in the pattern of future administrative reorganisation. Henceforth no government could introduce major reforms without due consultation with its employees. However, the 1919-20 reform has an even broader significance. The whole issue raised important constitutional questions concerning the respective roles of Parliament, trade unions, ministers and the Treasury in civil service matters. The episode is best interpreted as one of administrative reform in the broadest sense, and not merely as a chapter in the history of industrial relations.

By 1914 labour relations in the service were already in a state of flux and confusion. The traditional manner by which clerks sought to redress grievances or to better their position had been by petitioning the head of their department. However, this method had already become anachronistic by the later years of the nineteenth century. 'As the form of the Service changed from a collection of loosely connected departments to a highly centralized bureaucratic apparatus, so changed the Civil Servant's method of dealing with his employer.'[56] There developed first small associations of departmental clerks, and then, on a grander scale, bodies like the Writers Association and the Second Division Clerks Association, representing clerks across the board. However, the heads of the pre-war Treasury were reluctant to face the implications of the new developments and maintained a highly ambivalent attitude towards the new clerical associations. On occasions the Treasury recognised the right of civil servants to present claims through associations and dealt directly with them, as for example in its dealings with the Assistant Clerks Association in 1905. On the other hand it was extremely reluctant to 'recognise' any associations formally on the grounds that this might subvert the authority of departmental heads and encourage agitation in Parliament. A request by the Second Division Clerks Association for direct negotiating rights in 1911, for example, was turned down because 'in their Lordships' opinion ... it is essential to good order and discipline that the second division clerks should not be privileged to take action independently of the heads of their departments'.[57] However, in the Post Office, Sydney Buxton, Postmaster General in 1906, conceded full negotiating rights to the postal trade unions as a means of reducing friction within the department.[58] Official policy at this time was therefore singularly diffuse and elastic. Innovations and improvisations were made, but substantive changes were masked by an adherence to well-attested formulas and well-established conventions.

By 1911-14, however, the anomalies and confusions in grading and pay had reached the point where changes in policy and in structures were clearly needed. These were years both of marked inflation and of general industrial unrest. Agitation in the Post Office reached a new peak, while the Assistant Clerks Association, representing the junior clerks in the service as a whole, grew both in strength and militancy. A Civil Service Federation was founded as an umbrella organisation for the various independent associations. When the Treasury failed to respond satisfactorily to their claims, the associations demanded some kind of panel of arbitrators to judge the merits of their case. When this was refused they began successfully to whip up feeling in Parliament. Almost 400 MPs supported a demand for an enquiry, and at this point Asquith's government, in an effort to cool the situation, appointed the MacDonnell Royal Commission. This body in its turn highlighted the limitations of existing methods of Treasury control over establishments and in 1914 it was further proposed to set up an expert body to consider the future relations between the state and its employees.[59] The outbreak of war put a stop to these developments, but the war conditions quickly exacerbated an already tense situation. The new work, the influx of women and the recruitment of temporary civil servants threw most offices into confusion, while the increased cost of living caused great hardship and discontent. In the wartime emergency the Treasury was vulnerable to arm-twisting by a Cabinet anxious for industrial peace, and it was forced first to negotiate a cost of living bonus with the associations, and then, in December 1916, to set up an arbitration and conciliation board to settle claims for pay for all civil servants earning less than £500 per annum.[60]

By 1917-19, however, the tone adopted by the larger staff associations had become more militant. The early associations had not regarded themselves as trade unions, and in any case had possessed only rudimentary organisations. The leaders of the junior clerical unions who rose to power in the war years viewed matters differently. As Douglas Houghton recalls, 'they were rebels, fighters, strong personalities, egotistical, and fond of the limelight because publicity was propaganda'.[61] Many were convinced socialists, anxious to work within the context of the TUC and the Labour Party. Undoubtedly the most able was W.J. Brown, the Assistant Secretary of the Assistant Clerks Association, the forerunner of the Civil Service Clerical Association. Born in 1894, the son of a plumber, he had even before the war been responsible for founding the Boy Clerks Association and at the age of 19 had given impressive evidence before the MacDonnell Commission. Now he was determined to transform 'our well-meaning but innocuous little association into something like a Trade Union'.[62] The Assistant Clerks Association was established on a full-time basis after the war with Brown himself as its full-time paid officer. Membership and funds multiplied between 1918 and 1922, and an imaginative and lively magazine, *Red Tape*, was published. Another forceful leader, a great enemy of Brown, was G.H. Stuart-Bunning, who was a leading figure in the Postmen's Federation, the forerunner of the Union of Post Office Workers. Stuart-Bunning was largely responsible for the founding of the Civil Service Federation in October 1912 which embraced a composite membership of some 110,000 by May 1913.[63] Both the Federation and the rival Civil Service Alliance (spearheaded by Brown's Association) propounded radical policies for the future control of the civil service. The Federation called for thorough quinquennial investigations by the House of Commons and the establishment in every department of an advisory board of appeal comprising associations and permanent officials who should review 'all questions of urgency, appeals against punishments, passing over for promotion, disciplinary measures of any kind, and, in fact, any domestic matter'. This proposal, the Treasury considered, would constitute 'intolerable interference with the responsibility of the Head of a Department who might see his decisions overruled by a clique of his subordinates'.[64] The Civil Service Alliance, for its part, demanded a new controlling authority for the civil service, a board composed jointly of government appointees and nominees of the staff associations.[65] The Treasury was under open assault. 'Nothing less' demanded *Red Tape*,

> than the elimination of Treasury Control will do. These people at the Treasury serve nobody except their brothers, their cousins, and (nowadays) their aunts ... The Civil Service must achieve the right to make its own conditions (under Parliament) and nominate its own masters, who will be masterly men of affairs.[66]

Towards the end of the First World War, therefore, ideas about the control and direction of the civil service were in a peculiarly molten state. The existing pattern — or rather lack of pattern — pleased no one. The head of the Customs and Excise, L.N. Guillemard, vividly expressed the frustrations of all parties in a letter to Sir Thomas Heath of the Treasury in May 1918:

> What Ministers and permanent Heads alike want above all is *finality*, instead of interminable appeals to the House of Commons. What the Treasury wants is merely to retain its power of *veto*, by saying 'No money available at present'. What the men want is an appeal Authority *independent* of the Department.

Whether or not all three aspirations were reconcilable was debatable, but he believed the attempt ought to be squarely made.[67] But if solutions were to be sought, it was by no means clear what form they were likely to take. As Henry Parris has rightly pointed out, the administrative historian's hindsight may easily blind him to the fluidity of a particular circumstance. There was nothing inevitable about the development of the Whitley system. For contemporaries in 1917 many other courses seemed possible, and many questions needed to be asked. Were the staff associations prepared to forego the advantages of political agitation in order to work for improvements from within the administration? Would Parliament as the paymaster be content to let matters be settled 'within the administrative family'? Would the Government resist the temptation to set up some entirely new independent 'Commission' to superintend the civil service? The answers to these questions can have appeared by no means obvious at a time of unprecedented political as well as administrative upheaval.[68]

The initial momentum for change came from the civil service unions. In 1916 the government had become seriously alarmed at the high incidence of strikes and labour unrest in heavy industry which appeared to hamper the war effort. A sub-committee of the Reconstruction Committee was set up under the chairmanship of the Rt Hon. J.H. Whitley, Liberal MP for Halifax, to investigate the relations between employers and employed, and to make suggestions for their improvement. In its first Report published in June 1917, the Committee called for the creation by the government of standing industrial councils jointly made up of representatives of both sides of industry. These councils were to be organised on an industry by industry basis and were to operate in three tiers: at a national, district and works level. The new bodies were to bring about 'the regular consideration of matters affecting the progress and well-being of the trade from the point of view of all those engaged in it, so far as this is consistent with the general interest of the community'. The report went on to suggest eleven topics which the new bodies might discuss.[69] Here was indeed a bold and imaginative idea guaranteed to attract the support of a bold and imaginative premier and of the Ministry of Labour which he had created. The report was therefore widely circulated to trade unions and employers in June, and the Cabinet fully endorsed it in September 1917, seeing it as a means of simplifying the daunting problems of reconstruction after the war.[70] However, it soon became clear that the Ministry would have an uphill task in getting its vision translated into practice. For the Whitley Report, as Beatrice Webb pointed out straight away, took little account of existing British industrial and commercial organisation, and ignored the realities of trade union practice.[71]

This then was the context in which the civil service unions pressed for reform. It was ironic that whereas the normal trade unions, which the government sought to win over to the Whitley scheme, mostly remained obstinately suspicious, the civil service associations for which the report was considered unsuitable, immediately showed an unwelcome interest. As Whitley himself recalled

> the people in the Civil Service were among the first to prick up their ears, and I had, very speedily, an inquiry from the ranks of the Civil Servants as to whether or not what we had said was meant to apply also to the Civil Service.[72]

He and his colleagues quickly favoured the application of the scheme to administrative organisations, but the initial response in Whitehall was anything but encouraging. When, within a matter of weeks of the Report's publication, the Civil Service Clerical Alliance and the Civil Service Federation wrote respectively to the Ministry of Labour and the Treasury asking for the Report to be put into operation, they both received very dusty replies. Officials at the Ministry of Labour were at this time (summer 1917) every bit as hostile to the idea as their counterparts in the Treasury, since 'it would be undesirable to let the impression get about that the Whitley Scheme was intended to apply to commercial or clerical occupations, as in fact it was only framed with a view to organised industry'. 'It is clear that the Civil Service is not an industry, as it does not involve any association of capital and labour and is not concerned with the production or distribution of commodities.'[73] Within four months however the Ministry was singing quite a different tune, as a result of a determined campaign by the civil service leaders, who, despite their own bitter internal divisions, were determined not to let the opportunity for change slip by.

Their tactics were to exploit the government's eagerness for the Whitley system. 'The service associations', recalled W.J. Brown,

> jumped to the opportunity. Wherever a government speaker appeared to commend the scheme to employers and employed, there was a pertinacious civil servant blandly inquiring why, if the idea was so good, the government, which was the biggest employer of all, did not apply it in its own house?[74]

A series of embarrassing questions was asked in Parliament and pointed remarks made in newspapers. Meanwhile Whitley and his colleagues

issued a second Report in October 1917 advocating the extension of
the principle of joint councils to state departments and municipal
authorities who employed labour.[75] By December therefore the
Ministry of Labour began to bring pressure to bear on the Treasury.
The Permanent Secretary complained to his opposite number that his
ministry was under attack in Parliament and declared that his:

> Minister feels that it is a matter in which the Government are bound
> to set an example by giving the most careful consideration to the
> possibility of applying the principles of the Report to Government
> establishments ... He thinks therefore that a Departmental Com-
> mittee ought to be set up which would hear evidence from those
> who were interested. There has been a good deal of talk of schemes
> for organising the Civil Service on what purported to be the lines of
> the Whitley Report, and a thorough examination of these schemes
> by a competent Committee would probably do a great deal to clear
> the air and to make everybody understand what the real position is
> as regards the Government Services ... The Minister is convinced that
> pressure both in and out of Parliament will increase to such an
> extent that sooner or later the Government will be bound to take
> action on the lines suggested, and he thinks, therefore, that it would
> be better that the Government should act on their own initiative
> before they are driven to do so.[76]

Shortly afterwards G.H. Roberts, the Minister, sent a memorandum to
Stanley Baldwin, Financial Secretary to the Treasury, further arguing
the case for an initiative. The Whitley scheme was unsuited for purely
clerical work, but he could see no reason why it should not be applied
to the dockyards and other industrial establishments run by the
government. The scheme would certainly raise the question of negotiating rights for labour unions and associations, but this issue had
already been prejudiced by their recognition in the Board of Arbitration. 'There is no doubt', he warned, 'that a decision of the Treasury
that the Whitley Report is inapplicable to Government Departments
generally would only aggravate the present agitation unless it was
supported by a Report of a Committee specially appointed to consider
the whole question.'[77] Meanwhile those departments like the Post
Office and the Admiralty which superintended a large body of
employees began to draw up their own proposals. On 9 May 1918
Baldwin presided over a meeting of officials from the Treasury, the
Ministry of Labour, the Admiralty, the War Office, the Ministry of

Munitions and the Post Office when it was decided to submit the whole question to the War Cabinet.[78] When the matter was discussed in the Cabinet on 1 July Baldwin voiced the deep anxieties and apprehension felt by the Treasury. If joint committees were set up he believed:

> there should be as little interference as possible with Treasury control, and also with the responsibility of Ministers ... certain conditions ... should be insisted on in order to limit the subjects discussed in Committee. For instance, any Joint Committees set up should be purely consultative, and should not be vested with any executive powers. They should not be free to discuss questions of management or policy. Their scope should be strictly limited to matters which directly affect the conditions of service of the staff. Questions of discipline and promotion should be definitely excluded.[79]

He grudgingly conceded that discussion of wages would have to be included in order to render the new bodies acceptable; but such discussion 'may undoubtedly make the position of the Treasury more difficult, and will disclose to the staff any differences of opinion between the Treasury and the employing Departments'.[80] At this point the arguments of the War Office seem to have made considerable impact. In a strongly worded memorandum Viscount Milner, Secretary of State for War, pointed out the dangers of a decentralised or piece-meal approach in the face of increasing trade union pressure and organisation.

> The whole theory of the Whitley Report rests on the assumption that employers, as well as employees, will be adequately organised and will act together. In public establishments there is, as the Treasury paper says, only one employer, but experience makes it abundantly clear that the employer speaks with different voices. There is not any approach to a common basis of labour policy in the many Government Departments employing industrial labour, nor is there any effective co-ordination of action in such matters.

He and his financial secretary urged the setting up of a strong inter-departmental committee, rather than leaving the application of the scheme to *ad hoc* arrangements between the Treasury and different departments.[81] The Cabinet followed this advice and a committee was set up under the chairmanship of G.H. Roberts, the Minister of Labour.

This was announced in the House of Commons on 4 July 1918.

The Roberts Committee reported in October 1918. It advocated the creation of consultative joint councils in all departments which employed industrial workers along with national trades councils on an industry basis.[82] The Report was accepted by the Cabinet's Committee of Home Affairs the same month, and on 20 February 1919 a conference was called with the trade unions to work out ways of applying the scheme. At this conference Sir Malcolm Ramsay, who had recently been appointed to the new post of Controller of the Establishments at the Treasury, spoke in a conciliatory tone assuring his audience that the 'Treasury veto' would no longer be applied in the old manner.[83] In this way the government's policy towards industrial relations was applied among its own industrial employees. Whether the same principle could be applied to its clerical work-force was a different question, but, given the interest shown by the clerical unions, it was one that could not be ignored. Accordingly in October 1918 the Roberts Committee set up a sub-committee, chaired by Sir Thomas Heath, Joint Permanent Secretary to the Treasury, to consider the issue.

Leading Treasury officials, including Sir Thomas Heath, obviously felt uneasy at the turn of events. They were alarmed both at the strident tone of the clerical unions and the threat of political agitation from outside sources. Both the Federation and the Alliance, for example, argued for the introduction of MPs, prominent businessmen and even 'persons of public eminence' into any council or board which might be set up.[84] The Treasury retained unpleasant memories of the 1911-14 agitation and genuinely feared lest any such development would mark the effective end of the Treasury's financial control which had in any case already taken a battering as a result of Lloyd George's wartime improvisations. But if the Treasury was to be weakened what other discipline could be imposed? Employees in commerce or private industry at least faced the discipline of market forces, but in government offices this factor was non-existent. In reaction against these fears Heath and his colleagues adopted an unduly cautious approach, which only exasperated the staff leaders. In their Report they advocated the establishment of joint councils at national, departmental and office levels composed of two sides: an official side comprising senior civil servants, and a staff side representing the staff associations. The objectives of the new co-operative bodies were to promote efficiency and the well-being of all employees. The new councils were to have only consultative functions and were not to be invested with executive

powers. Discussion of administrative policy and of superannuation
would be out of order and only the principles of promotion and
discipline might be considered. Ministerial responsibility to Parliament
must remain unimpaired. It was possible, the Report austerely added,
that the Whitley scheme 'may have received support under the
impression that its adoption will give Civil Servants a deciding voice in
the settlement of their own remuneration and conditions of service'.
Such an interpretation would strike at the essential functions of
government.[85]

The staff association leaders received the report with disappointment.
It seemed like an attempt to muzzle them with an essentially ineffective
machinery. They might even be worse off under the new procedure
since they would not have the same freedom to appeal to Parliament,
once the new bodies were set up. The scheme, wrote Stuart-Bunning
later, 'looked like Whitley, smelt like Whitley, almost tasted Whitley,
but it was not Whitley'.[86] He and his colleagues felt the more aggrieved
because of the lack of adequate consultation. Although their associations had given written evidence to the Heath Committee, only Stuart-
Bunning had appeared in person:

> towards the end of the sittings I was given a hearing by a few
> somnolent gentlemen. I do not think any other staff representative
> was heard and, as I was told later that the Report was in print before
> I was called, the Committee had some reason for apathy.[87]

The Report put the staff leaders on the spot, for if they rejected it
outright, the Chancellor could have told the House of Commons that
the civil service had been offered the Whitley scheme only to reject it.
In the face of this dilemma there seemed no hope of their maintaining
a united front, which was difficult enough at the best of times. Moreover, in Stuart-Bunning's words:

> The Treasury was not without guile, for with the Report, came an
> invitation to meet the Chancellor of the Exchequer only two days
> later, when he would expound the scheme. This left no time for
> effective consultation and only with difficulty could we collect a
> skeleton committee.[88]

Stuart-Bunning responded by immediately dispatching telegrams to
every known association inviting them to a meeting on the eve of the
meeting with the Chancellor. At this he persuaded the delegates to

allow him simply to move an amendment to the resolution accepting the Heath Report. The effect of this amendment would be to refer the Report to a provisional joint committee of officials and staff to work out a more acceptable scheme.

The next day, 8 April 1919, Austen Chamberlain, the Chancellor of the Exchequer, along with leading Treasury officials and the heads of other departments, presided over a crowded meeting at Caxton Hall. In a graceful speech Chamberlain commended the Report's proposals as opening a door to a 'new era for understanding and contentment among the services of the state'. He was prepared to hear a discussion upon them and would answer questions. At this Stuart-Bunning rose and voiced the staff associations' objections. His account of the outcome of the meeting is worth quoting at length:

Chamberlain evidently thought I was a less experienced debater than I really was, for as soon as I launched my attack, he got up with well-simulated indignation and asked whether we had really discussed the Report without waiting for his exposition. I quietly reminded him that he had sent it to us; what did he think we were going to do with it? Put it under our pillows and dream sweet dreams like maids at Hallow-e'en? We had read, marked, and learned the Report and it had given us inward indigestion. I made great play with the fact that we had not been consulted and saw Chamberlain turn to Heath and obviously ask him whether that was so. The answer displeased the Chancellor, for he shook his head and made an impatient gesture. My seconder batted nobly – 'I formally second' – and then came two or three minutes of suspense, but no one rose, although Chamberlain twice asked for further speakers. For the first and perhaps the only time in its history, the Service was united, obedient and silent. Chamberlain saw that he was beaten, but it would never do for the Service to carry an amendment against the Chancellor of the Exchequer, and I have always admired the way in which he covered his retreat and, indeed turned it into a minor triumph. Speaking very slowly, he said that he had been thinking, and that as, above all, he desired an agreed scheme, he would accept the amendment. He would appoint a team and we could appoint ours. That fetched the biggest cheer of the day. Histrionically, the Chancellor stole the show, but we won the battle.[89]

As a result of the meeting, a joint committee, headed by Sir Malcolm Ramsay from the Treasury and Stuart-Bunning, was formed to modify the Heath proposals. The scheme drawn up by the Ramsay-Bunning Committee (as it became known) did not differ much in machinery from the earlier proposals. The difference really lay in the terms of reference of the proposed national council. According to the Ramsay-Bunning scheme the council was to 'determine' (rather than 'consider' as in the Heath Report) the general principles governing conditions of service, and any decisions were to be reported to the Cabinet 'and thereupon become operative'.[90] A further conference of representatives, presided over by Sir Malcolm Ramsay, met at the Treasury on 30 June where Ramsay did his best to 'thaw the frost and to dissipate the suspicion'. He managed to persuade the staff representatives that the Treasury men could be 'reasonable human beings'. The Treasury would do its best to make the new system, which was 'a very momentous departure', work, but he warned that the consequences of failure would be grave.[91] The Cabinet accepted the revised scheme, and it was publicly endorsed by another large assembly of civil servants addressed once again by Austen Chamberlain on 3 July. The Chancellor stressed the extent to which the official side had been prepared to compromise and pointed out the potential dangers:

> everything depended upon the spirit in which we come to our subsequent deliberations. If that spirit be right then the feature of the Scheme which I think to be dangerous will not in practice result in danger to the Public Services.[92]

The first meeting of the National Whitley Council was held only three weeks later on 23 July 1919.

The operation and development of the Whitley system which was set up as a result of all these negotiations has been fully described and analysed by L.D. White and more recently by Henry Parris.[93] In this study, which is essentially concerned with the dynamics of the administrative-reform process, it is necessary only to examine briefly the salient characteristics of the new pattern. Joint councils were established on the local, departmental and national levels. At the departmental level the conduct of the new bodies varied, but they seem very quickly to have provided a valuable mechanism for mutual understanding between departmental heads and their staff. When the Treasury investigated the working of the new bodies in 1921 it found that departmental heads were pleased with the new procedures, and the Tomlin Commission found the same satisfaction ten years later. The chief value of the new council, in the words of a spokesman for the

Ministry of Pensions, lay 'in the substitution of personal relationships
between the Head of a Department and his staff for the old system of
written memorial and written reply'; face-to-face discussions allowed
far franker exchanges of views and helped put 'various matters of real
or imagined grievances into their true perspective'.[94] Opinion was less
unanimous concerning the value of the National Council. The Council
itself was a rather unwieldy body of 54 members representing the
officials and representatives of the staff associations. The proceedings
of the Council tended towards intense formality. Relations tended to
be 'a blend of starch and dynamite'. After the first two years when
the Council played an important role in debating the reorganisation
scheme of 1920 it tended, in the words of Warren Fisher, to become
'more or less a debating society, rather academic and sometimes a little
oratorical, which is no doubt very good in its way, but does not have
much relation to practical business': a view which was more or less
upheld by most other heads of departments.[95] Much of the most
valuable work of the Council took place in standing sub-committees
or *ad hoc* committees. Both sides would meet on their own and work
out prepared positions which would then be the subject of negotiation.

What then were the chief effects of the introduction of the new
system? In the first place the reforms hastened the development of
representative associations and unions within the civil service. The
growth of such bodies was not merely tolerated but was actively
encouraged. For the effective working of the Whitley system depended
upon the co-operation of representative staff bodies. Although official
reaction to overt political affiliation by clerical unions remained
suspicious and hostile, the new system eased a development that might
otherwise have proved painful and complicated. The Whitley process
furthermore helped to alleviate much of the discontent of staff
representatives. Under the new system, declared Stuart-Bunning, staff
associations were transformed from 'somewhat vituperative and
protesting bodies into committees of negotiation and experiment'.[96]
Although militants among the trade unionists sometimes suspected
that the new machinery served to muzzle staff protest, the prevailing
feeling among employees was that it was preferable to the 'chaos which
is what reigned before'. The Councils could be plausibly seen as 'an
extension of our democratic rights', 'as indispensable to the wider
democratic process as a local council or Parliament itself'.[97] The staff
side soon recognised the great advantages of negotiating 'out of the
public gaze' with officials. For when decisions were made they were
really effective, since the official side had already cleared their position

with ministers. The necessity for achieving consensus was a price worth paying to secure effectiveness.[98] Without question the new procedures, although often costly in manhours, smoothed away a good many minor disputes and difficulties. After a year's experience of the Whitley system even so harsh a critic of the Treasury as W.J. Brown had become convinced 'that, to an immense extent, the *minor* grievances and anomalies which have been so prolific a source of irritation in the past have been due not so much to Treasury malignity as to Treasury ignorance'.[99] From the other side Sir Malcolm Ramsay, although disappointed at the continued prevalence of ill-will, pointed out that the Treasury no longer 'sat like the Gods upon Olympus where they were obscured by clouds from the people in the valleys below'.[100] The complex nature of the Whitley procedures, with their curious blend of formality and informality, provided the flexibility necessary to deal with the later problems caused by the Second World War. Once it was set up, the Whitley machinery, like so many organs of British government, proved it was capable of organic growth, adapting itself to the changes in the administrative and political climates.

The whole episode of the Whitley reforms is a good example of the way in which reforms in Britain, while often pressed upon the administration from 'outside', tend only to be effective when accepted by the bureaucracy itself, and when transformed to meet the requirements of those responsible for operating the administrative machine. For the Whitley reforms had originated from a demand for radical change from the service associations. During 1917-19 these saw a golden opportunity to change completely the system of control over the civil service. The movement was in part an attack upon the Treasury whose position at this time was peculiarly weak. Once the demands for change had been made they were quickly taken up by politicians and even more strongly by elements within the government itself, in particular those departments who saw a necessity for a change in the central direction of British administration. Austen Chamberlain, Malcolm Ramsay and Warren Fisher, on the other hand, proved that the Treasury was sufficiently flexible to stave off change that was in its view too radical. Moreover, once the reforms were instituted the Treasury proved adept at moulding the direction they would take. The official side of the National Whitley Council was selected by the Treasury and from the beginning dominated by it. The small number of 'outside' MPs, who in the early days served on the body, were never more than a mere appendix to a body which was essentially administrative rather than political.[101] Even the official representatives from other departments played a dignified rather than an efficient role. Their function 'resembled that of the witnesses to a medieval charter. They were there to lend weight and dignity to the proceedings, but not to discuss'.[102] The Treasury soon found that the new devices could be very useful. The Whitley machinery afforded

> a more satisfactory method of ventilating and settling grievances than the old system of Memorials by Associations, and ... acted as a useful safety valve in a period of considerable unrest, and ... has tended on occasions to remove difficulties and to promote harmonious working.[103]

The expectations held by many of the staff leaders that a new Jerusalem was about to be inaugurated were soon dashed. There was no chance that a rift might be forced between the government as employer and the government as sovereign. The new Council soon showed that it was not some independent commission or employing agency; and it was formally agreed in 1921 that 'the government has not surrendered, and cannot surrender, its liberty of action in the exercise of its authority and the discharge of its responsibilities in the public interest'. Ministerial responsibility to Parliament precluded any other interpretation.[104] Thus for the Treasury the Whitley machinery provided more of an opportunity than it imposed an obligation. In no way did it supersede other mechanisms for the redress of staff grievances.[105] Although Stuart-Bunning believed that at the Caxton Hall meeting on 8 April 1919 Austen Chamberlain, while stealing the show, had lost the battle, subsequent history suggests that the Treasury may well after all have won the war.

There was nothing inevitable about either the institution of the Whitley system or its subsequent development. Neither can be divorced from the general administrative development of the time. The Whitley ideas and the Whitley machinery struck root only because certain other contemporary developments had prepared the ground. By 1919 staff associations had evolved to the point where they could effectively represent most civil servants; civil servants had already recognised the benefits of negotiating through administrative channels rather than agitating politically; and the establishments side of the Treasury was already in a process of development. As Henry Parris has stressed, these factors made the development of Whitleyism possible, and the application of the Whitley philosophy 'had the effect of fusing these three developments into one'.[106] After 1919 Whitleyism flourished because it was intimately bound up with other developments of which it was at once a cause and an effect. These were: the general desire to remove staffing questions from the parliamentary arena; the development of a unified civil service with broad staff associations; and the efforts by the Treasury to secure greater uniformity in the civil service and more effective control. It is these latter reforms presided over by Warren Fisher at the Treasury to which we must turn next.

Reforms in the Treasury Control of the Civil Service in the Inter-War Years

The Victorian Treasury in reality was far from being the dominating force which legend would have us believe. Although the Treasury's own predilections for thrift, balanced budgets and *laissez-faire* were in line with the canons of orthodox economic thought, the department lacked the institutional apparatus to translate these ideals into continuously effective influence or control. It was — along with the Foreign Office — one of the two most prestigious of departments; but it is best pictured as being near the summit of a hierarchy of offices, rather than as lying at the hub of an integrated civil service. Its special ties with the Prime Minister and its hold over the purse strings ensured that it occupied a special position and had dealings with all other departments, but, with the exception of its own subordinate financial departments, these dealings were neither intimate nor sustained. Victorian Treasury officials were unable to exercise any general guidance or initiative in improving administrative machinery except when there were special political circumstances. Despite Trevelyan's efforts of the 1850s, the distinction continued to be made between 'economy' and 'efficiency'. Sir Reginald Welby, Permanent Secretary to the Treasury, was quite clear on this point when he gave evidence to the Ridley Commission in 1886: 'The Treasury is of course responsible mainly for economy, and the head of the department for efficiency; but the Treasury would not, I think, start an inquiry on the subject of efficiency'. The Treasury could have an effect upon policies of other departments only when an application was made for an *increase* in expenditure. Thus Treasury influence upon policy-making was both indirect and erratic. His successors, Sir George Murray and Sir Robert Chalmers, maintained an almost identical position before the MacDonnell Commission 25 years later.[107] As a result the Treasury had acquired a somewhat unenviable reputation for aloofness and for niggardly and negative economising. It was seen as an obstructive force not only by reformers but even by staid prime ministers like Lord Salisbury and Lord

Rosebery. Developments in the recruitment and grading of civil servants, it is true, had fostered the idea and then the reality of a single 'civil service'; and as a consequence the Treasury's position had taken on a new significance. But after 1870 there had not been any sustained effort to further the process. If the masters of the late Victorian Treasury had a priority, it was for economy rather than standardisation; and if this led to a proliferation of overlapping grades and to peculiar departmental practices, then it was a price worth paying.

Even before 1914 there was some dissatisfaction at this state of affairs and various commissions recommended the creation of some kind of controlling civil service authority to assist the Treasury, but most of these suggestions were stillborn. The war years at once intensified and identified the earlier deficiencies. Conventional Treasury restraints on expenditure went by the board in the face of the emergency. Everything was sacrificed to the speedy mobilisation of men and resources even if this meant enormous expenditure or the creation of whole new organs of government. Many perceptive observers soon recognised that there could never be a return to the old ways in the post-war world. Edwin Montagu, who as Financial Secretary to the Treasury had pioneered reconstruction work, openly criticised the old pattern of Treasury control in the Commons on 14 May 1917. 'The Treasury atmosphere', he confided to the Prime Minister at the end of the war, 'is wholly out of keeping in my opinion with the requirements of the moment.'[108] Sir Robert Morant believed that the Treasury 'must be drastically remodelled, in organisation, in personnel, in method of recruitment, in powers *vis-à-vis* the other Departments, and (most of all) in spirit, attitude and tone towards the work of all the other offices'. It was necessary to do away with the debilitating and

> wholly obsolete doctrine that only the cheapest method can be the best, and that every proposed expenditure averted is necessarily a wise economy, when in fact it is frequently the cause of the most grossly wasteful expenditure in the long run.[109]

The Haldane Report voiced the same feelings, although it was not as radical as Morant, one of its signatories, wished. It called for a closer relationship between the Treasury and the spending departments, the strengthening of financial control within government departments and the creation of a special 'establishments' branch which should cultivate expertise in administrative matters.[110]

It was against this background of discontent within some governing circles that external political pressures began to force the issue. Towards the end of the war denunciations of idleness, waste and over-manning in government offices became commonplace in newspapers, and the civil service became something of a scapegoat for the frustrations of the civilian population. By 1917 backbench MPs too were extremely restive at the course of events. They were alarmed at the apparent growth in executive power, and many were uneasy at the unorthodox expedients of the Lloyd George regime. Runaway expenditure in government offices was an obvious target and in 1917 187 MPs requested a special investigation by a House of Commons expenditure committee. A series of investigations were put in train, and in February 1918 an important Treasury Departmental Committee was appointed to enquire into the organisation and staffing of government departments. The members of this Committee were Warren Fisher, Frances Durham, a Chief Woman Inspector from the Ministry of Labour, Joseph Rostern, the Chief Goods Manager of the Great Central Railway who had served on various government railway committees, and Charles Wood. It was chaired by Sir John Bradbury, Joint Secretary to the Treasury.

The Committee worked extremely rapidly and efficiently. It set up a series of sub-committees to investigate the internal organisations of various departments, and issued a series of interim reports as it went along. In character it was similar to the Trevelyan investigations before 1853, and had nothing in common with the ponderous workings of the Ridley and MacDonnell Royal Commissions. In just a year it had completed its investigations and had produced a final Report. The picture which the Bradbury Committee drew was not altogether reassuring. The Committee recognised the difficulties of the situation and found much to commend. On the other hand there had all too often been a lack of systematic planning. The efforts of the various departments to recruit additional or temporary clerical labour directly, for example, had led to duplication and waste. In some instances departments were bidding against each other for the same staff or even enticing typists from each other's employment.[111] The organisation of most of the new departments was woefully inadequate. The Committee estimated that a thousand of the Ministry of Pension's staff of 5,714 were unnecessary. In the Ministry of Food no attempt had been made to pool typists and other junior staff, and this had led to gross inefficiency. In one branch the staff had been instructed to re-copy the ledgers of 1916-17 even though the originals were legible and had already been audited. In the Registration Clearing House several hundred clerks had for a few weeks been 'almost entirely occupied in knitting and reading novels' during an hiatus in work at the very moment when other sections of the same ministry were recruiting new labour.[112] The importance of the Bradbury Committee, however, lay in its ability to rise above the particular and draw useful general lessons from their investigations:

> as the effect of any *ad hoc* investigations such as we have undertaken must necessarily be transitory, and the defects which we have noted may occur indefinitely so long as the system is not improved, our terms of reference appear to require us to consider the system of staff management in the Public Service generally.

Here the Committee acknowledged its debt to the Haldane Report 'which came into our hands while we were formulating our conclusions'. The answer lay in a broader concept of financial control.

> The best guarantee of efficiency and economy in the actual administration of the Public Service ... is the possession, as a matter of course, by all officials in *every* department of the feeling that they are in the position of trustees for the public purse.

Co-operation between the Treasury and the departmental officials was therefore of crucial importance: only if 'a sense of trusteeship and responsibility' developed would such co-operation flourish and yield dividends. They recommended therefore the creation of an establishments branch in the Treasury along with high-ranking establishments officers in the departments of state. The latter were to meet in a Standing Committee of Establishment Officers which should advise the Treasury.[113]

The Bradbury Committee's final report of February 1919 could not have come at a more critical time. A general election had been held, and Austen Chamberlain had just become Chancellor of the Exchequer. Rationalisation of the now confused pattern of grading and remuneration was long overdue, and the various staff associations were agitating for some completely new negotiating machinery. The three joint permanent secretaries who had controlled the Treasury during the war were due shortly either to retire or to leave the service. Demands for economy and retrenchment continued to grow in intensity. The time was therefore ripe for a complete overhaul of the whole system of Treasury control. Twenty-three years later Lord Geddes gave the House

of Lords an account of how reform was initiated in 1919. Matters were
sparked off by the fact that a large number of permanent secretaries
were due to retire simultaneously, and there were not always suitable
successors available within their departments. Lord Milner, 'always
profoundly interested and very wise in all these matters of organisation
and control of the Government machine', began to work on a scheme
to overcome the difficulty. To help him Lloyd George appointed a
Finance Committee of the Cabinet comprising Milner, Sir Auckland
Geddes (as he then was), Bonar Law and Austen Chamberlain. It fell to
Milner and Geddes to do most of the work, 'the idea in Lord Milner's
mind was that we should get a powerful, strong, central Department
to be the Department of the Civil Service, and that is the Establishment
Division of the Treasury as it was created'. They recommended therefore that the Permanent Secretary of the Treasury should have a more
powerful position and be able to advise the Prime Minister on civil
service appointments. What was needed was some *esprit de corps* to
counteract the discontent widespread in the service. The idea of the
reform scheme was to 'provide a definite central figure who would ...
impersonate the Government as the employer in the vast extents of the
Civil Service which are not immediately under observation in
Whitehall.[114] As a result of the Finance Committee's deliberations the
Treasury was divided into three separate departments to deal with
Finance, Supply and Establishments. Each department was to be
headed by a Controller having the status of a permanent secretary.
Over them all a single Permanent Secretary was to hold sway having
general powers of co-ordination, supervision and direction. This new
Permanent Secretary was to take the title of Permanent (Official) Head
of the Civil Service and would advise the Prime Minister on all senior
civil service appointments.[115] This functional division of the Treasury
replaced the older pattern whereby different sections dealt across
the board with a group of departments; and although the three divisions
of the Treasury were once again closely integrated in a further
reorganisation in 1927, the 1919 arrangement remained the basis of
Treasury structure until the 1950s.

   The man chosen for the new task of heading the civil service was Sir
Warren Fisher, Chairman of the Board of Inland Revenue, who had
just turned 40 and who was to remain in the post during the whole of
the inter-war period, becoming in the process one of the most
influential men in British government. Hard-working, ambitious and
able, he had already carved out for himself a notable career principally
in the Inland Revenue but also as one of Morant's assistants in the work

to establish the National Health Insurance Commission in 1912. Lord
Bridges, one of Fisher's successors who worked under him at the
Treasury, described him as

> a man of enormous dynamic energy, quick to make up his mind and
> with a great capacity to get things carried through to their
> conclusion. He was fearless, restless in disposition, and rather
> impatient. He was given to quick enthusiasms, both for people and
> for causes ...[116]

The description reminds one of Charles Trevelyan, but Fisher, although
he made enemies, clearly had a greater sense of tact and proportion
than Trevelyan. At all events, both Fisher's outlook and experience
were very different from those of the ordinary Treasury clerk. He had
seen the department from the outside and disliked its aloof spirit and
its disdainful tone; ironically he had suffered personally from the latter
when his application for a transfer to the Treasury had met with a
brusque response a dozen years earlier. His service on both the Ramsay-
Bunning and Bradbury Committees had given him a deep insight into
the complex problems of the civil service, and his influence can surely
be traced in both Committees' reports. Over the next two decades he
was to have the opportunity to implement his ideas.

Between October 1919, when Warren Fisher took up his post, and the
appointment of the Tomlin Royal Commission a decade later four
major developments occurred in the civil service: first the consolidation
of the Whitley Council structures and the reorganisation of the classes
in the civil service; secondly the creation of a fully integrated class of
elite administrators; thirdly the fostering of closer relations between the
Treasury and the other departments; and finally the development of
establishments work within the Treasury. All four developments were
related; all were closely guided by Fisher, but all had roots in the years
before his appointment.[117]

The reorganisation of the clerical grades of the civil service was long
overdue. In mid-1919 both the Assistant Clerk's Association and the
Second Division Clerks Association pressed pay claims upon the
Treasury. The Treasury's position was that these claims were so bound
up with such questions as the reclassification of work, the reorganisation of the service and the employment of women that they could
only be dealt with in the context of the Whitley councils which were
then being established. The associations may have suspected that this
was a ploy to delay the issue, and so pressed at the first meeting of the

National Whitley Council for joint committees to be set up to review
the salary question. Meanwhile the Civil Service Alliance put before the
Official Side a proposal to consider the whole organisation of clerical
work in the civil service, and a 25-strong joint 'Reorganisation
Committee' of the National Whitley Council was set up which reported
in February 1920.[118] The 'Reorganisation Report' recommended that
clerical work throughout the service should be reclassified into four
comprehensive grades each having its own hierarchy. These were to be:
the Writing Assistant Class for simple mechanical work; the Clerical
Class for work consisting of the 'application of well-defined regulations,
decisions and practice to particular cases'; an Executive Class for those
concerned with 'the higher work of supply and accounting departments, and of other executive or specialized branches of the Service';
and an Administrative Class which would be concerned with forming
and administering policy and with the organisation and direction of
the business of government.[119] Although disputes immediately arose
concerning the adjustment of salaries and the position of women, the
Reorganisation Report was soon accepted by both the Official Side and
the great majority of the staff associations. The Reorganisation
Committee's fourfold classification was not particularly original. It
was adapted from a Treasury Committee into the Recruitment of Civil
Servants, chaired by Viscount Gladstone, which had reported the
previous year, and which in turn derived from the Minority Report of
the MacDonnell Commission of 1914.[120] Its chief significance lay in
that it represented 'the first occasion on which a body composed
entirely of present or past Civil Servants ... have been given an opportunity of framing a scheme for its reconstruction'.

The application of the Reorganisation Report, however, was not
without difficulty. The Treasury soon argued that certain departments
could not easily be assimilated to the new scheme, and over the next
few years various separate 'Departmental Classes' were introduced.
Special treatment also was meted out to some of the groups of
ex-servicemen. This aroused stiff opposition from the Staff Side, in
particular from W.J. Brown's Civil Service Clerical Association. The
Association maintained that the Reorganisation Report represented
some kind of a 'contract' between the government and its employees,
whereas the officials maintained that such an interpretation would
strike at the heart of ministerial responsibility. However, it was clear
that even if the Whitley procedures did not amount to 'joint control'
of the civil service, at least in the new order consultation was necessary
and valuable to both sides. The Treasury was no longer prepared to

give an absolute priority to cheeseparing on labour costs. Its leaders increasingly valued the 'evergrowing team sense in all ranks'. The *esprit de corps* which resulted could not do anything but good, maintained Warren Fisher:

> if the country is to go on getting in requisite measure the service it needs from the civil establishments of the Crown, the ideal of a Service must be fostered and supported in all ways possible and thereby traditions and experience be broader and deeper based.[121]

That this was not mere pious verbiage is indicated by the fate of the Reorganisation Committee's recommendations. In contrast to the short-lived attempts of Trevelyan and Lyon Playfair to rationalise grading, the Reorganisation Report's fourfold classification remained the basis of civil service classification for the following 50 years.

The same philosophy gave rise to the second major development in the inter-war years: the creation of an integrated elite of administrators. Already before 1919 administrative necessity had broken down a little the autonomy of the Victorian departments of state with their narrow horizons, idiosyncratic customs and almost family atmosphere. But the transfers which had taken place had been sporadic and in no way systematic. Fisher on the other hand pursued a deliberate policy of cross-fertilisation. One of his new duties as 'Head of the Civil Service' was to advise the Prime Minister on the appointment of permanent secretaries, and by 1930 14 of the 20 principal administrative posts in the service had been filled by transfer from other offices.[122] The ostensible reason for this policy was the need to secure the best man for the job. But Fisher made no secret that it also stemmed from a particular view of the nature of administration. There was, he told the Tomlin Commission in 1930, 'a good deal to be said for "musical chairs" '; the man 'who has travelled is far less rigid than the man who is *in situ*'. The permanent secretary was seen as a general manager; 'they are not experts', declared Fisher; 'let us guard ourselves against the idea that the permanent head of a department should be an expert; he should not be anything of the kind'. This high regard for the virtues of the 'all-round' generalist was to hold sway almost unchallenged until the 1960s.[123]

The third development, the fostering of closer links between the Treasury and the departments, was linked to the other two. If the civil service was to be truly a 'Service' comparable to the armed services, it ought to have not only an *esprit de corps* and a unified body

of officers but also a 'general staff '. Fisher saw the Treasury in this
role: 'a sort of clearing house or general staff '. The Treasury staff
therefore needed to have a direct experience of and sympathy for the
work in departments.

> I see every disadvantage in the Treasury taking people straight from
> the administrative class examination. If you do that, then they get
> to work and take their little pens in their infant hands and they
> write away little criticisms of every sort and kind, very clever ones
> no doubt, but there is no training for constructive work, or work
> that would enable them to get the practical experience that might
> make Heads of Departments.[124]

These views represented more than Fisher's mere personal prejudices:
his dislike of the clever but aloof 'Balliol first-class men' of the old
Treasury. They reflected the desire for a more sophisticated concept
of Treasury control. The new thinking in the Treasury is best expressed
in a letter Fisher sent in March 1921 to the House of Commons' Public
Accounts Committee. The new ideals were shared responsibility and
mutual comprehension. For too long the idea had existed:

> that the Treasury official was the sole watch-dog of the public purse
> – all other officials in charge of Departments being influenced by
> duty and inclination alike to raid the till. The fact that *every* official,
> inasmuch as he is handling other people's money, is a trustee, has
> been insufficiently emphasised; and the Treasury, realising that it
> could not successfully operate or criticise *in vacuo*, has endeavoured
> to find in the 'Accounting Officer' the means of approach to other
> Departments. The Accounting Officer has thus come to be regarded
> in not a few instances as in reality the Treasury's man – and the rest
> of the Department has tended to keep and be kept at arm's
> length.[125]

Such a conception was faulty. The very phrase 'Treasury control' was
a misnomer. Discussion of expenditure could not be divorced from
issues of public policy, and the 'control' of expenditure was a complex
operation which took place at different levels: the Cabinet, discussions
among official heads of departments, and lower down 'the continuous
search for shorter and more economical processes in giving the effect to
policies already settled'. Ultimately all responsibility for 'control'
rested with the Cabinet, and the Chancellor's control over finance

may most fully be achieved, not by a body of watchdogs with orders
to bite, but by a Service animated by a common understanding of
the objectives of its Government including the objective of
economy, and by a common desire to attain those ends.

In the past Treasury officials had been as guilty as anyone, 'conjuring
up a picture of themselves as the single-handed champions of solvency
keeping ceaseless vigil on the buccaneering proclivities of Permanent
Heads of Departments'. Happily, Fisher reflected in 1930, 'this state
of affairs is fast becoming a memory; and I only refer to it here to
express the sincere hope that it may be finally relegated to the limbo
appropriate to shibboleths'.[126]
The change in attitude was largely helped by a series of reforms in
the early 1920s. In the winter of 1919-20 Stanley Baldwin, Financial
Secretary to the Treasury, presided over a 'Council of Financial
Officers' which reported in favour of greatly strengthening the status
and position of Finance Officers in departments. Fisher wanted to go
even further and recommended that the permanent heads of departments themselves should have the responsibility for financial matters.
When the Public Accounts Committee of the House of Commons
considered the matter it questioned Fisher closely on the subject of
financial control. The Committee sat at a time when economy was
seen as an imperative necessity if national bankruptcy was to be
avoided; the Geddes axe which brought devastatingly depressing cuts
in the civil service was soon to be swinging. It concurred heartily in
Fisher's contention that the heads of departments would have to work
as a team in the pursuit of economy and that they had a special duty
to be vigilant in the spending of public money. The Committee
reported in favour of making the permanent heads of the armed
services' departments the accounting officers, and a few years later in
1925 recommended that the civilian departments should follow suit.
In this way the permanent heads of departments became directly
responsible for the financial aspects of policy changes.[127] The
significance of this was considerable. In Lord Bridges' words the
arrangement 'now corresponds to something quite fundamental in our
way of thinking: namely, that responsibility for policy and for the
financial conclusions of that policy go hand in hand'. Such an
arrangement 'not only makes departments think about finance from
the outset of the consideration of new policies, but also ensures that
the Treasury are brought into discussion at an early stage'.[128]
The fourth major innovation during Warren Fisher's time at the Treasury

was the development of establishments work in line with the recommendations of the Haldane and Bradbury Committees. Sir Malcolm
Ramsay had already been appointed the head of an Establishments
Division in February 1919, and, as we have seen, at once smoothed the
path for the introduction of the Whitley machinery. The development
of establishments work was in its turn encouraged by the Whitley
developments, since a united Staff organisation virtually necessitated
a strong Official organisation able to co-ordinate the official
position.[129] As part of the general reorganisation of the Treasury in
September 1919 an Establishment Department was set up as one of
the three constituent parts of the Treasury. This contained five
divisions covering the whole range of pay and organisation of the civil
service. Meanwhile establishment officers were appointed in all the
other major departments of state. Herman Finer gives an interesting
contemporary assessment of how the new procedures operated in a
short essay of 1927 designed to explain the British system to
foreigners. 'The members of the [Establishments] Branch have
obtained a profounder knowledge of the principles underlying their
work, and a much more intimate knowledge of the inside conditions of
other Departments. Both these advantages are fundamental to any
attempt at fruitful control.' Between the establishments officers of
departments and their counterparts at the Treasury 'there is practically
day-to-day consultation'. Often in departments there would be three-
cornered discussion as both officials would be keen to bring in a
representative of the departmental Whitley council. On occasions this
led to slowness, and tensions between the three parties often remained
'but consultation is surgical to much displeasure, and an anaesthetic of
the rest'.[130] The Association of First Division Civil Servants when
giving evidence to the Tomlin Commission in 1930, spoke in similar
terms of the substitution of 'a much more intimate relation between
the Treasury, the Departments and the representatives of the Staff ' for
'the remote, purely financial, and somewhat autocratic control of the
Treasury in pre-War days'. However, all did not become at once
sweetness and light: 'more intimate relations do not ... always mean
more comfortable relations'.[131] Difficulties stemmed in part from the
financial and economic constraints of the period. Nevertheless, there
can be no doubt that both the Whitley process and the more sophisticated establishments work of the Treasury encouraged far more
flexible attitudes than those which had prevailed before. In other
areas, however, change came more reluctantly. And since the reforms
which do not occur may reveal as much about the dynamics of reform

as those which do, it will be instructive to examine briefly one area
where no change occurred: organisation and methods.

One of the chief concerns of the authors of the Haldane Report had
been to stress the importance of systematic research. This was seen as
applicable as much to the internal administration of departments as to
the external policies which they implemented. Haldane, the Webbs and
Morant had looked forward to a time when advances in the social
sciences − in psychology, economics and sociology − might be applied
with profit to the art of management. Much could surely be done to
improve management techniques and they envisaged a cross-fertilisation
between the worlds of local government, business and the civil service.
According to this view administration, if not quite an exact science,
was at least an area of study able to sustain academic analysis. The
response in government was meagre to an extreme. A few officers were
introduced to the Treasury to advise on the use of labour-saving
machinery, but, in the words of a highly critical Commons Committee
of 1942, the concern of these 'organisational experts' 'seldom rose
above the efficient use of the machines which they had supplied'.
Henry Roseveare has likened the 'half-hearted employment' of this
'insignificant handful of technicians' to 'the furtive way in which, in
1889, two lady typists had been allowed to tip-toe into the Treasury
attics, past the dozing satyrs of the five divisions'.[132] No one in
authority at the Treasury in the inter-war period seems to have viewed
contemporary developments in America in public administration other
than with distaste or at best cynicism. The Tomlin Report of 1931
criticised the civil service for its failings in this respect. It called for the
use of specially-trained management officers on a systematic basis, and
suggested that 'outsiders' might be able to offer valuable advice. These
suggestions appear to have been ignored.[133]

The absence of development in this area is significant. In contrast to
the other reforms which we have considered, it ill-fitted the new
pattern of civil service control. The development of organisation-and-
methods work would have given a role to specialists and technicians of
one sort or another which would have been incompatible with Warren
Fisher's concept of administration. It would also have entailed fostering
links with administrative worlds outside the civil service: the business
community and local government. In this respect the prevailing
Treasury attitude to 'administration' was rather narrower than its
exponents sometimes liked to suggest. For despite the talk of administration as an 'art' in its own right demanding special practitioners −
'generalists' rather than 'experts' − the Treasury leaders were most

reluctant to allow that that 'art' might benefit from any kind of professional study. The attitude is succinctly expressed in the answer of Sir Russell Scott, Director of Establishments at the Treasury, to the sponsors of the proposed Institute of Public Administration after the First World War. Scott disliked the idea of a professional institute for the civil service.

> For the most part Civil Servants have no concern with Admini-
> stration. And so far as the administrators of the Civil Service are
> concerned, I should, myself, have thought that insofar as your
> Scheme was intended to provide for instruction in the theory and
> practice of administration, it was not much good attempting to
> apply it to the administrators of the Civil Service at this stage.
> They are, poor creatures, badly overworked already.

Doctors and lawyers, he believed, had need of 'professional etiquette' and therefore of professional institutes, but this did not apply to civil servants. 'The Civil Servant ... is an employee. He does what he is told, he cannot devise his own professional etiquette.' It was important to avoid the creation of a 'bureaucracy' or of anything which gave rise to that charge.[134] Fisher and his colleagues, in short, were far more concerned with developing the *esprit de corps* of the civil service than with administration *per se*.

There were insufficient external pressures from the academic, political or business worlds to alter this view before the Second World War. The chief external pressures which the Treasury faced were the apparently irreconcilable demands of the staff for improved conditions of service, and of Parliament and political parties for economy. The Treasury's efforts to change both the concept and the reality of its control took place against the background of these pressures, and proved capable of containing both demands. The various reforms of the 1920s all formed part of a harmonious conception, although all were subject to modification according to circumstances. The application of the Whitley system, the creation of systematic grading, the development of establishments work, the creation of a unified administrative class were all interdependent. One cannot be said to have 'caused' the other, all had repercussions upon each other. Warren Fisher played an important part, although his role was often less that of initiating change than of guiding developments already in train. Fisher was a conductor rather than an architect: his contribution was to orchestrate the reforms and to pull the discordant elements together, so that they all formed part of a harmonious whole. The idea that held them together was the concept of a 'Service' analogous to the armed services of the state. The Treasury was the key. Although Fisher's attempt to secure Treasury control of the Cabinet Office in 1922 was defeated by the redoubtable Sir Maurice Hankey, under his guidance the Treasury became without question the central co-ordinating department of policy-making in Britain.[135] All this occurred contemporaneously with the Treasury's increasing confidence and competence in economic management. The net result was an immense growth in power and prestige. Although the comparison may not be wholly fair, the contrast between the humiliating criticism meted out to the Treasury by Lord Salisbury, Prime Minister at the time of the Boer War, and the meek acceptance by the Ramsay MacDonald Government of 1929-31 of the department's unwelcome advice, is too striking to be passed over.[136]

The reforms of the 1920s had a profound effect upon the conduct and still more the spirit of central British administration. They helped to create that blend of intimacy and informality which has characterised the higher echelons of Whitehall. By the Second World War 22 out of the 31 most important Treasury officials had started their career in other departments, and 47 out of the top 103 civil servants had had experience of more than one department.[137] The Treasury and the spending departments had by this time become closely linked in a symbiotic relationship. Informal communications and procedures were the order of the day. Gone were the days of starchy correspondence between 'My Lords of the Treasury' and spending departments, which had been so characteristic of the period before 1914. When Sir Richard Hopkin, Permanent Secretary to the Treasury, was asked in 1943 wherein lay the ultimate authority in a clash on spending questions, he answered 'with a charming smile' that he would himself ' "write to the Permanent Secretary of the Ministry. If he doesn't do what we want, I'll ask him round here for tea and a chat. If it's an obdurate case, I'll send out and get a small piece of cake with the tea".'[138] The foundations had been laid for the post-1945 'Whitehall Village', with its informal contacts and its carefully coded language and behaviour, which has been so graphically described by Heclo and Wildavsky.[139]

None of these changes of the inter-war years was allowed to go unquestioned. Perceptive commentators realised the serious implications. For example, the Rt Hon. William Graham, a Labour MP and a former Financial Secretary to the Treasury described in *The Banker* in 1927 how Fisher and a group of leading civil servants were increasingly able to dispose of appointments. The new pool of their protégés were

to be circulated around departments. Graham believed the matter
ought to be discussed in Parliament since it raised grave issues concerning the sort of civil service which was desirable.[140] The question was
in fact debated several times in Parliament when criticism was directed
against the position of the Permanent 'Head of the Civil Service' with
his apparently large powers of patronage. However, the motives of
critics were extremely diffuse. Some were interested in attacking
Fisher personally; others were worried about patronage; others,
particularly from the staff associations, complained of the class
barriers and wanted more open promotion; others, on the left, wanted
a more radical view of the place of administration in the modern state;
whereas most merely felt vague distaste for 'bureaucracy' and a desire
to 'cut down' government. The whole question, however, raised
important implications concerning the place of the civil servant in
society, and the nature of British administration. Outside criticism,
however, was singularly ill-informed. It tended to take a highly
political and rhetorical form, consisting mostly of rather negative
left-wing condemnations of privilege and elitism or of equally
emotional right-wing denunciation of the 'new despotism' of bureaucrats. Part of the difficulty was that there was little tangible to attack.
The important changes occurred gradually and the working out of new
procedures or the implementation of reforms was as important as
their definition in circulars. The nature of British administration
therefore became all too easily intangible, and critics were left to tilt
at such windmills as the 'title' of the Permanent Secretary to the
Treasury. The reform of the Treasury during the inter-war period is a
good illustration of the way in which institutions and government
processes can be transformed from within.

Notes

1. Hans Daalder, *Cabinet Reform in Britain 1914-63* (OUP, London, 1964),
pp. 29-53; R.K. Mosley, *The Story of the Cabinet Office* (Routledge and Kegan
Paul, London, 1969), pp. 1-24.
2. K. Smellie, *A Hundred Years of English Government*, 2nd edn. (Duckworth,
London, 1950), p. 241.
3. Sir Edward Troup, *The Home Office* (Putnams, London, 1925), preface.
4. Minute of Warren Fisher to Chancellor of Exchequer, 9 December 1924,
PRO/T163/85/G1824. Marchant later worked in the civil service during the
Second World War, *The Times*, 22 May 1956, p. 11.
5. PRO/T163/85/G1824.
6. Margaret I. Cole (ed.), *Beatrice Webb's Diaries, 1912-24* (Longmans,
London, 1952), p. 83.

7. Ibid., pp. 68-9.

8. PRO/CAB21/72.

9. Memo by E.S. Montagu, 22 June 1916, PRO/REC01/655.

10. *Beatrice Webb's Diaries*, p. 82.

11. Minutes of First Meeting, Reconstruction Committee, 16 March 1917, PRO/REC01/664, also Passfield Reconstruction Papers, A, fo. 192. Lloyd George here was drawing heavily on phrases drafted by Montagu, T. Jones to Prof. Adams, 28 February 1917, Lloyd George Papers, F/81/20/1.

12. Memo by Montagu, Lloyd George Papers, F/81/20/1.

13. PRO/REC01/665.

14. *Beatrice Webb's Diaries*, pp. 84-6.

15. Memo by Vaughan Nash and minutes by Montagu, 23 March 1917, PRO/REC01/658.

16. *Beatrice Webb's Diaries*, p. 82.

17. 'Memorandum on the Work of the Reconstruction Committee, 1917, by Mrs. Webb', 31 July 1917, Passfield Reconstruction Papers, A, fos. 445-60.

18. Addison to Lloyd George, 17 July 1917, Lloyd George Papers, F/1/3/27.

19. Addison to Lloyd George, 25 October 1918, Lloyd George Papers, F/1/4/27.

20. S.R. Letwin, *The Pursuit of Certainty* (CUP, Cambridge, 1965), pp. 365-78.

21. 'Memorandum on the Reconstruction Committee, 1917', Passfield Reconstruction Papers, A, fos. 459-60.

22. Montagu to Lloyd George, 18 May 1917, Lloyd George Papers, F/39/3/13.

23. Memorandum by Montagu, 30 April 1917, Lloyd George Papers, F/39/3/13, quoted Hans Daalder, 'The Haldane Committee and the Cabinet', *Public Administration*, vol. 41 (1963), pp. 120-22.

24. *Beatrice Webb's Diaries*, p. 89.

25. Ministry of Reconstruction, *Report of the Machinery of Government Committee* (hereafter cited as *Haldane Report*) p. 4, *P.P.*, 1918 [Cd. 9230], XII.

26. V.R. Markham, *Return Passage* (OUP, London, 1953), p. 147, quoted Daalder, *Cabinet Reform*, p. 277; *Beatrice Webb's Diaries*, p. 138.

27. *Beatrice Webb's Diaries*, p. 98. On Morant see also *DNB* (1912-21) article by Sir Lucien Amherst Selby-Bigge.

28. R.B. Haldane, *An Autobiography* (Hodder & Stoughton, London, 1929); Haldane Centenary Essays, *Public Administration*, vol. 35 (1957).

29. Haldane to his sister, 23 July 1917, Haldane Papers, MS. 6012, fo. 210.

30. Daalder, 'Haldane Committee', pp. 124-5.

31. Montagu to Bonar Law, 8 August 1917, Bonar Law Papers, 82/3/11; Bonar Law to Addison, 8 August 1917, ibid., 84/6/107.

32. *Beatrice Webb's Diaries*, p. 98.

33. Notes on the Conspectus, n.d. but July 1917, Passfield Reconstruction Papers, A, fos. 388-93, quoted Daalder, 'Haldane Committee', p. 123.

34. *Haldane Report*, pp. 7-10.

35. Memo by Sir Edward Phipps on Establishment Work in Government Offices, 19 June 1918; John Anderson to Beatrice Webb, 16 July 1918; Morant to Beatrice Webb, 6 December 1918; Passfield Reconstruction Papers, A, fos. 1039-54, 1071-81. J.M. Keynes, on the other hand, drew attention to the enormous political prestige of the Treasury and counselled caution, Keynes to (?) Beatrice Webb, 11 March 1918, ibid., B., fos. 157-8.

36. Memo by Beatrice Webb, July 1917, Passfield Reconstruction Papers, A, fos. 372-3; Beatrice Webb to Herbert Samuel, 27 October 1917, Samuel Papers, A/54/3.

37. Memo by Lord Haldane, 11 January 1918, Passfield Reconstruction Papers, A, fos. 781-7.

116   *The First World War and the Inter-War Years*

38. *Haldane Report*, pp. 22-35.
39. Ibid., pp. 4-7.
40. Michael Heseltine (Secretary to MOG Committee), to Lord Haldane, 24 May 1918, Passfield Reconstruction Papers, A, fos. 1029-31.
41. Daalder, 'Haldane Committee', upon which this paragraph draws.
42. C.H. Wilson, *Haldane and the Machinery of Government* (London, 1956), p. 15.
43. Minutes, 14 July 1917, Passfield Reconstruction Papers, A, fo. 404.
44. *Westminster Gazette*, 7 January 1919, p. 1; *Manchester Guardian*, 8 January 1919, p. 4; *New Statesman*, 11 January 1919; *The Times*, 7 January 1919, p. 7.
45. Daalder, *Cabinet Reform*, pp. 133-4.
46. *Select Committee on Estimates*, q. 297, *P.P.* 1926, VI.
47. Eg. Sir Edward Troup of the Home Office and Sir Hubert Llewellyn Smith of the Board of Trade, Passfield Reconstruction Papers, A, fos. 699-706, 774-8, quoted, Daalder, 'Haldane Committee', p. 129.
48. Bernard Schaffer, *The Administrative Factor, Papers in Organisation, Politics and Development* (Cass, London, 1973), pp. 67-71.
49. Treasury Minute, 13 June 1925, appointing a Committee of Civil Research, *P.P.* 1924-25 [Cmd. 2440], XXIII.
50. Smellie, *Hundred Years*, pp. 253-4; Bridges, 'Haldane and the Machinery of Government', *Public Administration*, vol. 35 (1957), pp. 262-3.
51. W.J.M. Mackenzie 'The Structure of Central Administration', in G. Campion *et. al., British Government Since 1918* (Allen and Unwin, London, 1950), p. 58.
52. Rosamund M. Thomas, *The British Philosophy of Administration. A Comparison of British and American Ideas 1900-1939* (Longmans, London, 1978), p. 195.
53. R. Nottage and F. Stack, 'The Royal Institute of Public Administration 1922-39', *Public Administration*, vol. 50 (1972), pp. 281-9.
54. R.B. Haldane, 'The Constitutional Evolution of the Civil Service', *Journal of Public Administration*, vol. 2 (1924), p. 9.
55. L.D. White, *Whitley Councils in the British Civil Service. A Study in Conciliation and Arbitration* (University of Chicago Press, Chicago, 1933).
56. B.V. Humphreys, *Clerical Unions in the Civil Service* (Blackwell and Mott, London, 1958), p. 35.
57. MacDonnell, *Evidence*, pp. 30-31, *P.P.* 1912-13 [Cd. 6535], XV, quoted Humphreys *Clerical Unions*, p. 47.
58. PRO/T1/11057/15657.
59. Humphreys, *Clerical Unions*, pp. 59-77; *Introductory Memoranda Relating to the Civil Service Submitted by the Treasury*, (HMSO, London, 1930), pp. 74-8; *Royal Commission on the Civil Service 1929, Appendix 1*.
60. Humphreys, *Clerical Unions*, pp. 78-98.
61. D. Houghton, 'Whitley Jubilee – The First 20 Years 1920-1940', *Whitley Bulletin*, vol. 49, no. 6 (June 1969), p. 88.
62. W.J. Brown, *So Far ...* (Allen and Unwin, London, 1943), p. 85.
63. *The Civilian*, 17 May 1913.
64. PRO/T1/11783/1641/1915, quoted F. Stack, 'Civil Service Associations and the Whitley Report of 1917', *Political Quarterly*, vol. 40 (1969), pp. 284-5.
65. H. Parris, *Staff Relations in the Civil Service. Fifty Years of Whitleyism* (Allen and Unwin, London, 1973), p. 20.
66. *Red Tape*, November 1917, p. 10.
67. L.N. Guillemard to Sir Thomas Heath, 23 May 1918, PRO/T1/12308/15647/1919.
68. Parris, *Staff Relations*, pp. 15-17.

69. Sub-Committee on Relations between Employers and Employed, *Interim Report on Joint Standing Industrial Councils* (8 March 1917), *P.P.*, 1917-18 [Cd. 8606], XVIII.

70. *Report by the Ministry of Labour on the Attitude of Employers and Employed to the Whitley Report*, 26 September 1917, Paper G.T. 2176, PRO/CAB 24/27.

71. Memo by Mrs Webb on the Interim Report of the Sub-Committee on Relations between Employers and Employed, n.d. but c. March 1917, PRO/RECO 1/665.

72. *Civil Service Gazette*, December 1920, quoted White, *Whitley Councils*, pp. 4-5.

73. Letters Ministry of Labour to Treasury, 22 August 1917 and 5 September 1917, PRO/T1/12308/15647/1919.

74. Brown, *So Far*, p. 90, quoted Parris, *Staff Relations*, pp. 26-7.

75. Committee on Relations between Employers and Employed, *Second Report on Joint Standing Industrial Councils* (18 October 1917), *P.P.* 1918 [Cd. 9002], X.

76. Sir David Shackleton to Sir Thomas Heath, December 1917, PRO/T1/12308/15647/1919.

77. Memorandum by G.H. Roberts, 4 January 1918, Roberts to Stanley Baldwin, 30 January 1918, ibid.

78. 'Government Establishments and the Whitley Report', 21 June 1918, Paper G213, PRO/CAB24/5.

79. Minutes of War Cabinet, 1 July 1918 (W.C. 438), PRO/CAB23/7.

80. 'Government Establishments and the Whitley Report', Paper G213, PRO/CAB24/5.

81. 'Government Establishments and the Whitley Report', by Viscount Milner, Paper G214, PRO/CAB 24/5; War Cabinet Minutes, 1 July 1918 (W.C. 438), PRO/CAB23/7. See also 'War Office Note on the ... Whitley Report ...', 7 June 1918, PRO/T1/12308/15647/1919.

82. 'Interim Report no. 1 of the Application of the Whitley Report to Government Establishments', 4 October 1918, Paper G223, PRO/CAB24/5. See also minutes of the Committee, 23 July 1918, PRO/T1/12308/15647/1919.

83. Home Affairs Committee of Cabinet, Minutes 30 October 1918 (HAC 16th Minutes), PRO/CAB26/1; *The Times*, 21 February 1919, p. 12; *Red Tape*, March 1919, p. 44.

84. Stack, 'Associations and Whitley Report', pp. 290-1.

85. *Report of the Sub-Committee of the Inter-Departmental Committee on the Application of the Whitley Report to the Administrative Departments of the Civil Service*, 7 March 1919, *P.P.*, 1919 [Cmd. 9], XI.

86. Stack, 'Associations and Whitley Report', pp. 291-2; Parris, *Staff Relations*, pp. 28-9.

87. G.H. Stuart Bunning, 'Whitley Jubilee The Events of 1919', *Whitley Bulletin*, vol. 49, no. 4 (April 1969), p. 53.

88. Ibid., p. 54.

89. Ibid., p. 54.

90. *Report of the National Provisional Joint Committee on the Application of the Whitley Report to the Administrative Departments of the Civil Service*, 28 May 1919, paras 23 and 26, *P.P.*, 1919 [Cmd. 198], XI.

91. Parris, *Staff Relations*, pp. 30-1.

92. Report of Conference, 3 July 1919, National Whitley Council Staff Side Minutes.

93. White, *Whitley Councils*; Parris, *Staff Relations*.

94. PRO/T163/12/G567.

118   *The First World War and the Inter-War Years*

95. Warren Fisher, Tomlin Commission Evidence, q. 18752; Royal Commission on the Civil Service, *Report*, para. 49, *P.P.*, 1930-31 [Cmd. 3909], X; Parris, *Staff Relations*, p. 34.

96. G.H. Stuart-Bunning 'Whitley Councils in the Civil Service', *Journal of Public Administration*, vol. 2 (1924), pp. 179-80.

97. Houghton, 'Whitley Jubilee', p. 87.

98. Parris, *Staff Relations*, pp. 191-2.

99. W.J. Brown, *Whitleyism on its Trial, A Critical Examination of the First Year's Working of the Whitley System in the Civil Service* (W.J. Brown, London, n.d. but 1921), p. 5.

100. Tomlin, *Evidence*, q. 17948.

101. Parris, *Staff Relations*, pp. 37-40.

102. Ibid., p. 35.

103. Draft Treasury memo, 4 October 1921, PRO/T163/12/G567.

104. PRO/T162/72/E6599.

105. Parris, *Staff Relations*, pp. 32-3.

106. Ibid., p. 25.

107. Welby, Ridley, *Evidence*, qs. 8-9, *P.P.*, 1887 [C.5226], XIX, quoted, H. Roseveare, *The Treasury: The Evolution of a British Tradition*, (Allen Lane, London, 1969), p. 204; MacDonnell Commission, *Fourth Report*, pp. 85-86, *P.P.*, 1914 [Cd. 7339], XVI.

108. 93 H.C. Deb., 5s., cols. 1380-86 (14 May 1917); Montagu to Lloyd George, 16 December 1918, Lloyd George Papers, F/40/2/24.

109. Draft addendum to Haldane Report by Morant, Passfield Reconstruction Papers, A, fos. 1072-81.

110. Ministry of Reconstruction, *Report of the Machinery of Government Committee, P.P.*, 1918 [Cmd. 9230], XII.

111. *First Interim Report of the Committee Appointed to Enquire into the Organisation and Staffing of Government Offices, P.P.*, 1918 [Cd. 9074], VII.

112. *Third Interim Report*, ibid. [Cd. 9220].

113. *Final Report*, ibid., *P.P.*, 1919 [Cmd. 62], XI.

114. 125 H.L. Deb., 5s., cols. 284-91 (25 November 1942).

115. Treasury circulars, 15 September 1919, 12 March 1920.

116. Lord Bridges, *The Treasury* (Allen and Unwin, London, 1964), p. 171.

117. A good detailed account of Fisher's career at the Treasury is to be found in Sir H.P. Hamilton, 'Sir Warren Fisher and the Public Service', *Public Administration*, vol. 29 (1951).

118. Humphreys, *Clerical Unions*, pp. 117-21.

119. *Interim Report of the Reorganisation Committee of the Civil Service National Whitley Council* (HMSO, London, 1921).

120. *Report of the Committee on Recruitment for the Civil Service after the War, P.P.*, 1919 [Cmd. 34, 35, 36, 164], XI. See G.K. Fry, *Statesmen in Disguise, The Changing Role of the Administrative Class of the British Home Civil Service 1853-1966* (Macmillan, London, 1969), pp. 39-41.

121. Statement by Warren Fisher, paras. 5-6, Tomlin, *Evidence*, p. 1267.

122. Ibid., para. 20, p. 1269.

123. Fisher, Tomlin, *Evidence*, qs. 18695, 18556, 18805, quoted Fry, *Statesmen in Disguise*, pp. 57-8.

124. Fisher, q. 18787, ibid.

125. Quoted in Fisher's Statement to Tomlin Commission, para. 7, op. cit., p. 1267.

126. Ibid., paras. 29-31.

127. A detailed account is given in Hamilton, 'Warren Fisher', pp. 15-22, upon which this paragraph is based.

128. Bridges, *The Treasury*, p. 173.

129. See Memo on Treasury Establishment Department, n.d. but June 1923, PRO/T162/59/E5083.

130. Herman Finer, *The British Civil Service. An Introductory Essay* (Fabian Society, London, 1927), p. 31.

131. *Statement submitted by the Association of First Division Civil Servants* (Tomlin Commission Evidence, Appendix 8), (HMSO, 1930), p. 27.

132. *Sixteenth Report from the Select Committee on National Expenditure, P.P.*, 1941-2 (120), III; Roseveare, *Treasury*, p. 246.

133. *Tomlin Commission Report*, p. 172, *P.P.*, 1930-1 [Cmd. 3909], X.

134. Scott, quoted Nottage and Stack, 'Royal Institute', p. 284.

135. S.W. Roskill, *Hankey: Man of Secrets* (Collins, London, 1970) vol. 2, pp. 310-20.

136. Roseveare, *Treasury*, pp. 183-6, 264-9.

137. 125 H.L. Deb., 5s., cols. 238-9 (25 November 1942).

138. I.J. Pitman, MP, 'Organisation and Methods. An Important Select Committee Report', *Public Administration*, vol. 26 (1948), p. 4.

139. H. Heclo and A. Wildavsky, *The Private Government of Public Money. Community and Policy inside British Politics* (Macmillan, London, 1974).

140. *The Banker*, June 1927.

3

3 THE CIVIL SERVICE IN MID-TWENTIETH-CENTURY BRITAIN

In the period after 1939 war again had a fundamental effect on the service; many civil servants enlisted in the armed forces and were replaced by temporary staff who brought with them new attitudes to civil service work, who required training, and whose employment focused attention on problems of recruitment and career prospects. The war also stimulated public concern about the efficiency of the service and generated suggestions for reform. In addition, the informed public began to ask whether some war-time innovations in government could not be developed and consolidated into permanent peace-time features. These elements are all evident in the three topics selected for detailed analysis in this period: reorganisations in the machinery of government, the creation of the Civil Service College, and changes in the recruitment and classification of staff.

Some of the proposals for reform in these areas originated before 1939 and took years to implement; administrative reforms are often long in gestation and require appropriate political and social environments. Early thoughts about reform in the machinery of government, for example, involved referring back to the Haldane Report and thinking ahead to the post-war period. Parliament in wartime made changes in its procedures, nowhere more obviously than in establishing the Select Committee on National Expenditure, which acquired a significant cutting edge and positive role in relation to executive government highlighted, for example, in its 1942 Report on the Organisation and Control of the Civil Service. In addition to the impact of war there were also continuing changes in society of great importance to civil service reform. These included the expansion of higher education, relaxations in the social structure, a growing appreciation of the opportunities and rights of individuals and an increased awareness of the need for equality in treatment for all citizens in a parliamentary democracy intent on developing a welfare state. Such trends contributed to a social and political climate sympathetic to innovation and which enabled advantage to be taken of the post-war reconstruction period to realign the administrative system with the social and political systems.

It is interesting to observe the roles during this period of individual officials and the general influence of the bureaucracy. Some reform proposals were given impetus while others appear to have been effectively discouraged by officials. Perhaps in our system of government it is acceptable that more power and influence should be assumed by officials in wartime; indeed, it is inevitable when there is strong national unity and agreement on the main tasks of government. However, one must guard against overemphasising such contributions at that time compared with the later years in this period. Although official files up to 1949 are available in the Public Record Office, it will be the year 2000 before the first of those relating to the year 1970 become accessible. But even when allowance is made for this difference in the availability of information, the war years were undoubtedly rich as far as the origin of reform proposals is concerned.

The war also made its impact in other ways. One of these was in giving opportunities to certain individuals to gain practical experience in central government administration. Some were university teachers or businessmen who built upon this experience to make contributions to particular inquiries in subsequent years; examples in relation to public administration include D.N. Chester, W.J.M. Mackenzie, J.P.R. Maud and Lyndall Urwick. From their brief practical acquaintance they acquired insights and experience which enabled them to make well-received recommendations on various aspects of the British system of government. Towards the end of the period their most important contributions to administrative reform had been made and any successors they have in the role of intermediary between the practical and academic worlds of public administration will have to adopt different techniques acquired from different experience. It is, furthermore, remarkable to notice how many of the recommendations in reports as late as the Fulton Report originated in often unpublicised suggestions made in wartime discussions and developments. By 1970, however, wartime innovations and influences had worked their way through the system, and the origins and dynamics of reform from that time seem likely to reveal a new pattern in accordance with different influences and constraints.

Reorganisations in the Machinery of Government

'Machinery of government' is a term which is used in a number of ways. In the first place it generally refers to the arrangements for dividing work between departments. In the British system of government ministers ultimately decide how the functions of government are to be arranged, and, since such decisions may affect more than one department, this means at Cabinet level. This was probably one of the reasons why questions concerning the machinery of government were outside the terms of reference of the Fulton Committee on the Civil Service, 1966-8 (it was not a Royal Commission but a departmental committee which brought flexibility in other respects). It should therefore be noted that where machinery of government is used to refer to the distribution of functions between departments, it is a topic for consideration and decision primarily at ministerial rather than official level. Secondly, the term is used to refer to the way in which departments are organised and structured internally with a view to implementing various policies. Officials are expected to play a prominent role in determining such questions, and their work here may well have repercussions on the distribution of functions between departments. They are also important for facilitating co-ordination between departments both formally and informally. Thirdly, machinery of government also involves questions of management efficiency. This includes techniques for ensuring that resources are used for maximum economy, and that objectives are effectively achieved. Since 1939 a good deal of attention has been given to management techniques; one example of this is the development of Organisation and Methods ('O & M') work in the Treasury. All three facets of the machinery of government are interconnected. Moreover, they all relate to the general question of 'efficiency' within government which in the last resort cannot be distinguished from broader political judgements.

There are therefore considerable difficulties to be faced in presenting a clear account of reorganisations in the machinery of government. One reason for this is the absence of any sustained attempt – before 1970 – to apply general principles to the problems of the organisation of government, although it has been said that 'the English have generally been more theoretical than they care to admit' on this matter.[1] Another is that the various committees which contributed to reforms in this area had other responsibilities, so it is difficult to isolate organisational questions from other specific concerns. Thirdly, the machinery of government is an area where the relations between politics and administration become particularly cloudy. Our object here is not so much to discuss in detail all the structural changes in the organisation of central government, which have already been studied in depth by Chester and Willson,[2] but to discuss the various pressures for reform which have borne upon it.

It is possible to distinguish two general considerations which have affected the question. The first has been the desire for management efficiency. The influence of this is to be traced in the background to the Haldane Report, to the Anderson Committee on the Machinery of Government during the Second World War, and to the 1970 White Paper on *The Reorganisation of Central Government*. Secondly, one can trace the influence of broader policy considerations, which are conditioned by the political environment. An example of this is the desire after 1945, inspired by memories of the slump after 1919, to improve the machinery of government in order to avoid economic depression.

What has happened in practice, therefore, is that changes in the machinery of government are influenced by policy considerations as well as by the desire for internal management efficiency; and the principles which are recommended as guides to action are not the only, nor necessarily the primary, reasons for structural changes. Often governmental structures are changed by a large number of pragmatic decisions, and, as they constitute the framework within which civil servants work, administrative processes cannot be understood without appreciating them. Changes in structures may also have implications for morale and efficiency far beyond the intended consequences of particular structural changes.

The Second World War stimulated as much discussion about the administration of central government as the First, and the results of the discussion may be considered in relation to changes in the structure of organisations and in the growth and development of the 'O & M' division which, in September 1941, was formally created out of the Investigating Section of the Treasury. The Anderson Committee and the Select Committee on National Expenditure stimulated thought and focused attention on both these areas.

One of the main characteristics of the Haldane Committee was that it was a body of 'outsiders', but the officials in charge in the Second World War wished to learn from the experience of their predecessors. It was felt that Haldane's emphasis on general principles was a typical product of external theorising which neglected current practice and had no impact on government, and that a committee of 'insiders' would be in a stronger position to influence day-to-day events. The committee appointed in 1942, under the chairmanship of Sir John Anderson, the Lord President of the Council, was in fact a Cabinet committee and the scope of its enquiry was intended to be broadly similar to that covered by the Haldane Committee; it had no formal terms of reference laid down. As J.M. Lee records in his recently-published authoritative study, it 'began its life not with a survey of constitutional problems but with assorted items put together from notices then appearing in newspapers, pamphlets and journals. The civil servant who prepared Sir John Anderson's brief for the first meeting attached copies of small booklets and articles.'[3] These included copies of the Report of the Haldane Committee, PEP *Planning* No. 173, and a Liberal Party Pamphlet on the Civil Service.[4] The Anderson Committee met first in November 1942 but by that time parallel inquiries were being conducted into reform in the Foreign Service and Colonial Service (the Robertson Report, January-May 1941) and by the Colonial Service Committee (June-October 1941). In addition, A.P. Waterfield, First Civil Service Commissioner, broached the subject to the Treasury in April 1941. The Government, Lee concludes, 'did not lack internal prescriptions for reform, and found it easy to reach agreement that what was needed was an internal assessment of the problems then being debated'.[5]

The machinery of government inquiry under the Anderson Committee was a direct product of Sir Stafford Cripps's personal ambition – Lee comments that at the time he seemed to many people to offer a sensible alternative to Churchill's leadership – and it was set up solely in response to a specific proposal from Cripps, supported by Cabinet colleagues who had come to believe that some kind of review was needed. Churchill tolerated the exercise but did nothing to promote it.[6] The decision to set up the Committee was taken in principle by the Cabinet on 24 August 1942 with Attlee in the chair and after Cripps had been persuaded by Anderson to change his original proposal from an 'outside' to an 'inside' inquiry. Sir Edward Bridges wrote to the Prime Minister on 26 August 1942 about the Cabinet decision, making suggestions for its membership. He said 'Sir Kingsley Wood wants to be on the Committee, partly because of the Treasury interest in Civil Service administration', and commented that the Home Secretary, Herbert Morrison, 'has more administrative experience than the Lord Privy Seal, but there is a risk that on matters of this kind he might be influenced by the rather theoretical views of, e.g. Mr Harold Laski and Mr Kingsley Martin, Editor of "The New Statesman" '.[7] The Prime Minister, Churchill, issued a Personal Minute on 27 August in which he said that he hoped 'these speculative inquiries will not be allowed to distract the attention of any of the Ministers concerned from the urgent war tasks with which they are charged. Such academic and philosophical speculations, ought, in these times, to be the province of persons of leisure',[8] but Laski wrote to him on 1 October to try to persuade him to take action on the Cabinet decision and it seems he was finally persuaded to act by Sir Kingsley Wood, then

Chancellor of the Exchequer. Lee concludes that by early October 'the real initiative for proposing a machinery of government inquiry lay in the hands of those ministers and senior civil servants who saw practical problems in any future government organisation which they thought no Haldane type committee of "outsiders" could appreciate'.[9] The Prime Minister was then approached by Anderson (who was receiving advice from Norman Brook, his former personal assistant, and from principal officials in the Cabinet Office and Treasury) who said he thought the Chancellor of the Exchequer should be consulted, and Wood then stirred the Prime Minister into action so that the Prime Minister's directive setting up the Committee was issued on 19 October 1942.

Although the Anderson Committee was a Cabinet committee its existence was fairly widely known; it was mentioned in the press and in 1944 the *Political Quarterly* published a series of articles to mark the progress of its work. In 1942 Sir Horace Wilson retired as Permanent Secretary to the Treasury and Head of the Civil Service, and Churchill promoted Sir Richard Hopkins, with whom he had worked when he was Chancellor in 1924, to succeed him. Although Wilson, it seems, lost influence and devalued the power of the Treasury in the years before his retirement, Hopkins helped to restore the standing both of his department and of his position as Head of the Civil Service. Bridges, who succeeded him in 1945, became the Head of the Civil Service who contributed most to considerations of machinery of government questions.[10]

Lee thinks that Cripps was strongly influenced by the PEP inquiry into the machinery of government conducted by three study groups set up in August 1940, and that the principal report, *Planning* No. 173, was probably drafted by Michael Young, then Director of PEP, with help from Sir Henry Bunbury and David Owen, a former lecturer at Glasgow University who became the full-time secretary of PEP in 1940 and later, in 1942, became Cripps's private secretary. Owen was particularly well placed to secure publicity at this time, Laski was using his contributions on machinery of government in the *New Statesman*, and he may also have been the author of anonymous articles in newspapers on the organisation of government and related matters.[11]

The Anderson Committee essentially supervised a survey for practitioners by practitioners.[12] It was nominated by the Prime Minister on 19 October 1942 and comprised the Lord Privy Seal (Cripps), the Lord Chancellor (Simon), the Chancellor of the Exchequer (Wood), the Home Secretary (Morrison) and the Lord President (Anderson). It was appropriate for Anderson to be chairman as he was assuming increasing responsibilities for the 'home front', and in January 1943 he became chairman of the Reconstruction Priorities Committee, which was to consider the implications of the Beveridge plan. The first joint secretaries of the Committee were Thomas Padmore and E.C.S. Wade (the Cambridge constitutional lawyer then on attachment to the Cabinet Office).

The Ministerial Committee was paralleled by a small official committee of three senior civil servants, chosen by Anderson himself for their special qualities of judgement. This collated the views of people who were referred to as 'great and wise men'[13] and gave ministers the benefit of their own advice in confidence. The three officials were Sir Alan Barlow, the Treasury's Second Secretary on machinery of government and establishment matters, Sir Robert Wood, the Second Secretary in the Board of Education (whose name was proposed by Brook), and Percivale Liesching, Second Secretary in charge of external commercial policy at the Board of Trade. Anderson specifically said at a meeting on 23 November 1942 that the Official Committee should get contributions from people like Lord Hankey, Sir Horace Wilson, Sir William Beveridge, Sir Cyril Hurcomb, and Professor Harold Laski.[14]

Both the committee of ministers and the committee of officials were served by part-time joint secretaries from the Treasury and the Cabinet Office. Cripps was unsuccessful in trying to get David Owen appointed as an additional secretary to the Anderson Committee. Later, when Brook became Woolton's Permanent Secretary, he was added to the officials' committee and Bruce Fraser, a Principal in the Treasury, became the Anderson Committee's full-time official, with supporting staff. Another influence on both ministers and senior officials at this time came from the United States. Anglo-American joint planning had already introduced them to American approaches to problems of government; and efforts to relate Cabinet committees to federal agencies or bureaux stimulated thoughts about Cabinet reform. At the same time, the Treasury was itself moving towards reconstruction policies for the civil service by stimulating discussion on the differences between private and public sector management techniques, and by arranging courses of lectures for establishment officers; also, its own O and M officers were making contact with other organisations and other countries. In July 1942 a committee had been set up under Sir Harry Crookshank, Financial Secretary to the Treasury, with Sir Alan Barlow as one of its members, to consider civil service reform including the proposal for a civil service college.

When the Anderson Committee set about its work, it was generally presumed that there would be a published report, a sort of practitioners' equivalent to Haldane, but this expectation was not fulfilled. Bridges wrote to the Chancellor of the Exchequer about this on 5 March 1945 and said it was 'increasingly difficult to find time for MG matters on the War Cabinet agenda and any attempt to achieve, within the lifetime of this Government, a document which can be published on the full authority of the Government ... would almost certainly fail'.[15] The Anderson Report itself was never published. Anderson submitted it to the Prime Minister after the caretaker administration was announced and the published equivalent to the Haldane Report became in fact Sir John Anderson's Romanes Lecture, 1946, at the University of Oxford.[16]

The Machinery of Government Committee was not formally reconstituted after the 1945 election, but the new Prime Minister asked those members of his Government surviving from the Committee under the Coalition Government (Morrison and Cripps) to join the new Chancellor (Dalton) in completing the 'unfinished business'. This was done by separate *ad hoc* committees. Thus the Committee on Future Scientific Policy produced the 'Barlow Report'[17] on Scientific Manpower and recommended the appointment of the Advisory Council on Scientific Policy, and a separate committee dealt with the details of the Cabinet's decision to replace the Ministry of Information with 'a central office'. Lee comments that 'what held all these different discussions together was the interlocking membership of the committees, particularly at the official level where Bridges, Barlow and Brook played a prominent part'.[18]

Bridges played a very important personal role in guiding developments in the machinery of government and, according to Lee, 'played his cards close to his chest' and 'tried to retain the initiative whenever he could'.[19] He appears as an astute tactician, particularly sensitive to political pressures which at that time were primarily expressions of anxiety about the size of the civil service and demands for greater use of business methods in government. It was mainly in response to widespread public criticisms of the civil service on grounds of inefficiency that the Treasury transformed its management investigation section into a full-scale O and M advisory service – but the independence of departments and the constitutional conventions of personal ministerial responsibility meant that it could do no more than offer advice when asked.

In 1946 the Select Committee on Estimates decided to inquire into Organisation and Methods in central government. When Bridges gave evidence he told them he was setting up a standing committee of permanent secretaries, to be called the Government Organisation Committee (with membership which overlapped with two other committees of permanent secretaries, the Economic Development Committee and the Civil Service Manpower Committee), and that henceforth machinery of government work would become part of the departmental Treasury, under the supervision of the Director of Organisation and Methods, so that there would be a more coherent approach to such problems. From 1946 to 1949 William Armstrong was Assistant Secretary in charge of the Machinery of Government branch and, although he was not hard pressed with his duties, Lee notes that much of the work of the branch at that time was in fact initiated by the enterprise and imagination of (usually) senior officials. When an initiative originated from someone lower down the hierarchy it had normally to have a recognised appeal to a senior official, if not to the Head of the Civil Service himself.[20] In 1947, following the 'manpower ceilings' which ministers had inaugurated in 1946, Bridges conducted a campaign to instil a greater sense of management economy through special meetings with groups of permanent secretaries in October and November 1947. Lee records that he 'caught the mood of different feelings inside and outside the service and provided a mixture of internal endeavour to satisfy the somewhat resentful attitudes of civil servants under attack, and external projection to meet the criticisms of public commentators from both the Left and the Right'.[21]

The war, therefore, stimulated a great deal of discussion about a whole range of matters concerning the organisation of government departments, which continued after 1945. In March 1946, for example, the meeting of permanent secretaries called by Bridges set up five working parties of higher civil servants to examine headquarters accommodation, recruitment, training and posting, business efficiency, and the staffing of public boards.[22] The contrast with the First World War lies in the fact that ministerial and parliamentary concern with the question had deeply influenced official thinking. Added momentum to the process of change was provided by Bridges and others who felt that there was a clear need for greater liaison between O and M questions and the work of the machinery of government in the broader sense.

Moreover, major questions relating to the distribution of work between departments were also closely considered at the official level. The

organisation for defence, the future of the supply departments and
necessary machinery for scientific policy were each dealt with by *ad
hoc* inquiries and held together at the official level by Bridges and
Barlow at the Treasury.[23] The government proposals on defence were
later published as a White Paper in November 1946 and the creation
of a Ministry of Defence and the merging of the Ministry of Aircraft
Production with the Ministry of Supply necessitated a review of
Cabinet committee organisation. The Ministry of Production was
merged with the Board of Trade. Machinery dealing with scientific
advice became the responsibility of the Lord President's Office or the
Ministry of Defence.

By mid-1949 ministers' minds were turning towards preparations for
the forthcoming general election and allegations of bureaucratic
incompetence had become a political issue. This had been stimulated
in part by the inquiry into Sidney Stanley's activities and the role of
intermediaries in government,[24] by the unsuccessful groundnuts
scheme in Tanganyika sponsored by the Overseas Food Corporation,
and by the devaluation of the pound in September 1949.

During the war instruments for control and regulation could change
the structure of departments, and the most important of these were
made under the Ministers of the Crown (Emergency Appointments)
Act 1939, which authorised the creation of new departments and the
transfer of functions. However, the initiatives in this respect came from
individual departments, and were never part of an overall plan; minor
accommodations were brought about by agreements achieved through
liaison between departments without requiring Cabinet approval. In
addition, responsibility for some non-departmental organisations could
be transferred from one department to another with the minimum of
fuss. But Lee makes the important point that without a strong
ministerial interest in reform, central officials would have made little
impact in bringing major questions up for decision, and that the
agreements on minor changes tended to be the result of ponderous and
protracted negotiations.[25] He also draws attention to an aspect of
reform in central government that seems similarly to apply at other
times and in relation to other changes. 'Without ministerial backing
the MG branch was reduced to asking departments what they wished
to see done, and to engaging in often fruitless dialogue with reluctant
opposite numbers.'[26] The independence of departments has always
been a constraint on implementing proposals for reform but Bridges,
when Head of the Civil Service, made a significant impact in a number
of ways, particularly in securing the co-operation of departments for

the creation of common services for which there was no formal
provision or legal sanction.[27]

Perhaps the most important machinery of government legislation to
result from this period was the Ministers of the Crown (Transfer of
Functions) Act. The bill was published in August 1945, enacted in
1946, and was the result of two years of discussions on the future of
war-time departments in the Lord President's office. It enabled the
executive to transfer functions between existing departments and to
suppress departments by transferring their functions elsewhere.
Although there was opposition in the House of Commons the
provisions in the Act became permanent and the first orders under it
were made in 1946. It was in pursuance of this Act that the Minister
for the Civil Service Order enabled functions to be transferred from
the Treasury to create the Civil Service Department in 1968.

The pound was devalued in September 1949 and ministers in general,
and in particular Cripps, then Chancellor of the Exchequer, were
concerned to make savings in public expenditure. They thought there
could be reductions if certain departments were amalgamated. Cripps's
officials had, in 1948, at his request, considered whether it was
necessary to maintain the Ministry of Works and the Ministry of Town
and Country Planning as separate departments. There was an important
ministerial meeting to discuss such possible amalgamations in
December 1949.[28] Although some of the suggestions made at the time
were in due course put into effect this was not done immediately.
Indeed, some of the most important amalgamations such as the
abolition of the Ministry of Supply, which featured in the Conservative
election manifesto in 1950, did not take place until after the 1951
general election when Churchill again became Prime Minister.

Lee's general comments and conclusions on his study of the Anderson
Committee and its successors are particularly valuable for being based
on comprehensive research into the official files. The evidence, he
says,

> betrays ... many inside concerns with tactics and personality ...
> Ministers and senior civil servants were confident of their ability
> to adapt British institutions to post-war concerns without any
> radical changes ... The history of MG work is more interesting for
> the light which it throws on contemporary uncertainties than for
> the concrete reforms which its deliberations achieved.[29]

The discussions betray 'the realism which ministers and civil servants liked to cultivate when faced with pressure for greater government intervention', 'a sensitivity to the costs of administration', and 'an awareness of the changes in Britain's standing as a world power'.[30] But they also reflect inhibitions arising from the association of the science of public administration with socialism, and 'insiders often found that the comments of outside academic specialists in public administration were too naive and idealistic to carry conviction within the civil service'.[31]

It seemed to some people at the time that there might be a middle ground between the specialists inside government and what were regarded as the propagandists outside. Anderson became President of the Institute of Public Administration in 1944 and the Institute received its first Treasury grant in 1948. However, it may be that such apparent encouragement of the Institute was in fact designed partly to keep its activities under control, for the revision of the Whitehall series of histories of individual departments, proposed by the Institute in 1949, was authorised only on condition that they were written in departments under the guidance of each permanent secretary: so that – to quote Bridges – they could be 'satisfactory, consistent, and unembarrassing'.[32] Evelyn Sharp is on record as regretting that the distribution of functions in government proceeded not on the basis of analysis and judgement, but on the basis of guesswork and personalities, and she pressed for 'a permanent-and very powerful-Commission' into machinery of government matters, which 'should be so conducted that parliamentary and public opinion would compel acceptance of its conclusions'.[33] Bridges and Barlow, on the other hand, preferred to move more cautiously, considering a number of separate problems, rather than support a full-scale investigation. The general Treasury attitude is perhaps well typified in an article published in the *O and M Bulletin* in 1951 where Louis Petch, then an Assistant Secretary in the Machinery of Government branch of the Treasury (and later, Second Permanent Secretary, Civil Service Department, 1968-9), argued that 'it is clearly best that all machinery of government investigations should be undertaken from within the Government service ... in fact a full-scale investigation of the present administrative organisation from outside would be most unlikely to find any weaknesses or faults previously undetected'.[34] Meanwhile, the university teachers who had been temporary civil servants during the war presented their reflections in a number of books, pamphlets, lectures and articles after they had returned to their universities.[35]

The inquiry into O and M in 1953 was the last item to be considered by the Government Organisation Committee and by the time Bridges retired, in 1956, approaches to reviewing the machinery of government by ministerial committees and committees of permanent secretaries had both been generally discredited. There was no longer the same faith in the capacity of ministerial or official committees to review the machinery of government. Moreover, the political climate had changed both nationally and internationally. The mood of the country was more optimistic and no longer so concerned about the dangers of post-war slump and unemployment. The Festival of Britain had marked the end of the post-war grey period, a new Conservative Government was elected, and there were the beginnings of a period of economic stability and affluence that was soon to stimulate Harold Macmillan to tell the nation 'You've never had it so good'. There was a lull in enthusiasm for avoiding economic depression by means of reforms in the organisation of government.

In fact the period of ten years from about 1953 was fairly quiet as far as developments in the machinery of government were concerned. Churchill's administration may have provoked a certain amount of controversy by his introduction of 'Overlords', but this was more a matter of political change in relation to machinery of government than a matter of administrative reform. The Priestley Royal Commission on the Civil Service, 1953-5,[36] came and went almost unnoticed by the public at large. It was only a partial inquiry which made a number of recommendations on superannuation, hours of work, leave and other matters, mainly on the basis of what is known as the principle of fair comparison; and the most important innovation following the report (which was never debated in either of the Houses of Parliament) was the creation of the Pay Research Unit as a means for determining the pay of civil servants when comparable work outside the civil service is also considered.

In 1957-8 one of the sub-committees of the Select Committee on Estimates examined Treasury control of expenditure covered by the Estimates,[37] but they found that a comprehensive survey of the system of Treasury control or, as they put it, the 'complex of administrative practice that had grown up over the centuries', was beyond them. Their one firm recommendation was that a small independent committee, with access to Cabinet papers, should be appointed to report on the theory and practice of Treasury control of expenditure. However, events did not develop in quite the way that the Estimates Committee intended. As Lord Bridges has explained:

The Treasury, in their observations on the Report ... stated that the Government could not accept the Estimates Committee's recommendation in favour of an outside committee, but had decided to set in hand ... an internal inquiry under the authority of the Chancellor of the Exchequer ... by a group consisting of Sir Edwin Plowden (now Lord Plowden) and three other persons from outside Government service, and senior officials drawn from departments, including the Treasury.[38]

Plowden had been a temporary civil servant in the Ministry of Aircraft Production during the war, and from 1954 to 1959 was Chairman of the Atomic Energy Authority. The civil servants who were members of his group remained anonymous, but the three persons from outside the service were named. These 'outsider' colleagues were Sir Sam Brown, who had been a temporary civil servant during the war and when he left in 1954 was Under Secretary in the Ministry of Aircraft Production, Sir Jeremy Raisman, who had retired from the Indian Civil Service in 1945, and J.E. Wall, who had been Under Secretary in the Ministry of Food when he left the service in 1952.

The Plowden Report[39] contained various recommendations. One led to the creation of the Public Expenditure Survey Committee (PESC) – the committee of principal finance officers of the major spending departments, chaired by a Treasury deputy secretary – which considers reports from the Treasury on the forecasts of departmental expenditure. Another was that the organisation of the Treasury should be reviewed; this led in 1962 to a reallocation of functions within the Treasury. From this date the Treasury was organised in two sides, each under a Permanent Secretary – a 'Finance and Economic' side, and a 'Pay and Management' side. Consequently, for the first time (according to Bridges)[40] the distribution of duties in the Treasury between divisions and groups became almost entirely on a functional basis. Although Lord Bridges had retired from his post as Permanent Secretary to the Treasury in 1956, he subsequently stated that the Plowden Report was 'a most important and helpful document'; that the reorganisation introduced in 1962 was 'on the right lines'; and that he was particularly glad that the management side was not taken out of the Treasury and made into a separate department.[41]

At this point the whole question became affected by the broader political climate, which had once again shifted. The early 1960s witnessed the growth of interest in the machinery of government among politicians and writers. It became fashionable to explain the post-war economic failures of Britain in terms of a faulty administrative structure. In 1963 Harold Wilson inspired the delegates at the Labour Party Conference with his vision of 'the Britain that is going to be forged in the white heat of the scientific revolution', and in 1964 the new Labour Government set up the Ministry of Technology ('Mintech') 'to guide and stimulate a major effort to bring advanced technology and new processes into British industry'. As Tom Lester recalled in an article in 1973, 'the Ministry was to take on a wider and wider responsibility for increasing productivity and efficiency, particularly within those industries in urgent need of restructuring or modernisation'.[42] Another creation thought to be important by the Government was the Department of Economic Affairs (DEA), which it was envisaged would have responsibility for long-term planning and for bringing about 'structural' changes in the economy while leaving financial management to the Treasury. The new government appears to have rushed into these changes without paying sufficient attention to the implications in Whitehall. In the event, the work of the DEA and Mintech was adversely affected by economic forces which the Labour Government proved quite incapable of controlling.

It was, however, not only the distribution of functions among ministries which attracted attention. Other moves toward administrative reform under the post-1964 Labour Government also fitted the mood of the time. In the mid-1960s there was a spate of books and articles critically analysing various British public institutions. They included analyses of Parliament, British industry, hospitals, the Church, and institutions in both central and local government. Many of the established public institutions and procedures had been in operation, essentially unchanged, since the nineteenth century, and it was increasingly felt that they should be re-examined and brought into line with changes in other parts of the social system. This general attitude for reform overrode party political considerations and it was therefore hardly surprising that formal and official inquiries were instituted to examine areas for potential administrative reform in both central and local government. Some (like the Maud and Mallaby Committees on local government) were established by the Conservative Government before it went out of office in 1964. Others (like the Fulton Committee on the Civil Service, the Seebohm Committee on Personal Social Services, and the Royal Commissions on Local Government and the Constitution) were set up after the Labour Government came to power in 1964.

However, the civil service, for long the subject of music-hall jokes, was

the target of a more consistently academic attack than other
institutions. One of the first and most significant publications in the
pre-Fulton decade to criticise the civil service in a stimulating way was
the essay by Thomas Balogh (now Lord Balogh) entitled 'the
Apotheosis of a Dilettante', published in *The Establishment*, a
symposium edited by Hugh Thomas.[43] Balogh criticised the service
for being 'the establishment of mandarins' and found its basic weakness
in its structure which, he said, favoured centralism and dilettantism.
Following that essay the next critical piece of writing to make a similar
impact was Brian Chapman's *British Government Observed*, in which
the author explained his contention 'that the source of many of our
present ills is institutional, and lies in a mistaken veneration of old
ideas, and a refusal to examine them coolly and objectively'.[44]
However, in terms of pre-history to the Fulton Committee the Fabian
tract *The Administrators*[45] is particularly notable. The group
responsible for this included R.R. Neild, subsequently a member of
the Fulton Committee, Shirley Williams and Lord Balogh; in addition
some civil servants are believed to have taken part in the work. The
tract has a number of basic similarities with the scope, approach and
style of presentation of the Fulton Report.[46] About the same time,
in 1964, Harold Wilson was interviewed by Norman Hunt for the BBC
and asked about his plans for the modernisation of Britain. He said the
Labour Government would 'make government more efficient. As the
tasks of government grow more numerous and more complex the
machinery of government must be modernised ...'[47] However, the
main precursor to the Fulton Report was the 'Recruitment to the Civil
Service' Report of the Select Committee on Estimates, published in
1965,[48] which recommended a committee to initiate research upon,
to examine and to report upon the structure, recruitment and management of, the civil service. The Report of the Estimates Committee will
be considered further in the last section of this chapter.

The Fulton Committee, then, was set up partly in response to public
pressure, stimulated by academic publications and a rather special
interest which had become apparent in the Labour Party and its allies
including the Fabian Society. Another factor was the expectation that
there should be a major inquiry into the civil service about once in
every generation of civil servants. However, internal factors played a
part because civil servants and their associations, always wary of the
Treasury, were becoming increasingly restless about the management
divisions. These, they felt, had never assumed a very active role in
central management and had had insufficient resources. Nor had they

shown enough interest in the career-management of scientists, engineers, accountants and lawyers.

The Committee well fitted the prevailing mood and it was widely welcomed in the press and by the unions.[49] *The Economist*, 12 February 1966, referred to its members as 'three dons, four very able top civil servants (at least three of them rather unconventional), two extremely intelligent MPs, two leading industrialists, and the statutory white collar trade unionist'. It is obvious that a number of its members were very sympathetic to the Labour Party and its approach to problems of government of the 1960s; this particularly applied to Norman Hunt (now Lord Crowther-Hunt) who devoted a year working full time for the Committee and who, with the Committee's Secretary, drafted the Report.

The Committee encouraged the submission of evidence from individuals and interested bodies; sponsored six research projects conducted by several academics and a management consultancy team; and stimulated a number of government departments to produce evidence on what were thought to be relevant topics. The Fulton Committee was the first official committee or Royal Commission investigating the British civil service to commission research from persons outside the service. Some of the research papers were extremely modest in scope, others were delivered very late, and there is little evidence that the Committee was much influenced by the research except, perhaps, through the management consultancy team which included Norman Hunt. Clearly, the official bureaucracy played a considerable role in the scope and manner of the research, as well as in the presentation of various departmental viewpoints. The Treasury had particularly close contact with the work of the Committee both formally (it was a departmental committee) and informally, and this was helped by the fact that its able and industrious Secretary, Mr. R.W.L. Wilding, was previously a principal in the Treasury.

Problems of machinery of government were largely beyond the Committee's terms of reference, though some aspects were considered because they related to the structure of the service. Sir Laurence Helsby, then Head of the Civil Service, presented a personal paper on central management of the civil service. Other bodies submitting evidence specifically on this topic included the Labour Party, the TUC, staff associations and several individuals. The general, but not unanimous, weight of opinion was in favour of a change, either to a Public Service Commission or to a new department. The Report recommended that the Civil Service Commission and the work of the Pay and

Management group of divisions of the Treasury should become part of a new Civil Service Department. The suggestion for a Civil Service Department had been raised in various forms on a number of previous occasions. For example, in a paper considered by a sub-committee of the Select Committee on National Expenditure (1941-2), Lyndall Urwick had argued that there should be a member of the Cabinet responsible for the whole civil service,[50] and W.J. Brown argued in the parliamentary debate on the Expenditure Committee Report that control of the civil service should be taken out of the hands of the Treasury.[51]

On the day the Report was published the Prime Minister announced that the Government accepted the proposal to establish a new Civil Service Department, as recommended in the Report. The new department was, in fact, established from 1 November 1968 by an Order in Council[52] in pursuance of the Transfer of Functions Act. The Lord Privy Seal (Lord Shackleton) was appointed by the Prime Minister to assist him in the day-to-day operation of the department and the Permanent Secretary became Head of the Home Civil Service. Setting up the Civil Service Department in this way may be considered a somewhat dubious use of the Transfer of Functions Act which, bearing in mind the development intended for the transferred functions, has bestowed on the department a doubtful pedigree. That Act made provision for dissolving a department and transferring its functions elsewhere by an Order in Council subject to the affirmative resolution procedure, transferring functions between departments, and changing the title of a department. However, the Act was a specific outcome of the process for reducing government activity after the war and did not confer powers for the creation of new ministries. Indeed, in the House of Commons debate on the Bill the Solicitor-General emphasised that it contained no provision to increase the number of ministers or to create a new ministry.[53] Nevertheless the Order, which transferred to the Minister for the Civil Service a number of Treasury statutory functions, was not challenged, and there can be little doubt about the CSD's well-established existence − it now has about five times the number of staff in the Treasury.

The White Paper, *The Reorganisation of Central Government*,[54] published in 1970, was the result of a four months' review of the machinery of government by officials. In some respects it was intended to complement the investigations into the Home Civil Service conducted from 1966 to 1968 by the Fulton Committee. The Fulton Committee considered whether it should propose a major review of the whole machinery of government but did not examine the question in detail as it was outside their terms of reference. However, they said that if the review of 'hiving off', which they proposed, recommended substantial changes, this would also provide the opportunity for simultaneous consideration to be given to a general review of the machinery of government.[55] In the House of Commons the Prime Minister, Mr Harold Wilson, said that reviewing the machinery of government had been, and would continue to be, a continuing process, but it was impossible to refer the subject to outside inquiry because so much depended on the way the Government was working and the personalities and working methods of prime ministers and their colleagues.[56] Impetus was given to the publication of the Reorganisation White Paper by the determination of the new Conservative Government to undertake a systematic review of the organisation of government. Mr Edward Heath, the new Prime Minister, had devoted considerable time and effort in opposition to reflecting upon what he saw as the failings of Conservative governments before 1964, and upon the difficulties which seemed to bedevil successive administrations. In his view insufficient weight was given to longer-term planning, which suffered at the expense of short-term expediencies. He had encouraged the Conservative Research Department to produce proposals which a future Conservative government could implement. The White Paper, therefore, was produced because the new Conservative Government had pledged itself in its election manifesto to introduce 'a new style of government' with 'a fresh approach to the taking of decisions' which would involve improving the efficiency of the machinery of government to ensure that its aims were achieved.[57] It was an attempt to ensure that the broad framework of the machinery of government complied with the Government's strategic policy objectives, and sought to apply the functional principle as the basis for the allocation of responsibilities. It said 'government departments should be organised by reference to the task to be done or the objective to be attained, and this should be the basis of the division of work between departments rather than, for example, dividing responsibility between departments so that each one deals with a client group'.[58] It added that the basic argument for this functional principle is that the purpose of organisation is to serve policy. However, it is immediately apparent that this principle made no great advance in terms of administrative theory on the principle enunciated by the Haldane Committee over half a century earlier. Clearly, not all functions of modern government fit easily into this approach, much depends on how functions are defined or delimited, and much more depends on the relative political sensitivity of functions, policies and client groups at any particular time. The Conservative Government later became increasingly aware of the constraints imposed by the circumstances it was to encounter.

In relation to this present study the publication of the White Paper was important for two reasons. One was that it announced the intention of the Government to create the Central Policy Review Staff as part of the Cabinet Office with clearly defined tasks,[59] making it available to study inter-departmental issues which could include investigations into the machinery of government. The other was that it preceded the setting up of the 'giant' departments which, as Sir Richard Clarke subsequently explained,[60] reflected the thought that it is more efficient to operate with ten large departments rather than with over 20 small ones. The main advantages hoped for in the reorganisation were that the 'giant' can develop its own strategy and decide its own priorities, it can settle problems itself instead of through lengthy discussion in interdepartmental committees, it is big enough to have specialised services, it can support a clearer strategy at the centre, and it might result in a reduction in the size of the Cabinet. It can be argued, in addition, that in practice the creation of 'giant' departments is associated with a change in the balance of power from the legislative influence to the executive influence in policy making; that it may result in a reduction in sensitivity to the needs or demands of client groups; and that it may also have an unfortunate effect, at least in the short term, on the morale and efficiency of civil servants.

Although major machinery of government issues in Britain are primarily the responsibility of ministers, our study reveals that a significant role in the reform and development of the machinery of government was, in fact, played by civil servants. Sir N.F. Warren Fisher once wrote that 'the last word in shaping the machinery of Government (as with policy) rests with the political management and ... the Civil Servant, however progressive the individual might be, is a servant'.[61] Perhaps our study of this topic suggests there is sometimes a weakness in the political system which has an effect on the administrative system. If, in any form of government, the political management does not exert itself and perform its intended functions, the work of government does not stop but the vacant functions are performed by another element; in this particular case civil servants not only ensured that the administrative system suffered no irreparable damage but also were able to introduce modest administrative rationalisations.

Anyone who looks for a clear pattern in reforms in the machinery of

government after 1939 will be disappointed. A number of pressures
bore on the question – economic, political and administrative – but
there was insufficient agreement among politicians in Parliament to
provide clear political direction. In the 1940s and 1950s although there
was concern to reduce waste in government expenditure, little further
thought was given to the meaning and practice of efficiency. During
the 1960s there was a change, as complacency concerning the merits
of British government gave way to a mood of self-doubt and criticism.
Emphasis was then placed on wholesale reform of British institutions
and 'institutional change came to be widely seen almost as a panacea
for arresting national decline'.[62] Most important public institutions
were subjected to examination and review in the 1960s and 1970s, but
proposals that were implemented as a result were piecemeal rather than
as a part of a carefully considered overall design. Sometimes it is
possible to trace the incremental stages through which pressure towards
the achievement of a particular change was built up, but somewhat
disappointingly this has the flavour of *post hoc* rationalisation rather
than the uncovering of details of prior agreement on a particular
objective. Nevertheless, it will be instructive to turn our attention
from such a broad area as the machinery of government to examine in
detail the history of a more specific proposal: the creation of the Civil
Service College.

The Civil Service College

The idea of a Civil Service College had been first mooted soon after the
end of the First World War,[63] but although certain official reports[64]
had advocated improvements in training they stopped short of
recommending a staff college.[65] However, the Sixteenth Report of the
Select Committee on National Expenditure for the Session 1941-2 was
much more specific in its analysis of contemporary problems and in its
recommendations. It commented that 'the period from 1919 to 1939
was marked by an almost complete failure to foster the systematic
study of organisation as applied to Government Departments',[66]
recommended the reorganisation of establishment work in the
Treasury, and was impressed by the need for the kind of post-entry
training that would involve the creation of a Civil Service Staff College.
The Committee reported that they looked forward

> to the creation of a Staff College to which picked members of the
> Administrative and Professional Grades, as well as promising
> members of the Executive and Clerical Grades, could be sent after a

few years' service. The syllabus might include courses in public administration and in modern developments in trade and industry, economics, social services, etc.[67]

In a particularly interesting section of the Report the Committee added that 'The experience of the last twenty-five years suggests ... that ... such recommendations are frequently shelved and that continuous and authoritative stimulus is required if effect, in the spirit as well as in the letter, is to be given to needed changes ... [and] that stimulus can be most effectively applied by Parliament itself.'[68]

The selection of this topic for consideration was consistent with the general approach of the National Expenditure Committee. The Committee was the war-time successor of the Select Committee on Estimates (which disappeared for security reasons; estimates give valuable information to the enemy, so during war-time the estimates were prepared but not published) and was established every year during the war 'to examine the current expenditure defrayed out of moneys provided by Parliament ... and to report what, if any, economies ... may be effected ...' The Committee worked through sub-committees with a staff of eleven clerks drawn from the House of Commons offices, and the Chairman of this particular sub-committee of four members was Arthur Woodburn.[69] The subject for investigation was presumably chosen as a result of initiative by the Committee and because, as Woodburn put it, 'the Civil Service is the pivot on which the whole management of the war and of war production really turns'.[70] It is difficult to be more specific about influences on the Committee because, for security reasons, it was not customary for minutes of proceedings to be subsequently published and the recently available Committee records (in the Victoria Tower) contain no helpful indications.

However, the PEP broadsheet *Planning* (No. 173) of 15 July 1941, reviewing problems of machinery of government in relation to the war effort, specifically recommended the establishment of a Staff College for the higher training, at a suitable age, of men and women destined for higher administrative or executive responsibilities. Also, the National Administrative College Group, one of the most significant initiatives in management training during the war, was formed about this time, in 1942, and may well have influenced the Committee. It consisted of a large number of interested individuals, acting in their private capacities, from industry, the universities, politics and the civil service, among whom the moving spirit seems to have been Major

Lyndall Urwick (who was also a member of the Liberal Party
Committee on the Civil Service, a majority of which had advocated the
creation of a Staff College for the civil service). Other leading
individuals from the public service who supported the proposal
included Professor Henry Clay (Bank of England), Sir William Jowett
(Paymaster General), Sir Richard Livingstone (President of Corpus
Christi College, Oxford), Sir Kenneth Lee (Ministry of Supply), Harold
Macmillan (Parliamentary Secretary to the Colonies), R.A. Butler
(President of the Board of Education), Sir James Irvine (Principal and
Vice-Chancellor, University of St Andrews), Lord Woolton (Minister
of Food), Sir Stafford Cripps (President, Board of Trade), Sir Walter
Citrine (General Secretary, TUC), and Field Marshall Lord Milne,
together with a large number of leading figures from local government
and the largest industrial companies. Although the group had good
contacts with the Treasury, mainly through Sir Donald Banks, who
was the Director-General, Petroleum Warfare Department, the Treasury
seems to have been positively discouraging. As a result of a submission
from the National Administrative College Group to the Paymaster
General, the proposal to establish an Administrative Staff College was
considered by the Cabinet's Advisory Panel on Home Affairs on 26
October 1942.[71] A Treasury minute by Sir Richard Hopkins,
Permanent Secretary, recording one of his discussions with Banks,
refers to Urwick 'as a man who must be conceded to be an expert
in his own line', says that 'although the proposal has the blessing of
many distinguished people, including Ministers, I do not think it can
be claimed to be put forward by an authoritative body', 'the
establishment of such an institution must come as a deliberate
decision of the Government of the day and not as a by-product of
certain outside enthusiasts, whatever their motives, and whatever their
expert knowledge of organisation' and 'we ought not to prejudice the
issue by light-hearted acquiescence in the project'. Another Treasury
minute recommends that contributions for establishing the College
should *not* be allowed as business expenses for excess profits tax
purposes.[72] Despite this lack of interest from central government the
Administrative Staff College, without the assistance of public money,
was established at Henley-on-Thames soon after the end of the war.

The Report from the National Expenditure Committee could hardly
have been more specific and forceful either in its analysis or in its
recommendations and it was well received. *The Times*, for example,
noting that the Committee's recommendations were on the same lines
as suggestions recently made in its columns, gave it a warm welcome in

a leading article.[73] However, there was not unanimous approval for its recommendations. A minute of 4 January 1942 from BDF (probably Bruce Donald Fraser, later Permanent Secretary of the Ministry of Health) to Sir Richard Hopkins said: 'I was much struck by the differing views on an administrative staff college expressed by Heads of Department at your meeting in November. Everyone, was, of course, very wise – Sir Thomas Gardiner, I thought, was the wisest – and of course their views were much more weighty than those of the Select Committee and other outsiders.'[74] On 31 December 1942 Clement Attlee, Deputy Prime Minister, sent a note to the Machinery of Government Committee under the chairmanship of Sir John Anderson, in which he asked the Committee to consider *inter alia*, 'the desirability of establishing a Civil Service College'.[75] This initiative, however, did not progress far. On 9 January 1943 H. Wilson Smith wrote a minute to Sir Richard Hopkins in which he pointed out that there was nothing new in the points raised by Attlee and that the possible establishment of a Civil Service Staff College was 'a matter which has been engaging the closest attention of the Financial Secretary and those associated with him in examining the problems of the post-war Home Civil Service'.[76] The Minutes of the meeting of the Committee on 22 April 1943 state that the Committee agreed to await the report of the Committee on Training of Civil Servants before discussing post-entry training.[77] In the House of Lords debate (26 November 1942) on the Headship of the Civil Service various appreciative remarks were made about the Report and Lord Winster said the suggestion to establish a Civil Service College was a very important one, 'but such a staff college must not be an extension, for instance of the London School of Economics, although no doubt economics should be taught at it if it is established'.[78] The debate in the House of Commons was similarly appreciative and Sir Kingsley Wood, Chancellor of the Exchequer, acknowledging that a Civil Service Staff College had been advocated in a number of quarters for some time, welcomed the recommendation and proposed 'at once to start an investigation into the general question of the training of civil servants, including the question whether a staff college could be established and, if so, the particular form and character that that establishment should take'.[79] In one of the concluding speeches in the debate Sir John Wardlaw-Milne commented on the attitude of officials to the work of the Select Committee and said that in his opinion 'the investigations made by the Committee are not only not resented by Departments but are very often strongly supported and encouraged by them ... The senior members of the Civil

Service show no resentment; rather do they think that these inquiries have been helpful to them'.[80] Whilst the recommendation for a Staff College received some support from within the civil service,[81] some of the strongest criticisms also came from civil servants. For example, W.J. Brown, speaking in the House of Commons debate[82] and drawing upon his 30 years' experience of the civil service, said that he was against the recommendation, mainly, it seems, because he thought that the Hendon Staff College for policemen did more to demoralise the London police than even Home Secretaries did; and L.C. White, General Secretary of the Civil Service Clerical Association, wrote that the idea of a Staff College 'had a very unenthusiastic reception in the Civil Service, where it is regarded, particularly among the middle and lower grades, with a good deal of suspicion',[83] because it was thought the College would be small and elitist.

As a direct result of the work of the Select Committee on National Expenditure, early in 1943 the Chancellor of the Exchequer set up a Committee on the Training of Civil Servants under the chairmanship of Ralph Assheton, Financial Secretary to the Treasury.[84] The Committee received memoranda from a number of sources including several government departments, the Joint University Council for Social Studies and Public Administration, and the National Administrative College Group. It also heard oral evidence from a number of witnesses including D.N. Chester, then Chief Economic Adviser, Offices of the War Cabinet, Professor Lionel Robbins, Director of the Economic Section, Offices of the War Cabinet, J.P.R. Maud, then Master of Birkbeck College and Second Secretary, Ministry of Reconstruction and Professor Harold Laski of the London School of Economics who had recommended the creation of a Staff College for the administrative class, in his Introduction to J.P.W. Mallalieu's book *Passed to You, Please.*[85] The civil service representatives were not very enthusiastic for a Staff College but seemed more interested in periods of secondment for civil servants who could spend a year on a course at a university or in industry or local government. A.J.T. Day, Chairman of the Staff Side of the Civil Service National Whitley Council and a member of the Assheton Committee, thought the College would be 'a high-faluting academic institution designed for a corps d'elite'. Most of the academic witnesses favoured more use of university resources rather than the creation of a new college. Like Robbins, they doubted whether there was a body of administrative doctrine to be taught and also could see no solution to the practical difficulties of finding qualified staff to teach at a new college.[86]

On 28 October 1942 the Paymaster General, Sir William Jowett, wrote to the Chancellor of the Exchequer:

> On Monday I submitted the proposals for an Administrative Staff College, which we discussed the other day, to the Panel which advises me informally on internal reconstruction matters. This body includes such people as Mr. Simon Marks, Sir John Greenly, Sir Samuel Beale, Mr. Seebohm Rowntree, Mr. S. Courtauld, Mr. H.U. Willink, Sir William Beveridge, Mr. G.D.H. Cole and Mr. John Maud, all of whom from their various standpoints are well qualified to speak on this subject. I was impressed, therefore, to find that it was their unanimous opinion that a college to bring together able young administrators from the services, the civil service, from business, and from local and central government was a very real need.
> ... [but] they were agreed it was totally impossible to achieve [the broadening of outlook] in a course of the kind proposed. In short the institution of an Administrative Staff College was approved, but not one of the type originally envisaged by Sir Donald Banks and his group.[87]

The Assheton Committee noted that 'neither inside nor outside the Service has there been much systematised post-entry training in peace time',[88] and made a number of recommendations for post-entry training of civil servants at various levels and in particular for new entrants. However, as the Committee's ideas did not coincide with those of the advocates for a Staff College, it could not recommend the Government to associate itself with the establishment of such a college; it also said that 'the idea of a central institution where the training of all civil servants would be carried on has only to be mentioned to be seen to be impracticable'.[89] It seems that to some extent the Committee had not fully appreciated the previous proposals which were not wholly inconsistent with its own ideas. Whereas, for example, Arthur Woodburn, in the House of Commons debate, was arguing primarily for 'a director of studies to decide how people in the Civil Service could gain expertise' and for arrangements 'so that the civil servant can know not only how the Civil Service works but how business works',[90] the Assheton Committee was firmly saying that it could not conceive of 'a method of teaching administration common to both business and the Civil Service',[91] though they also stated that 'While administration can be represented as being primarily a matter of commonsense, we believe that the achievement of the balanced judgement which is the real meaning of commonsense in this connection can be hastened and facilitated by a well thought-out training scheme.'[92] The Committee therefore recommended that the civil service should have its own central organisation for training administrative cadets, which 'might serve a number of purposes connected with background training and be a centre for bringing together administrators from the Service and from outside to discuss common problems'.[93]

The Report was sympathetically received. *The Times*, in a leading article on 18 May 1944, referred to its detailed recommendations as 'a sincere and meritorious effort to adapt the traditional methods of the public service to new conditions' and said that 'In general, the present report may be looked on as a first fruit of the new public demand for continuous revision and improvement in the machinery of government.' Nevertheless, there was no debate on the Report in either of the Houses of Parliament.

However, within the civil service consideration of the Report had been proceeding in the usual manner. On 3 July 1944 the Chancellor of the Exchequer told the Machinery of Government Committee that the Report of the Committee on the Training of Civil Servants had received preliminary consultations between the Treasury and more than 20 heads of departments. He said that 'two or three Heads of Department' had been doubtful of the proposed centralised course of training for entrants to the administrative class (these are not named in the minutes). The Chancellor proposed that the Committee should accept the recommendations in principle and that the Treasury, with other departments and the staff associations, should be instructed to work out the steps necessary to implement the recommendations and that, at a suitable moment an announcement of the Government's attitude towards the report should be made in the House of Commons. The Committee agreed.[94]

The main recommendations of the Assheton Committee, together with the traditions and experience of the civil service, became the basis for training in the immediate post-war period. The Training and Education Division was set up in the Treasury in 1945, under the directorship of an Under Secretary, to co-ordinate departmental training and run a variety of central courses, and a National Whitley Council Joint Committee on Training was formed to assist the Treasury in formulating training policies. But due to 'shortage of staff' the two to three months' part-time course for Assistant Principals recommended by the Assheton Committee became, in practice, a two-week full-time

course on the 'Machinery of Government'.[95] In 1946 a working party
of senior civil servants was set up to consider training for higher
administration, and in their report recommended a break from normal
work to broaden the experience of senior staff by way of secondment
to posts in government service abroad, to international authorities,
short-term attachment to industrial and commercial firms, sabbatical
leave to undertake administrative studies and attendance by selected
officers at the Imperial Defence College.[96] Analogous recommendations, not for a Civil Service Staff College, but for secondments and
attendance at courses in other Staff Colleges including the Administrative Staff College, were proposed in 1947 by a Fabian Committee
chaired by Professor W.A. Robson.[97]

The Conservative Government which came to power in 1951 was
pledged to reduce public expenditure and this led first to a Treasury
review of training arrangements, then to drastic cuts in departmental
training programmes, although the two weeks central training course
for Assistant Principals and induction training were allowed to
continue.[98] The expenditure of the Training and Education Division
of the Treasury was reduced by one-half, the staff was cut down and
put in charge of a Principal.[99]

This retrenchment, however, led to rethinking within the civil service
and to considerable criticism from the informed public outside it.
Robson, for example, wrote in *The Political Quarterly* in 1954 that
'our central training arrangements are very weak' and compared the
superficiality and inadequacy of the Treasury's two-week course for
Assistant Principals with the three-year course for recruits to the
French administrative elite at the Ecole National d'Administration or
the one-year course offered at the Indian Training School.[100]

During the late 1950s thinking on the training of civil servants was
affected by the prevailing mood critical of British institutions in general
and of the civil service in particular. As we have already seen, in
connection with the machinery of government, the Plowden Committee
stimulated a good deal of discussion on the organisation of government.
This Committee had been set up as a result of the 1957-8 Report of
the Select Committee on Estimates ('the most famous and probably the
most influential report produced by the Committee'[101] – Nevil
Johnson). It specifically stressed the importance of training as a tool of
management. The widely-felt unease was reflected in the thinking of
informed people. Increasing disquiet was felt about the nature of
training in the civil service, especially for the administrative class. There
had been no fundamental changes in the training of Assistant Principals

since the inception of the two-week course in 1946, except for the addition of an extra week in 1957. In 1961 Robson gave an address as Chairman of the Executive Council of the Royal Institute of Public Administration, in which he referred to the absence of a central staff training college and said there was 'a crying need for a centre which would serve as a focus for training in public administration'.[102] Also in 1961 Sir Maurice Dean, Permanent Under Secretary for Air, argued[103] for a reconsideration of the proposal for a Civil Service Staff College, and during 1960 and 1961 articles, letters and comments appeared in the journal of the First Division Association showing over-whelming support from Assistant Principals for more training for recruits to the administrative class. Shortly after this, in 1962, the meetings began of the Committee of Fabian Socialists whose report *The Administrators*, published in 1964, had been prepared, according to Anthony Sampson,[104] with the help of several civil servants and in consultation with Harold Wilson, George Brown and James Callaghan.

Outside pressures had therefore built up over the years for improved training facilities in the civil service, with a number of significant people pressing for a Civil Service College. The idea for the creation of a Centre for Administrative Studies (CAS), however, seems to have originated from other, internal sources. Gabriel Iglesias in his study of this has pinpointed three particularly significant factors in the decision to create the CAS. First, there was the idea, expressed in a minute of 20 March 1962 which W.A.B. Hopkin, Deputy Director of the Economic Section of the Treasury, sent to Sir Alec Cairncross, Director of the Economic Section and Economic Adviser to HM Government. He proposed a centre to stimulate research into economic policy-making and to provide training in economics for administrative civil servants. The centre would also be of indirect assistance to developing countries. Cairncross, who was known to favour the creation of 'some kind of college',[105] liked the idea, which was then discussed at a meeting of officials from the financial side of the Treasury, chaired by Sir Frank Lee. Lee, Iglesias writes, 'was initially sceptical about the need for training in economics, but was finally convinced after his informal discussions with Cairncross and Armstrong, both of whom were in favour of improving the competence of administrators in economics'.[106]

Secondly, W.W. Morton, of the Home Civil Service side of the Treasury, who was concerned with training and establishment matters, and who was aware of the debate among Assistant Principals about the existing training provided for them, was appointed to chair a Treasury Committee on the matter. By this time the Treasury was virtually committed in principle to establish a centre which would offer training for administrative recruits. Morton himself drafted the terms of reference for his committee, which was to recommend how the centre would operate and what it would teach. It met in private on a number of occasions, on one of which Professor W.J.M. Mackenzie attended – the only academic invited to meet the committee.

Thirdly, the Executive Committee of the First Division Association in April 1962 instructed its Sub-committee on Assistant Principals to consider and report on the problem of AP training. It reported in December recommending more formal central training and in the same month, at the request of the Staff Side, the National Whitley Council Joint Committee on Training considered the need for a Civil Service Staff College.

Lord Helsby told Iglesias that after the reorganisation in the Treasury in 1962 (when Helsby and Armstrong became joint Permanent Secretaries) he was under the impression that Treasury officials had already 'decided in principle' to set up the AP training centre, and that the problem was 'not whether it should be set up but how it should be set up'.[107] Departmental support and co-operation for the project was later achieved at one of the Sunningdale meetings of Permanent Secretaries.

The idea was formally proposed to John Boyd-Carpenter, Financial Secretary to the Treasury, in early 1963 (though he was already aware of the discussions that had been going on), but even before the centre had been formally approved, Ian Bancroft, an Assistant Secretary in the Treasury, was instructed by Philip Allen to find a suitable site for it.

The Centre for Administrative Studies opened in December 1963. It provided courses which developed into those lasting three weeks on the structure of government intended for Assistant Principals after they had served for about six months in a government department, and courses lasting 20 weeks on economics, statistics, new management techniques, government and industry, and the operation of business companies, for Assistant Principals in their third year of service. The centre ran two of each of these types of course in each course year.[108]

There was still concern about the lack of training for the large numbers of executive and professional civil servants, and in June 1963 the Joint Committee on Training set up a working party under the chairmanship of S.P. Osmond of the Treasury, to review the general question of civil service training in the light of developments since the Assheton Committee had reported, 'including the question whether a Central Staff College should be established'. The working party became concerned about the probable cost of establishing a Staff College and in their report, submitted in September 1964, concluded that an extension of short intensive courses for middle grades of all classes might constitute the better use of resources. They did, however, consider that 'the value of a centre for new thought and doctrine, and for the research on which valid doctrine can be based may, in time, be found by means of the extension and development of the recently founded Centre for Administrative Studies',[109] and recommended that 'further and more detailed consideration should be given to the possibility of a central institution for the higher training of – but not exclusively of – civil servants'.[110] The report of the working party was therefore submitted only about three months after the publication of the Fabian Tract, *The Administrators*, which had proposed a post-graduate School of Administrative Studies that would be 'altogether more formidable and prestigious than the CAS'.[111]

In November 1965 Osmond was appointed by the Chancellor of the Exchequer to chair another working party, to consider 'the training needs for middle and higher management ... taking account of the long term future of the Centre for Administrative Studies, and the desirability or otherwise of setting up a Civil Service Staff College'. The working party included among its members Professor Jean Blondel, Professor of Government, University of Essex, Professor D.C. Hague, Professor of Applied Economics, University of Manchester, C.D.E. Keeling, Director of the Centre for Administrative Studies, and C.H. Sisson, a senior civil servant and author of *The Spirit of British Administration*.[112] Its report was made available in the first instance to the Fulton Committee on the Civil Service which had been set up by the Prime Minister in February 1966. The working party drew attention to the inadequacies of the arrangements for training through the Centre for Administrative Studies and recommended that future training should be planned and directed by a single civil service organisation operating in two centres, a non-residential London centre developed out of the CAS and a residential centre out of, but with good communications to, London. Such an organisation, the working party concluded, 'though perhaps under another name, will give the Civil Service a Staff College, which many have advocated over twenty or twenty-five years'.[113]

Other evidence to the Fulton Committee also favoured the creation of a Civil Service Staff College. The evidence from individuals most relevant for this topic included three papers from academic specialists in public administration. Nevil Johnson, of the University of Warwick,[114] argued for an expanded Centre for Administrative Studies; Professor P.J.O. Self, of the University of London, made a strong case for a post-graduate School of Public Administration to be established in a British university as well as an expansion of training at the CAS;[115] and Trevor Smith, on behalf of the Acton Society Trust, argued that the case for a Civil Service Staff College was stronger than it had ever been.[116] There was also an interesting short paper from R. Turvey, member of the National Board for Prices and Incomes, formerly a university teacher and civil servant, who thought that the CAS should be renamed and its functions extended.[117] Perhaps more significant were the almost unanimous strong feelings of the staff organisations. The Institution of Professional Civil Servants said 'The need in the Service for management training is so great that we believe it is essential to set up a Civil Service Management Institute.'[118] The Association of First Division Civil Servants envisaged 'the CAS playing an increasingly important part in the training of graduate entrants'.[119] The Society of Civil Servants 'endorsed unreservedly' the Osmond working party's approach to training for management.[120] The Labour Party favoured 'a greatly expanded CAS which should have the size and status of a Graduate School of Government'.[121] The Trades Union Congress drew attention to the need for a National Planning College to develop a better approach to economic and social priorities in our society — and it specifically drew attention to the inadequacies of the CAS for the task it had in mind.[122]

In their Report, published in June 1968, the Fulton Committee recommended the creation of a Civil Service College which should provide major training courses in administration and management, a wider range of shorter training courses, in both general management and vocational subjects, and research into problems of administration and the machinery of government. They envisaged the college becoming 'a focus for the discussion of many of the most important problems facing the Civil Service as a whole'.[123] The Committee also recommended that the courses provided by the college should not be restricted to civil servants. They considered that the college would have 'an important part to play in laying the foundations for a greater under-standing between civil servants and the outside world'[124] and so recommended that outsiders should be able to make use of its facilities.

In the debates on the Fulton Report in the House of Commons and the House of Lords, the recommendation for a Civil Service College was well supported from all political parties. In the Commons Harold Wilson foresaw it as becoming 'the centre and focus of training in the Civil Service' and added 'the teachers it will attract will provide a centre for research into training needs and methods, and the study of public administration itself',[125] and Edward Heath, Leader of the Opposition, said he fully supported the Civil Service Staff College.[126] In the outstandingly well-informed debate in the Lords a few speakers were critical of the proposal; they included Lord Robbins and Baroness Sharp who thought there were already enough suitable education and training institutions to do the work recommended for the college and, if the recommendation was implemented, the Civil Service College would be 'an enormous affair and very mediocre';[127] but most speakers were strongly in favour, including Lords Trevelyan, Cumnor, Gladwyn and Redcliffe-Maud.[128]

Harold Wilson, then Prime Minister, speaking in the House of Commons on behalf of the Government on 26 June 1968, accepted a number of the Fulton Committee's recommendations including the creation of a Civil Service College. It was later decided that the college would have three centres, a non-residential centre in London, a residential centre close to London, and a provincial centre at a considerable distance from London. Dr Eugene Grebenik, the first Principal, was appointed in June 1969 and the main premises at Sunningdale were opened when the college was inaugurated by Edward Heath, the new Prime Minister, on 26 June 1970.

Since 1970 the Civil Service College, at its three centres in London, Sunningdale and Edinburgh (the Edinburgh centre closed for economy reasons in 1977), has provided a large number of courses for civil servants at all levels. It currently provides central training for nearly 10,000 students a year, in various aspects of management, administration, management techniques and foreign languages. College training is of two kinds. Some training is related to specific topics or techniques of management which are common to a number of departments; other training is of a background nature, intended to provide an understanding of the intellectual disciplines underlying work in the public services or to bring together for seminar purposes senior officials from a number of departments so that they can discuss among themselves and with outside specialists some of the problems they face in their work. The college is staffed by a mixture of civil servants, who are seconded from their departments for a period of two or three years and people recruited from the universities and other educational establishments. Following widespread criticism both within the service and outside, a Management Review Team considered the work and internal organisation of the college. Grebenik, who as Principal had the grade of Deputy Secretary, retired from the public service in the autumn of 1976, and the college became part of the new Training Group of the Civil Service Department. The Head of the Training Division, Mrs M.B. Sloman, an Under Secretary, who was already Deputy Principal of the College, then added the duties of Principal to her other responsibilities. The post of Principal was in effect downgraded from Deputy Secretary to Under Secretary; no new Deputy Principal was appointed, and there were also other changes simplifying the hierarchy within the college.

Although the case for a Civil Service Staff College was first unambiguously and officially proposed in a Report of the Select Committee on National Expenditure it is difficult to know for certain where the idea originally came from. The history of the proposal indicates the emergence of a pattern of diffused power where no progress in administrative reform could be made until there was an acceptable consensus among the most significant groups.

One interesting feature about this particular proposal is that although the initial recommendation for a college was well received outside the civil service, similar enthusiasm was not expressed within the service. Perhaps that was why the Chancellor of the Exchequer, after receiving a clear recommendation from the Select Committee, set up the Assheton Committee on training which was specifically asked to consider not how or when, but *whether* a Staff College should be established. When the Assheton Committee was set up it included several civil servants in its membership and they were not reticent in expressing their doubts about the value of the proposal, especially as they felt it would create a new elite within the service, so it was therefore hardly surprising that the Committee did not recommend the Government to establish a Staff College. The Select Committee consisted only of Members of Parliament and it became clear that they alone could not push forward an administrative reform that did not have the support of the official bureaucracy. Almost as if to re-emphasise this point, the Report of the Assheton Committee was not debated in either of the Houses of Parliament; it would be interesting to know whether any attempt was made to introduce a debate and if so by whom.

By the mid-1950s a number of leading members of the informed public were expressing criticism of civil service training, both because the academic study of public administration was establishing itself after the war and because there was a growing atmosphere critical of British institutions. This critical atmosphere seemed to thrive on comparisons of Britain with other European countries whose economy and institutions had been as severely hit by the war as Britain's but which had joined together in the new European Common Market.

The effective impetus for the creation of the college is to be found in the pre-history of the Centre for Administrative Studies. In the early 1960s, when Hopkin wrote his Minute to Cairncross, he already knew Cairncross's views and could be fairly certain that it would be well received. The idea then took off because the emphasis was placed on the importance of economics rather than administrative studies or training for management, and that fitted in with the high regard for economics that was fashionable at the time. The idea also gained credence because of the skilful 'closed politics' of the officials involved. The decision emerged and was made effective wholly within the administrative system and in an environment so confident that the most significant details of the CAS were all arranged, or were in the process of being arranged, before it was publicly announced through the political system that the centre was to be created.

Once the CAS had been set up on a fairly small scale and was well regarded, it was no longer very radical to propose a Staff College. The Fabians recommended it, the Labour Party supported the idea, and Harold Wilson, then Prime Minister and Leader of the Labour Party, who had been in touch with the work of the Fabian Committee, set up the Fulton Committee which included a number of Labour Party supporters whose opinions he could predict and whose support he expected. The political environment was therefore wholly sympathetic to recommendations for a Staff College, and its creation no longer involved a radical or unexpected decision. As Lord Shackleton explained the position in the House of Lords debate:

> whether we like it or not ... we are virtually advancing to the point where we have a college in one form or another. The Centre for Administrative Studies ... with a considerable range of improved courses for other civil servants, including some senior ones, already has provided the nucleus. And, of course, a training college, one way and another, is now something normal in all large organisations. I should find it very surprising and there would have to be most powerful reasons, if the Civil Service should not have such a college.[129]

Perhaps the main differences, or the most significant changes between the time of the Assheton Committee and the time of the Fulton Committee were that the attitudes of the staff associations had changed completely and the Government, at the time when the Fulton Committee reported, included a significant number of ministers who had taken part in proposing the creation of a Civil Service College. Furthermore, the proposal for a Civil Service College had, by the mid-1960s, become part of a non-partisan approach to administrative reform in the public services.

The establishment of the Civil Service College may also be a case of the creation and manipulation of the consensus that was necessary both for the acceptance of the idea and for its implementation. It was clear that no adequate consensus existed when the Select Committee on National Expenditure recommended the creation of a Civil Service Staff College, so a new committee was set up to reconsider the proposal. By the time the Morton Committee was set up in 1962 it was accepted that a centre would be established and the Morton Committee was concerned with how the centre would operate and what it would teach. So secure was the consensus for the Centre for Administrative Studies that by the time it was formally proposed to the minister the officials were already looking for accommodation – and it was such a short step from the CAS to the creation of the Civil Service College that by the summer of 1968 Lord Shackleton could present the decision, not by reviewing and emphasising the arguments for creating the college, but by saying that if it was not to be set up there would have to be very powerful reasons against it. It was no longer a matter for deciding *whether*, but when, to formalise the setting up of the college.

The Recruitment and Classification of Staff

During the inter-war period the pattern of recruitment and classification of staff in the civil service, which had been established after the First World War, was not greatly changed. The Tomlin Commission endorsed the main principles while recommending modifications in detail. However, although leading politicians, administrators and educationists were generally satisfied, there existed an undercurrent of discontent among the staff associations. The professional and technical classes were dissatisfied at their status, pay and conditions, and advocated the interchange of staff with other areas in the public service. Representatives of the executive and clerical classes, for their part, wanted to see far more flexibility in matters of promotion and a wider social base for recruitment. In addition to this groundswell in favour of change from within the ranks of the service, there developed during the post-war years a changing climate of opinion in academic and political circles which favoured improving the status and opportunities for specialists and the loosening of class divisions within the civil service. However, although the general feeling was more sympathetic to change, the original impetus for reform in the pattern of recruitment and classification came primarily from high-ranking civil servants themselves.

The first moves for change can be traced back to the early years of the Second World War. A.P. Waterfield, First Civil Service Commissioner, at this time gave much thought to civil service recruitment in the post-war reconstruction period. He felt this was vitally necessary 'if we are to avoid the disastrous consequences to the Service which followed from our state of unreadiness after the last war'.[130] In May 1941 Waterfield received a long and thoughtful letter from a colleague, H. Parker, about post-war recruitment to the civil service. This was following an earlier conversation they had had on the subject, and fitted in with a letter Waterfield had previously written to E.H. Ritson, at the Treasury. Waterfield wrote again to Ritson on 28 November raising further questions and re-emphasising points he had earlier made, including, it seems, the suggestion for a committee to consider the matter officially. Ritson replied unenthusiastically on 17 December 1941 that he was all in favour of dropping the suggestion for a committee at that stage: 'I think that all we can usefully do at the moment is to consider the sort of problems which will arise and to note them for future consideration. It seems quite impossible to me to think of the correct answers at present'.[131] However, in May 1942, while Waterfield was visiting Sir Alfred Hurst in the Offices of the War Cabinet to discuss the question of post-war recruitment to the civil service during the reconstruction period, he saw a copy of the report of Sir Alan Barlow's committee on the further education of demobilised members of the armed forces and civil defence services. The papers in the Treasury files suggest that Waterfield was upset because he had not been consulted by the Barlow Committee. He expressed his feelings to Hurst and pursued the matter by writing him a letter on 5 May, with copies to Barlow and Ritson, suggesting that, because it was so closely linked with general demobilisation policy, Hurst's minister might suggest that the Chancellor should set up a committee to inquire into recruitment to the civil service during the reconstruction period after the war. Ritson evidently consulted his

permanent secretary, Sir Horace Wilson, because on 11 May Wilson
sent a note to Waterfield rebuking him for his action:

> ... it must be remembered that the Treasury are primarily responsible
> for the recruitment policy of the Civil Service and if you wished to
> secure a revision of the Treasury view ... that a committee would be
> inappropriate at the present time, your proper course was surely to
> put your views to the Treasury rather than to Hurst — who in any
> case could not fail to be embarrassed by a suggestion on your part
> that his Minister should move the Chancellor to do something
> against the advice of Treasury officials.[132]

Waterfield called on Wilson on 3 June to discuss the letter he had
received, and, although there is no account of what was said on that
occasion, after the meeting Wilson minuted that the meeting had taken
place and that no positive further action should be taken. It may not,
therefore, have been entirely coincidence that, in June 1942, the
Chancellor of the Exchequer invited the then Financial Secretary,
Harry Crookshank, to conduct a general survey of problems that would
face the civil service after the war. Crookshank was assisted in this by
two permanent heads of departments, Sir Thomas Gardiner and Sir
Donald Fergusson, by Waterfield and by Wilson Smith of the
Treasury.

The Crookshank Committee was exceptionally vigorous and produced
an incisive but unpublished report. By February 1943 it had held 16
meetings on an entirely informal and confidential basis, involving
discussions with Lord Woolton, Lord Kennet, Sir Harold Hartley, Sir
Kenneth Lee and various other past and present members of the
Treasury Establishment staff. They considered the Report of the Sub-
committee appointed by the Liberal Party, PEP pamphlet 173,
Professor Laski's Twenty Point Plan written in his Introduction to
Passed to You, Please, by J.P.W. Mallalieu,[133] and Professor G.D.H.
Cole's article 'Reconstruction in the Civil and Municipal Services',
Public Administration, vol. 20 (1942). The Committee also considered
in detail the suggestions for a civil service training college which had
been put forward in the Report of the National Expenditure
Committee, 1941-2, with all the implications such a development might
have for the selection, training and promotion of staff. In addition,
Waterfield, on behalf of the Civil Service Commission, pursued the idea
of adopting for the civil service the psychological tests of the War
Office Selection Board. The Crookshank Committee's Report was

considered by the Machinery of Government Committee under Sir John Anderson and its paragraphs on post entry training were also referred to the (Assheton) Committee on the Training of Civil Servants. The Report concluded that 'If the Treasury is to continue to be the central authority ... there is scope for improvement in its attitude and policy,' it should encourage more contact between officials of its Establishments side and their opposite numbers in other departments, with greater flexibility and more time being spent by Treasury officials co-operating in the solution of problems on the spot. It added: 'there is scope for greater foresight and more lively imagination in detecting general service problems and in grappling with them even though such action carries with it no immediate reward by way of economy ...'[134]

The Treasury reacted to the suggestions being considered by the Crookshank Committee by putting its own proposals before a series of meetings with Staff-Side representatives and then, in July 1943, to special meetings of permanent secretaries. About this time the proposal for 'one class' was first considered within the service, long before it was publicly discussed. It would have involved abolishing the distinctions between administrative, executive and clerical classes and was consistent with the growing feeling for greater flexibility in the deployment of staff. For example, a letter from the Ministry of Health to the Treasury on 2 March 1943 drew attention to the distinction between the clerical and executive grades which 'leads to extravagance in numbers and, what is worse, to real waste of human material ...' However, the Staff Side of the National Whitley Council had yet to be persuaded though they were beginning to show signs of flexibility. At a meeting in the Treasury on 27 August 1943, A.J.T. Day, their Chairman, said that '... the Staff Side wanted to maintain the purity of the administrative conception though this did not mean the maintenance of the pre-war conception of the Administrative class'.[135] Although the meetings of permanent secretaries turned the idea down in June 1943 and it was abandoned as a reconstruction proposal,[136] it was not entirely cast aside; discussions about it continued within the service up to the point where, in an address to the Institute of Public Administration in 1948, R.A. Butler said he would value anything members of the Institute could tell him 'about the best method of creating a single unified service, that is to say of linking up the clerical and executive grades with the administrative grade by the ladder of opportunity'[137] — and it is worth noting that he was not asking *whether*, but *how*.

Meanwhile the staff of the Treasury Solicitor and Parliamentary Counsel were becoming increasingly restless about their status and pay, and Barlow had presided over a separate committee which investigated the position of scientific staffs. This further Barlow Committee, like the Crookshank Committee, was an 'inside inquiry' apart from the inclusion of W.F. Lutyens, a chemist from ICI.[138] The Treasury considered its report in April 1943 and decided to use existing pay scales to reward individuals who made outstanding contributions to the war effort and to defer until after the war further consideration of such matters as pay and equality of opportunity with the administrative class.[139] Barlow went on to chair another small Treasury committee on legal departments which reported in 1944.[140] All these committees reflected the dissatisfaction expressed and tensions felt among the various professional groups in the civil service; feelings which had been exacerbated by the influx of temporary professional civil servants during the war. There were similar tensions among other professional groupings, perhaps encouraged by the influx of a number of temporary professional civil servants appointed for the duration of the war.

Meanwhile, the Committee of Officials supporting the Anderson Machinery of Government Committee was receiving more and more evidence about personnel management in the civil service.[141] For example, at the Committee's fourth meeting, on 11 December 1942, Sir Donald Fergusson, of the Ministry of Agriculture and Fisheries, contended that the criticism that the administrative class was not wholly adequate for its present duties was justified. He felt that the highly trained mind which was produced by the competitive examination was apt to be narrow in its outlook and suffered from too little contact with the outside world, and he believed that more emphasis should be placed upon testing a candidate's personality in the open competition for recruitment. At the sixth meeting, on 30 December 1942, Barlow outlined the results of the inquiry which he had been conducting into the conditions of employment of specialists in the government service, but Wilson was doubtful whether a system of transfer from scientific grades in the civil service to the administrative class in middle life would be in the interests of the service – or, indeed, of the individuals – except in relatively rare cases. At the eighth meeting Gardiner voiced an opinion that the Treasury had achieved practically nothing in the way of general establishment work. This was partly because departments were not always receptive of ideas passed to them by the Treasury, but also because this side of the Treasury work had been consistently understaffed and was too hard pressed with day-to-day problems to tackle other work. Moreover, there was still a tendency, natural to Treasury officials, to think more of

economy than efficiency – they tended to give a chilly reception to
ideas which had no immediate economy value and which might involve
actual expenditure which could not be expected to bear fruit for many
years: for example on training. At subsequent meetings the whole
question of establishments organisation and the relationship between
the various classes of the service were considered, and much criticism
was directed at prevailing Treasury attitudes and the working of
Treasury control.

The debate on staffing questions soon spread outside the civil service
to a more public forum. A letter from three leading scientists was
published in *The Times* on 19 June 1943 which said: 'The claim that
the scientist, as scientist, is entitled to some position of exceptional
authority in deciding the policies of Governments, is one that cannot,
and should not, be accepted in a democratic community ... No social
problem can be solved solely by the methods of science ... A scientific
and soulless technocracy would be the worst form of despotism'. The
secretariat drew this to the attention of the Committee of Officials
supporting the Machinery of Government Committee, adding: 'These
words, in our opinion, apply with even greater force to the economist,
whose claim to specific authority is less clear than that of the scientist.'
Economics was 'concerned more with scientific theory than with
facts ascertained by scientific methods ... The subject is so close to
politics that there is a temptation for the economist to identify himself
with a partisan point of view ...'[142] The paper by the secretariat went
on to recommend the retention of the War Cabinet Secretariat after the
end of hostilities, and noted that recent changes in the civil service
examination might be expected to produce a larger recruitment for the
administrative class of personnel with an expert training in economic
statistics. Meanwhile Professor Robbins, at the twentieth meeting of the
Machinery of Government Committee, on 15 July 1943, had made
proposals for recruitment from the universities, intended to give
professors an opportunity for short spells of work at the centre of
government. Fergusson then argued that a central group of economic
advisers might be a threat to the sole right of ministers to co-ordinate
policy. Bridges and Brook disliked the presentation of a polarisation
between Robbins's statement and Fergusson's view and asked the
Chancellor of the Exchequer, Sir Kingsley Wood, to avoid any prema-
ture consideration of the Economic Section.[143]

Towards the end of the war the Treasury's position as the government's
central department with control over establishment matters was therefore under attack both from within the civil service and from sections

of opinion outside. The Treasury officials consequently began to defend their position. In a document, Memorandum 101 for the Committee of Officials supporting the Machinery of Government Committee, it outlined the development of the Treasury's position. The evolution of the Treasury had 'been as gradual as the evolution of the civil service itself from the days of patronage and peculation'. The MacDonnell Royal Commission, the 1917 Select Committee on National Expenditure, the Haldane Committee, and the Bradbury Committee on the Organisation and Staffing of Government Offices had all pressed for the strengthening of Treasury control not its replacement. It drew attention to the Treasury Circular issued in 1923 with Cabinet approval, that referred to the Treasury as the 'central' department of government.[144] This memorandum was circulated to departments for comments which in due course were reported to the Committee of Officials, including one from A.F.B. Fforde, a temporary under-secretary in the Treasury, who referred to the link between the problems then being considered and the suggestion that there should be a Civil Service Staff College. A later Treasury paper (MGO 74, June 1945) summarised these comments as providing:

> overwhelming support for the view, which we share, that control of establishment matters should continue to be vested in the Treasury. The main arguments for leaving this function with the Treasury are that removal to another Department would inevitably lead to duplication and delay, and that central establishment control by a Department without the Treasury's practical knowledge and experience of Departments' work and needs would be academic and unreal and would rapidly forfeit the confidence of other Departments.[145]

The Treasury's wisdom in taking steps to consolidate its support within Whitehall became evident in the context of the radical political climate of the years immediately after 1945. For it was during this period that civil service developments were increasingly becoming the concern of outsiders, a situation which was not exactly welcomed by Treasury officials. In this context a minute of 17 May 1947, from 'H.J.W.' to Padmore in the Treasury is worth quoting. The minute reads:

> The Financial Secretary had an interview with Wing Commander Cooper who is the Head of the Labour Party Group on the Civil Service which he himself has formed. He is the sort of slick business

executive type, and his whole attitude to the Civil Service is that it is an old-fashioned machine which needs a breath of good business methods air to get it right. There will be very considerable pressure on his part to get a whole enquiry instituted into the Civil Service, something like the Tomlin Commission, though possibly not a Royal Commission, with the object in particular of getting an investigator who is outside the Civil Service and therefore not tainted with our prejudices.

At the interview I tried to point out that we had already gone a long way towards setting our own house in order, and I said, whether rightly or wrongly, that the various Working Parties had taken evidence from a number of business concerns with a view to adopting their methods where practicable. The Financial Secretary is due to see the party again and it will be important for us to be ready with a somewhat stronger defence than I was able to put up on the last occasion. I hope that you may be able to put me on to some lines of research.[146]

There was a later meeting between the Financial Secretary and two other members of the Labour Group, though the Financial Secretary could only spend a couple of minutes with his visitors before he was called away and left 'H.J.W.' to deal with the interview. After the meeting 'H.J.W.' minuted that he felt the two representatives had been pacified by his remarks and by his offer of showing them some papers and he felt that they would not cause further trouble.

Radical criticism of the civil service and especially of its management was alleviated to some extent by the announcement about reform of the selection procedures. It was therefore this important, but specific, area which saw the most striking developments rather than the broader and more complicated issues concerning the classification of staff and the overall control of the service. In the war years general discussion about methods of selecting administrative class civil servants had been stimulated by developments at the War Office Selection Board. A number of people had thought a similar approach should be applied to civil service selection. Lord Winster, for example, in a House of Lords debate felt 'the examinations ought to be based upon the type of work which the candidate is going to perform in the Civil Service if he is successful'.[147] Sir Percival Waterfield, the First Civil Service Commissioner, whom Sir Edward Bridges referred to on one occasion as 'easily bitten by the psychological and psychiatric bug'[148] told the joint Official/Staff Side Committee on Post-War (Reconstruction)

Recuitment that the Commission had learned a good deal about psychological or intelligence tests since the First War and he was inclined to favour them.[149] However, all was not plain sailing. A press report on the Civil Service Selection Board headlined 'House party will be Cisby Test', in the *Daily Express* 20 February 1945, gave popularised details of an announcement the previous day by Waterfield. This was drawn to the Prime Minister's attention by one of his officials and led him to call for reports from senior civil servants and the Chancellor of the Exchequer. They were very apprehensive about misleading elements in the report and felt that 'such publicity may well put off serious applicants for [the] Civil Service who thought it [a] career for integrity and intelligence', 'publicity may well affect university opinion for years' and 'Why call it Cisby and so invite Music Hall jokes?'. On 18 March Churchill decided that the matter should be considered at Cabinet level,[150] but this did not stop the development.

In the immediate post-war years the Civil Service Commission was faced with the task of filling the vacancies which had accumulated since 1939 and permanent recruitment was carried out under the Reconstruction Regulations, in conformity with the recommendations of the National Whitley Council and approved by the House of Commons.[151] Under these regulations a system of selection for the administrative class was introduced depending on a qualifying examination, a residential Civil Service Selection Board 'house party' and an interview with a Final Selection Board. The new recruitment system and the work of the Civil Service Selection Board, specially instituted to play an important role in it, attracted the attention of the Select Committee on Estimates in 1947-8,[152] which was primarily concerned with the financial implications of its development within the Civil Service Commission Vote. The normal pattern of recruitment through open competition based on an academic examination was resumed in 1948 and became known as Method I. However, the reconstruction style of competition was retained, largely unchanged, to form the Method II system of selection, although after 1950 non-residential premises in central London were employed rather than the Manor House at Stoke D'Abernon, Surrey.[153] This method of selection, brilliantly caricatured in A.P. Herbert's novel *Number Nine*,[154] was reviewed internally in 1957 and from that time assistant principals were recruited by both methods.

Developments relating to the more general aspects of the classification and grading of civil service staff were, however, less clear-cut because they could not easily be separated from the more immediate concerns relating to pay and conditions of service and there was no consensus about how to proceed. Both during and immediately after the Second World War a number of changes, which were approved by 'inside' committees along these lines, had originated from pressure exerted by heads of departments whose staff included a large proportion of specialists. This pattern of *ad hoc* change to deal with individual problems continued up to and beyond the time of the Priestley Royal Commission, 1953-5. Although the scientific classes had been re-organised on the basis of the recommendations of the Barlow Committee and the Government's white paper published in 1945,[155] in other areas changes had been more unco-ordinated: for example the abolition of the grades of higher clerical officer and principal assistant secretary.

Scepticism was expressed, in Parliament and elsewhere, when the Government announced the setting up of a new Royal Commission under the chairmanship of Sir Raymond Priestley. R.A. Butler, Chancellor of the Exchequer, maintained in the House of Commons that the time had come for a comprehensive review of the pay and other conditions of service since the last Royal Commission, the Tomlin Commission, a generation previously. But Attlee, for the Opposition, wondered why a Royal Commission was needed, seeing that for many years these matters had been dealt with by Whitley Councils; and Douglas Houghton pointed out that the Chancellor had given Whitley Council members only a week to consider his intentions and the Staff Side had declared the proposed Royal Commission to be un-welcome.[156] At a later date Bridges indicated some of the background to the decision when, in his opening words of oral evidence before the Commission, he explained that the Whitley machinery was no longer capable of resolving the conflicting demands of various classes as championed by their staff associations. Some kind of comprehensive review of the structure as a whole was needed to ensure that changes proposed 'were carried out with general approval and in an objective and non-political atmosphere'.[157] The Commission was therefore concerned primarily with conditions of service; it considered comparisons with similar work outside and also comparisons of pay and conditions of service for staff in various classes within the service. This was indeed a sensitive problem area, illustrated not only by the great volume of written and oral evidence from interested parties, but also by the content of replies given by officials to questions put by the commissioners. For example, one question put to Sir Thomas Padmore,

Second Secretary at the Treasury, related to the suggestion being considered by the Commission that the experimental officer grade had substantially worse career prospects than the executive officer. In his reply Sir Thomas said '... it is very difficult to find an answer to that question, but if I were pressed for an answer I would say that, so far as we can see, taking it rather by and large, taking one time with another, and taking the average of Departments, it is probable that there would not be found to be very much in it either way'.[158]

The recommendations in the Report of the Commission[159] were mainly concerned with specific details about pay and conditions of service, and its most important general recommendation was for the creation of what became known as the Civil Service Pay Research Unit. However, its recommendations only dealt with the symptoms of far more intractable problems: the classification of the service and the career prospects for different categories of staff, and the need to establish what Professor W.J.M. Mackenzie subsequently referred to as 'a new "bench-mark" in dealings between the Treasury and the Staff Associations'.[160] Not surprisingly, the Commission received conflicting views from the various interested parties and their representatives. In its Report it noted the claims of representatives of specialist groups to be accorded parity with the administrative class but also noted that its 'official' witnesses on this topic (who all happened to have been permanent secretaries and therefore in the administrative class) thought that the existing relativities between the specialist classes and the rest of the service were about right.[161] The Report regarded the opportunities for scientific and professional staff to transfer to administrative posts 'as a matter of importance not only in the interest of providing careers but also as a means of ensuring that those who are responsible for policy in Departments such as the Ministry of Supply or the Post Office are able by educational background and previous civil service experience, fully to appreciate the technical issues involved in the formation of policy'[162] – a somewhat cautious recommendation on a topic that was subsequently to receive much more attention and to become increasingly controversial.

These were important matters of concern to the interested parties and especially to the staff associations that were acting on behalf of their members. The views of academics of the stature of Graham Wallas and Harold Laski from time to time were mentioned. Also, from the end of the war one group outside the civil service, the Fabians, kept up a fairly regular flow of recommendations and suggestions, originating from usually anonymous individuals, through the medium of tracts and reports of committees and study groups. However, for the first time in the history of the civil service academic social scientists made a significant contribution in the shape of the book *Higher Civil Servants in Britain* by R.K. Kelsall. This book on the social background of administrative class civil servants, published in 1955, was important because although minor comments and studies may have been previously presented in this area by academics, taken all together their impact was not at great as that of this book alone. It originated in the growing confidence and research ambitions of social scientists, especially sociologists. As Kelsall explained in his preface, the book was based upon a study forming part of a wider research programme, the first main results of which were published in 1954 in a symposium, *Social Mobility in Britain*, edited by D.V. Glass. This programme was concerned with general problems of social selection and differentiation in Britain, to show broad trends in educational opportunity and the relation of that opportunity to movement on the social ladder. It is obvious from the contents of the book as well as from the acknow-ledgements in the preface that Kelsall received encouragement from leading social scientists and also significant (and, as far as we are aware, unprecedented) help from officials in the Treasury and the Civil Service Commission.[163] A considerable amount of information was made available from official sources for use in the study.

Subsequently some of the officials may well have regretted their helpfulness since the book was critical of aspects of the higher civil service and in particular of the methods of selection, methods which had enabled the officials who had co-operated with the researchers to reach their important positions in the service. No attempt was made by the Civil Service Commission to pursue these ideas further, and Kelsall felt that the commissioners were 'not altogether happy about the book, in that they regarded it ... as critical of their procedures'.[164] Some of the reviews of the book were very critical and resulted in wider discussion of the points Kelsall made; for example, the review written by Kenneth Robinson, an ex-civil servant, in *Public Administration*, which was followed by a rejoinder and further comment in that journal.[165] As the first major academic study to be published on part of the contemporary British civil service it made the impact it deserved and now has an established place in the history of literature on the civil service. Its sharp criticisms from an outsider's perspective set people thinking and discussing important problems in a more informed way than had previously been possible, and it stimulated people in circles not really affected by

H.E. Dale's *The Higher Civil Service,*[166] which was in fact an insider's account of higher civil servants, their backgrounds and their work — a book critical by civil service standards but bland by academic standards. Unfortunately, however, Kelsall's was only a partial study, concerned with the social background of the administrative class and with looking at problems which related to the wider research programme of which it was part. The study drew attention to the advantages enjoyed by those candidates for the civil service who had been to public schools and Oxford or Cambridge Universities and pointed out that even when reforms had been introduced at various times in the history of selection, these advantages remained.

The wealth of information on these points presented in the book, together with the comments of reviewers stimulated further academic discussion outside the civil service. These led, a few years later, to three publications of particular importance in the academic debate on reform proposals. Thomas Balogh wrote a provocative attack on the civil service in an essay entitled 'The Apotheosis of the Dilettante', published in 1959 in a symposium edited by Hugh Thomas.[167] Balogh noted that recruitment to the administrative class had, 'in its time given rise to passionate feelings expressed mainly in letters to *The Times*, the Tories attacking and Labour defending the new method because it sounded un-English and odd to the one, and progressive to the other'. His view was that the Method II qualifying examination was too weak to exclude feeble intellects, it favoured the grasshopper mind and the exhibitionist, and 'the interview is so heavily weighted ... that the effective choice .. is made by the interviewing board on which prejudice is only too well represented'. The contentious essay of Professor Brian Chapman, *British Government Observed*, which we have seen focused attention upon the machinery of government, was highly critical of aspects of the British civil service. It described it as 'an over-specialised, parochial, closed corporation'; compared with their European counterparts 'senior British civil servants are sheltered spinsters' and 'ministers' private secretaries in Britain give the appearance of unwise virgins'.[168] In comparison with these two essays, the Fabian tract, *The Administrators*,[169] published in 1964, was a less flamboyant, more conservatively reasoned analysis and its publication well timed, whether by accident or design, to build upon the on-going debate and have an important influence on administrative reform. It criticised the concentration of Oxford and Cambridge graduates in the administrative class, drew attention to the serious feelings of frustration and grievance among scientists, engineers and other professional people in the civil service, and said the time had come to review the class structure between administrative, executive and clerical ranks. It proposed wider recruitment, 'a searching and independent investigation into selection methods to settle once and for all whether they are not only unbiased, but as efficient as they can possibly be made', and a complete ironing out of all grades so as to produce common levels throughout the whole service from the level of assistant secretary and equivalent upwards.

In the 1964-5 parliamentary session the Estimates Committee once more turned its attention to recruitment for the civil service. The subject was still topical and the Committee found that, as the memorandum of evidence from the Civil Service Commission stated, since the war it had been difficult, especially in the field of graduate and professional recruitment, to obtain as many recruits as the service required,[170] and appointments were consistently falling below the vacancies announced. The Sub-committee considering the matter was chaired by Dr Jeremy Bray, a graduate of Cambridge University, previously (1962-4) a member of the Select Committee on Nationalised Industries and subsequently (1971-2) Chairman of the Fabian Society; its members included Sir Edward Boyle, a graduate of Oxford University and subsequently member of the Fulton Committee. It received evidence from a number of senior officials and a few outsiders including, among the academics, Professors R.K. Kelsall and W.J.M. Mackenzie. The Sub-committee was concerned about the problems already being experienced in recruitment and it spent a great deal of time inquiring into the high proportion of successful candidates for the administrative class who had been to Oxford or Cambridge universities and public schools. It was also concerned about the inadequate remedies which the Treasury and Civil Service Commission were attempting to apply. The Committee created a precedent in its approach to its subject. It concentrated on aspects of the Estimates other than the merely financial, it received evidence from a number of outsiders, and most important of all, for the first time it had, in D.N. Chester, a virtually specialist adviser — as Bray put it, 'a step towards having a specialist in the subject of the inquiry sitting in on the whole inquiry'.[171] Chester, the Warden of Nuffield College, Oxford, and a leading academic specialist in public administration, had been a civil servant during the war, had since served on a number of official committees and also served on civil service Final Selection Boards. Towards the end of its work he presented a memorandum to the Sub-committee which contained his own ideas and comments on the other evidence presented, and the Committee's Report indicates that he made an important contribution to its thoughts and recommendations. One of the Committee's main recommendations was for a further inquiry to examine and report upon the structure, recruitment and management of the civil service, a recommendation which was to lead to the appointment of the Fulton Committee in 1966.

It is easy to trace some of the origins of the Fulton Committee recommendations concerning recruitment and classification of staff. The links between the Committee and the Fabian Society have already been mentioned, together with the publication of the Fabian tract on the administrative class, 'the governing class of the Service', which criticised amateurism and made recommendations for wider recruitment, better training and more movement into and out of the service. There was also the public attitude of the time, as expressed through various books and pamphlets, which was critical of the civil service and other public institutions, and in particular of its recruitment and classification system. However, there were other influences, too, upon the Committee. It was the first major inquiry into the civil service to sponsor research from outsiders and it regarded highly the contributions to its work made by its Management Consultancy Group headed by Dr Norman Hunt and the social survey conducted by A.H. Halsey and I.M. Crewe into the main general classes of the civil service. On recruitment the Treasury proposed a wider graduate entry to administrative work and the Civil Service Commission suggested a method for achieving this; there were also substantial comments by the staff associations and individuals. On classification, the Treasury proposed the merger of the administrative and executive classes and the formation of an integrated structure at the top of the service down to the salary level of the maximum of the assistant secretary grade; the Civil Service Clerical Association proposed the addition of the clerical classes to the merger proposed by the Treasury, and the Treasury agreed. The Institution of Professional Civil Servants proposed similar mergers of the scientific and of the professional (works group) and technical classes into a Science Group and a Technology Group respectively, and later the creation of a Social Scientist Group but the Treasury disagreed. The IPCS also proposed that the integrated structure at the top of the service should be extended downwards to the maximum of the principal scale. The First Division Association supported the merger of the administrative and executive classes, but opposed the integrated group structure. Other staff associations made proposals relating to their particular parts of the service, those

representing departmental classes for the most part strongly in favour
of their preservation.

In its Report[172] The Fulton Committee criticised the administrative
class for being the most evident embodiment of 'the philosophy of
the amateur', said that the system of classes in the civil service seriously
impeded its work, and found that many members of specialist classes
did not get the career opportunities they ought to have. The Report
called for 'new principles' to be applied to the selection, training and
deployment of all administrators; in essence these were for specialisa-
tion in administrative work giving what they called 'preference for
relevance', greater mobility into and out of the service, and the
abolition of classes. The Report said that the basis of divisions between
higher and lower classes was no longer valid because the work of
government had changed so much since the system was introduced; it
prevented the best development of individual talent and the adaptation
of the service to new tasks and restricted career opportunities, and the
Committee found the word 'class' to be no longer acceptable because
it produced feelings of inferiority. It therefore recommended abolishing
the divisions between higher and lower classes and replacing them with
a single, unified grading system; it also recommended a further inquiry
to consider the Committee's criticism of recruitment of graduates and
ways of reducing the subjective element in the Method II system of
selection. The number of candidates entering the Method I competition
had declined greatly since it was reintroduced in 1948; in 1968 there
were six successful candidates by Method I and 97 by Method II.
However, questions of bias in the procedure or on the part of the
selectors themselves continued to be raised about Method II.

A committee of inquiry into the Method II System of Selection for the
Administrative Class of the Home Civil Service was therefore set up by
the Prime Minister in October 1968, in accordance with a recommendation in the Fulton Report, to inquire 'into the methods of selection to
consider ways of making the process of selection more objective in
character'. In their Report the Committee found that 'In the United
Kingdom no other post-war development in the field of selection ... has
had so strong and so pervasive an influence'; 'Method II is a selection
system to which the Public Service can point with pride.'[173] The
content of the Report did not attract much critical public attention
when it was published. The main criticisms to which it gave rise were
about the membership of the Committee which cast doubts in the
minds of some people on the impartiality of its conclusions. Although it
appeared to be a committee of outsiders its members were not quite as

obviously independent as some critics of the Method II system had hoped. The Committee had a considerable amount of personal experience in personnel selection. It was chaired by J.G.W. Davies, a Cambridge graduate who had worked in the War Office Directorate for Selection of Personnel during the war and who was Secretary of Cambridge University Appointments Board, 1952-68; two of the other four members were also Cambridge graduates and members of the Final Selection Board. Method I was phased out quickly after publication of the Davies Report, the last examination being in 1970, and on 1 January 1971 the new grade of Administration Trainee was introduced to replace the grade of assistant principal.

In the period 1939-70 problems of the recruitment and classification of staff were complicated. It was difficult for those involved to separate the various facets, the constraints of resources and time had become more pressing, and unlike the mid-nineteenth century there were no clear-cut political principles nor any consensus about what should be done. There were, however, unprecedented changes in society, especially in relation to the pay and status of some professions and groups, a revolution in technology and management techniques, and the challenging opportunity for a new start to be made at the end of the war. Towards the end of the period the Fulton Committee hoped their report would have as great an impact as the Northcote/Trevelyan Report, but although the Fulton Report contained some strong expressions calculated to have a political appeal, few of its recommendations were in fact as new as they appeared in the publicity of 1968. This was especially noticeable in its recommendations on recruitment and classification of staff. Most of the recommendations in the Fulton Report had been already considered years before within the confidentiality of the service and among the informed public. Reforms in this area that were easy to implement and on which there was general agreement in the service were discussed by individuals and committees of insiders and implemented with little fuss. During this period there were dozens of committees and working parties concerned with different issues, sometimes overlapping, but also contributing to internal debate, acting as media for communication, and performing an important function in the formation of consensus.

There are two facets of changes in recruitment and classification of staff that are perhaps worth stressing. One concerns the changing position of academic commentators and the attitude of officials towards their proposals. Academics who seem to have been well received by insiders and whose comments were valued, tend to have had some experience in the practice of administration. Others, without that experience, seem to have found it difficult to get on the same wavelength as civil servants and have therefore rarely succeeded in putting their ideas across. The other facet, related to this, concerns openness in government. In the period 1939-70 there was a tendency for officials in central government to become more accessible and for more information to be published. This has been more obvious in matters of recruitment and classification than in other areas of greater party-political sensitivity or where state security could be involved. *The Times*, for example, in a leading article on 20 April 1948 complained 'What is happening now to candidates for a life in Whitehall is wrapt in unnecessary mystery', but *The Times* was only reflecting general attitudes, raising fundamental questions about what was being done on behalf of citizens in a parliamentary democracy, and making its own contribution to growing pressures for more open government.

Notes

1. W.J.M. Mackenzie, 'The Structure of Central Administration', in Sir Gilbert Campion, *et al*, *British Government Since 1918* (Allen and Unwin, London, 1950)

2. D.N. Chester and F.M.G. Willson, *The Organisation of British Central Government 1914-1964* (Allen and Unwin, London, 1968 ed.).

3. J.M. Lee, *Reviewing the Machinery of Government 1942-1952, An essay on the Anderson Committee and its successors* (Birkbeck College, London, 1977), p. 8.

4. PRO/T 222/71: OM 290/01.

5. Lee, *Machinery of Government*, p. 11.

6. Ibid., p. 146.

7. PRO/Prem 4/63/2.

8. PRO/Prem 4/63/2.

9. Lee, *Machinery of Government*, p. 16.

10. Ibid., p. 147.

11. E.g. 'The Administrative Machine', *The Times*, 27 April 1942.

12. Lee, *Machinery of Government*, p. 18.

13. PRO/T222/71: OM 290/01.

14. PRO/CAB 87/71.

15. PRO/T222/71: OM 290/01.

16. Sir John Anderson, 'The Machinery of Government', *Public Administration*, vol. 24 (1946), pp. 75-85.

17. *Scientific Man-Power, Report of a Committee appointed by the Lord President of the Council, P.P.*, 1946 [Cmd. 6824].

18. Lee, *Machinery of Government*, p. 30.

19. Ibid., pp. 41 and 144.

20. Ibid., pp. 36 and 142.

21. Ibid., p. 143.

22. Ibid., p. 44.

23. Ibid., p. 80.

24. *Report of the Committee on Intermediaries, P.P.*, 1950 [Cmd. 7904].

25. Lee, *Machinery of Government*, pp. 85, 87 and 88.

26. Ibid., p. 88.

27. Ibid., p. 147.

28. Ibid., p. 101.

29. Ibid., p. 139.

30. Ibid., p. 139.

31. Ibid., p. 140.

32. Ibid., p. 148.

33. Sharp to Barlow, 12 and 17 August 1947, PRO/T222/41/OM 355/01.

34. L. Petch, 'The Study of the Machinery of Government', *O and M Bulletin*, vol. 5, part 6 (1950), pp. 3-12.

35. For example, K.C. Wheare in Oxford and Denis Brogan in Cambridge made the machinery of government the subject of their inaugural lectures. See K.C. Wheare 'The Machinery of Government', *Public Administration*, vol. 24 (1946), pp. 75-85; H.R.G. Greaves, *The Civil Service in the Changing State* (Harrap, London, 1947); and Sir Oliver Franks, *The Experience of a University Teacher in the Civil Service* (OUP, London, 1947).

36. *Royal Commission on the Civil Service, P.P.*, 1955 [Cmd. 9613].

37. *Sixth Report from the Select Committee on Estimates, Session 1957-58, Treasury Control of Expenditure, P.P.*, 1958 [254-1]. See also *Seventh Special Report from the Select Committee on Estimates, Session 1958-59, Treasury Control of Expenditure (Observations of the Treasury), P.P.*, 1959 [227].

38. Lord Bridges, *The Treasury* (Allen and Unwin, London, 1964), pp. 137-8.

39. *Control of Public Expenditure, P.P.*, 1961 [Cmd. 1432].

40. Bridges, *Treasury*, p. 141.

41. Ibid., p. 203.

42. Tom Lester, 'The Unmaking of Mintech', *Management Today*, November 1973, pp. 91-3, 198, 200 and 204.

43. Hugh Thomas (ed.), *The Establishment* (Anthony Blond, London, 1959).

44. Brian Chapman, *British Government Observed, Some European Reflections* (Allen and Unwin, London, 1963).

45. *The Administrators, the Reform of the Civil Service*, Fabian Tract 355 (Fabian Society, London, 1964).

46. *The Civil Service, Vol. 1, Report of the Committee, 1966-68, P.P.*, 1968 [Cmnd. 3638].

47. *Whitehall and Beyond, Jo Grimmond, Enoch Powell and Harold Wilson: Three Conversations with Norman Hunt, with a Comment by Lord Bridges* (BBC, London, 1964).

48. *Sixth Report from the Estimates Committee together with the Minutes of Evidence taken before Sub-Committee E, Session 1964-65, P.P.*, 1965 [308].

49. See Richard A. Chapman, 'The Fulton Committee' in Richard A. Chapman (ed.), *The Role of Commissions in Policy Making* (Allen and Unwin, London, 1973).

50. House of Lords Record Office: FE/M/41-42/27.

51. 386 H.C. Deb., 5s., col. 677 (28 January 1943).

52. The Minister for the Civil Service Order No. 1656 (1968) in pursuance of section 1 of the Ministers of the Crown (Transfer of Functions) Act, 1946 (9 and 10 Geo 6, c. 31).

53. 418 H.C. Deb., 5s., col. 483 (25 January 1946). See also L. Petch, 'Changes in the Machinery of Government since 1945', *Public Administration*, vol. 29 (1951), pp. 383-92.

54. *The Reorganisation of Central Government, P.P.*, 1970 [Cmnd. 5406].

55. *The Civil Service*, vol. 1, p. 96, para. 293.

56. 773 H.C. Deb., 5s., col. 1563 (21 November 1968).

57. *A Better Tomorrow* (Conservative Party, London, 1970).

58. *The Reorganisation of Central Government*, para. 8.

59. Ibid., paras. 46-8.

60. Sir Richard Clarke, *New Trends in Government* (HMSO, London, 1971).

61. N.F. Warren Fisher, Preface to W.J. Brown, *The Civil Service, Retrospect and Prospect* (W.J. Brown, London, 1943).

62. G.K. Fry, *The Growth of Government* (Cass, London, 1979), p. 208.

63. See E.S. Byng, 'Post-Entry Training for Administration from the Industrial Aspect', *Public Administration*, vol. 21 (1943), p. 12.

64. For example, *Final Report of the Committee Appointed to Inquire into the Organisation and Staffing of Government Offices, P.P.*, 1919 [Cmd. 62]; and *Report of the Royal Commission on the Civil Service, 1929-31, P.P.*, 1931 [Cmd. 3909].

65. *Sixteenth Report from the Select Committee on National Expenditure, Session 1941-42: Organisation and Control of the Civil Service, P.P.*, 1942 (120).

66. Ibid., para. 121.

67. Ibid., para. 124.

68. For further details of the work of the Select Committee on National Expenditure, see Sir Ivor Jennings, *Parliament*, (CUP, Cambridge, 1957 ed.), ch. 11.

69. The other members of the sub-committee were James A.E. de Rothschild, Sir Edward Cadogan and Donald L. Lipson.

70. 386 H.C. Deb., 5s., col. 643 (28 January 1943).

71. PRO/CAB 117/269: APH (42) 11.

72. PRO/T162/806/4787/06.

73. *The Times*, 4 November 1942.

74. PRO/T162/806/47687/06.

75. PRO/CAB 87/74 (MG(42)6).

76. PRO/T162/806/47687/06.

77. PRO/CAB 87/73.

78. 125 H.L. Deb., 5s., col. 306 (26 November 1942).

79. 386 H.C. Deb., 5s., col. 695 (28 January 1943).

80. Ibid., col. 714.

81. See, for example, A Temporary Civil Servant, 'Post-War Machinery of Government: III Government Administration and Efficiency', *The Political Quarterly*, vol. 15 (1944), and Sir Gwilym Gibbon 'The Civil Servant: His Place and Training', *Public Administration*, vol. 21 (1943), pp. 85-90.

82. 386 H.C. Deb., 5s., col. 674 (28 January 1943).

83. L.C. White, 'Post-War Machinery of Government: I The Civil Service', *The Political Quarterly*, vol. 15 (1944), p. 6. See also L.C. White, 'Post-Entry Training for Administration from the Public Services Aspect', *Public Administration*, vol. 21 (1943), pp. 24-30.

84. The other members of the Committee were Sir Harold Hartley, Vice-President, London Midland and Scottish Railway Company, Sir Kenneth Lee, Chairman, Broadhurst Lee Company Ltd, Miss Myra Curtis, Principal, Newnham College, Cambridge, A.J.T. Day, Chairman, Staff Side, National Whitley Council, A.L.N.D. Houghton, Staff Side, National Whitley Council, Sir Thomas Gardner, Director-General, General Post Office, Sir Robert Wood, Deputy Secretary, Board of Education, and H. Wilson Smith, Under Secretary, Treasury.

85. J.P.W. Mallalieu, *Passed to You, Please* (Gollancz, London, 1942).

86. PRO/T162/752; T162/805/47687/01/1,2,3; T162/806/47687/01/4,5; and T162/806/47687/06.

87. PRO/T162/806/47687/06.

88. *Report of the Committee on the Training of Civil Servants, P.P.*, 1944 [Cmd. 6525] para. 8.

178   *The Civil Service in Mid-Twentieth-Century Britain*

89. Ibid., para. 45.
90. 386 H.C. Deb., 5s., col. 651 (28 January 1943).
91. *Training of Civil Servants Report*, para. 46.
92. Ibid., para. 91.
93. Ibid., para. 10.
94. PRO/CAB 87/73.
95. H.M. Treasury, Training and Education Division, *Annual Report*, 1945-6. Quoted by Gabriel Iglesias, 'A Case Study of British Administrative Decision Making: The Setting up of the Centre for Administrative Studies in 1963', unpublished Ph.D. thesis, Sussex University, 1971.
96. See 'Review of Civil Service Training Since the Publication of the Assheton Report, Report of a Working Party appointed by the Joint Committee on Training of the Civil Service National Whitley Council' (Osmond Working Party Report), *Whitley Bulletin*, vol. 44, No. 10 (1964).
97. *The Reform of the Higher Civil Service, A Report by a Special Committee of the Fabian Society* (Fabian Publications and Gollancz, London, 1947).
98. 'Manpower and Efficiency Considerations', 26 September 1951, *Establishment Circular 75/51* and 'Retrenchment in Civil Service Training', 14 March 1952, *Establishment Circular 22/52*, quoted by Gabriel Iglesias, 'Case Study'.
99. *Osmond Working Party, Report*, para. 26.
100. William A. Robson, *The Political Quarterly*, vol. 25 (1954), pp. 344-6. See also Frank Dunnill, *The Civil Service, Some Human Aspects* (Allen and Unwin, London, 1956).
101. Nevil Johnson, *Parliament and Administration, the Estimates Committee 1945-65* (Allen and Unwin, London, 1966), p. 40.
102. William A. Robson, 'The Present State of Teaching and Research in Public Administration, *Public Administration*, vol. 39 (1961), pp. 217-22.
103. Sir Maurice Dean, 'The Public Servant and the Study of Public Administration', *Public Administration*, vol. 40 (1962), pp. 17-28.
104. Anthony Sampson, *Anatomy of Britain Today* (Hodder and Stoughton, London, 1965), p. 265.
105. Alec Cairncross, 'The Higher Civil Service After the War', *Public Administration*, vol. 20 (1942), pp. 61-7.
106. Iglesias, 'Case Study', p. 86.
107. Ibid., p. 137.
108. C.D.E. Keeling, 'Treasury Centre for Administrative Studies', *Public Administration*, vol. 43 (1965), pp. 191-8.
109. Quoted by P.D. Lindley, 'The Origins of the Civil Service College', in R.V. Heaton and Sir Leslie Williams, *Civil Service Training* (Civil Service Department, London, 1974), p. 35.
110. Osmond Working Party Report, paras. 100 and 102.
111. *Administrators* (Fabian Tract 355), pp. 29-31.
112. C.H. Sisson, *The Spirit of British Administration* (Faber and Faber, London, 1952), C.H. Sisson, was also at the Ministry of Labour.
113. 'Manpower Training in the Civil Service, Report of a Working Party', Memorandum No. 13 submitted by Her Majesty's Treasury to the Committee on the Civil Service, *The Civil Service, vol. 5 (1)*, pp. 60-93, para. 96.
114. *The Civil Service, vol. 5(1)*, p. 957, paras. 44-52.
115. Ibid., pp. 1115-23, paras. 36-79.
116. Ibid., pp. 1144-6, paras. 36-43.
117. Ibid., pp. 1165-6.
118. Ibid., p. 321, para. 112.
119. Ibid., p. 144, para. 33.
120. Ibid., p. 411, para. 7 *et seq*.
121. *The Civil Service, vol. 5(2)*, p. 669, para. 83.

122. Ibid., pp. 799-800, paras. 22-5.
123. *The Civil Service, vol. 1*, paras. 99-103.
124. Ibid., para. 111.
125. 773 H.C. Deb., 5s., col. 1549 (21 November 1968).
126. Ibid., col. 1570 (21 November 1968).
127. 295 H.L. Deb., 5s., cols. 1133 and 1087 (24 July 1968).
128. Ibid., cols. 1137 and 1138 (24 July 1968).
129. Ibid., col. 1190 (24 July 1968).
130. PRO/T162/931/E 45491.
131. Ibid.
132. Ibid.
133. Mallalieu, *Passed to You, Please*.
134. PRO/T162/931/E45491.
135. Minutes of 10th Meeting of the Committee on Post-War (Reconstruction) Staffing Problems, with the Staff Side, PRO/T162/748/E45491/02/1.
136. PRO/T162/870/E45491/09/1.
137. R.A. Butler, 'Reform of the Civil Service', *Public Administration*, vol. 26 (1948), p. 169.
138. PRO/T162/802/E45662/1-4.
139. Lee, *Machinery of Government*, p. 78.
140. PRO/T162/808/E48680/01/1.
141. PRO/CAB 87/71.
142. PRO/CAB 87/72 (MGO 32).
143. Lee, *Machinery of Government*, p. 79, PRO/T222/135: OM 202/82/03.
144. PRO/CAB 87/72.
145. PRO/CAB 87/72.
146. PRO/T162/931/E45491.
147. 125 H.L. Deb., 5s., col. 308 (26 November 1942).
148. Bridges to Phillips, 12 June 1944, PRO/CAB 21/808.
149. PRO/T/162/748/E45491/02/1. For an account of the procedures used and the results obtained in the British forces during the Second World War see Philip E. Vernon and John B. Parry, *Personnel Selection in the British Forces* (University of London Press, London, 1949).
150. PRO/Prem 4/8/13 (20 February 1945) and PRO/CAB 21/808. See also Lee, *Machinery of Government*, pp. 79-80.
151. *Civil Service, Recruitment to Established Posts in the Civil Service During the Reconstruction Period. Statement of Government Policy and Report of the Civil Service National Whitley Council, P.P.*, 1944 [Cmd. 6567].
152. *Ninth Report from the Select Committee on Estimates, Session 1947-48, The Civil Service Commission, P.P.*, 1948 [203].
153. *Memorandum by the Civil Service Commission on the use of the Civil Service Selection Board in the Reconstruction Competitions* (HMSO, London, 1951).
154. A.P. Herbert, *Number Nine* (Methuen, London, 1951).
155. *The Scientific Civil Service. Reorganisation and Recruitment during the Reconstruction Period, P.P.*, 1945 [Cmd. 6679].
156. 513 H.C. Deb., 5s., col. 1536-1540 (30 July 1953).
157. *Minutes of Evidence taken before the Royal Commission on the Civil Service* (HMSO, London, 1954), q. 1.
158. Ibid., q. 3221.
159. *Royal Commission on the Civil Service 1953-55, Report, P.P.*, 1955 [Cmd. 9613].
160. 'Recruitment to the Civil Service', memorandum submitted by Professor W.J.M. Mackenzie to Sub-committee E of the Estimates Committee; *Sixth Report from the Estimates Committee, Session 1964-65, Recruitment to the Civil Service*, pp. 128-39, *P.P.*, 165 [308].

161. *Royal Commission on the Civil Service 1953-55, Report*, para. 529.

162. Ibid., para. 531.

163. Help in the same direction though not, it seems, to the same extent, was previously given to the Fabian Committee which produced the report *The Reform of the Higher Civil Service* (Fabian Publications and Victor Gollancz, London, 1947).

164. Evidence taken before Sub-committee E, *Sixth Report from the Estimates Committee Session 1964-65, Recruitment to the Civil Service*, q. 376.

165. See *Public Administration* vol. 33 (1955), pp. 383-8 and vol. 34 (1956), pp. 169-74.

166. H.E. Dale, *The Higher Civil Service*, (OUP, London, 1942).

167. Thomas Balogh, 'The Apotheosis of the Dilettante, The Establishment of Mandarins', in Hugh Thomas (ed.) *The Establishment*.

168. Brian Chapman, *British Government Observed*.

169. Fabian Tract, *The Administrators*.

170. Memorandum by Civil Service Commission, *Evidence to Sub-Committee E of the Estimates Committee, Session 1964-65*, p. 21.

171. *Evidence to Sub-Committee E of the Estimates Committee, Session 1964-65*, q. 1100.

172. *The Civil Service, Vol. 1, Report of the Committee 1966-68, P.P.*, 1968 [Cmnd. 3638].

173. *The Method II System of Selection for the Administrative Class of the Home Civil Service, Report of the Committee of Inquiry, 1969*, paras. 1.11 and 9.2, *P.P.*, 1969 [Cmnd. 4156].

4

4 THE DYNAMICS OF ADMINISTRATIVE REFORM

Administrative Reform in Britain

Administrative reform is the process of making changes in administrative structures or procedures within the public services, because they have become out of line with the expectations or values of the social and political environment. This means that the process itself is not necessarily a developmental one towards a clearly defined goal known in advance, but a complex matter of acceding to pressures, communicating and discussing ideas, stimulating comments from groups with potential interests, and making judgements within the administrative system about tactics and timing for the introduction of particular changes. This implies a number of differences between reform and other processes with which it may be closely related and or with which it may overlap. Changes may be introduced into an administrative system which do not result from tension between the administrative system and the expectations and values of the social and political environment. Changes may be neutral in comparison with administrative reform (though the study of them might nevertheless provide valuable insights into administrative decision-making); examples of such changes are the transfer of the collection of national insurance contributions from stamped cards to deductions from pay similar to income tax, minor transfer of functions between departments, and the abolition of resale price maintenance. Innovation may be part of administrative reform, as it has been in developing countries where administrative structures have been created in the public sector where none previously existed. Evolution may be another closely related process when it refers to structures or procedures in public administration that were at first simple but have become increasingly sophisticated and elaborate.

The essential feature, then, of administrative reform is the relationship of administrative changes to characteristics or pressures from the broader social and political environment. This is clearly illustrated in the reform topics analysed in this study. In the latter part of the nineteenth century the introduction of open competition may be seen both as an adjustment to changing social, political and educational conditions outside the civil service, and as part of an effort

183

by liberal reformers to mould the political structure. As Jean Holmes has noted, 'Ideally administrative reforms ... seek to structure changing social perspectives as well as follow them.'[1] In particular, open competition played an important part in the movement towards a politically neutral civil service and was consistent with the general political climate in the country at that time. This was later followed by growing attention to the democratic implications when certain social groups in the twentieth century appeared to be at a disadvantage in relation to particular methods of selection.

It is sometimes said that administrative reform is, in the end, a political process and some writers have seen reform proposals as waiting on political will.[2] Our study shows that this approach may be over-simplifying the position and that in Britain, in the period we have studied, it is much more than this. We agree that it *is* in part political (involving 'inside' politics as well as politics on a wider spectrum), but it is also a management process, and any appreciation of administrative reform must, therefore, allow for both its political and managerial elements. In our period the growth of more positive government gave rise to questions concerning the relationship of management efficiency to the political goals and objectives of government. This was expressed in the early part of the twentieth century in conceptions of government in mechanistic terms, as in the Haldane Report, and in the mid and late twentieth century in fundamental rethinking of the principles influencing the number and structures of major departments of state. A great deal of emphasis has been placed by some reformers on making government more efficient, but little attention has been paid to the meaning of such terms in the theoretical writings of British specialists in public administration. Indeed, this serves to re-emphasise what Gerald Caiden has called the underdeveloped nature and infancy of the study of this aspect of public administration.[3]

Furthermore, the management element in administrative reform is more than a question of formulating bold proposals for change and of working up strategies for reform. One aspect of the art of administration is to be found in the judgements of individuals and groups about tactics and timing, deciding how and when changes should be introduced. This has been observed in two ways. The first is appreciation of the situation: assessing whether a consensus for change already exists; whether the opinions of important groups have had sufficient time to be formulated and expressed; and whether all interested parties have had an adequate hearing. The second concerns the manner in which proposed changes are introduced: deciding the right moment for proposals to gain the widest possible acceptance in order to ensure that agreed aims are achieved. In the reconstruction periods which followed both world wars committees were created to consider particular problems, then further committees were appointed to gather together and assess the work of the specialist committees, to review and co-ordinate policy proposals. Some proposals in the early years of our period appeared too radical at the time because they disregarded or jeopardised the autonomy of departments, but in later years they were more readily acceptable. It is, however, remarkable that there was so very little awareness in the 1950s and 1960s of previous discussions concerning almost identical specific proposals for reform.

Throughout this period the civil service unions initiated the momentum for change in some areas but imposed vetoes in others. Few, if any, proposed changes were implemented at any time during the period unless they were accepted by senior officials in the civil service as well as by the unions. If proposals for administrative reforms are to be implemented it is therefore essential for them to be supported by an appropriate consensus. Sometimes the consensus or a sympathetic environment is naturally formed and the administrative system has to consider it and take advantage of it. At other times particular strong pressures or opinions may exist indicating a potential consensus that can then be realised by activating groups previously silent. Both of these require the practice of administration, characterised in British government by the political sensitivity of senior officials and their skill in guiding the situation to the point where decisions are formulated and supported. This has been evident in the period covered by this study. Indeed, there is clear evidence of civil servants assuming the initiative in the formation of consensus. For example, when A.P. Waterfield, in discussion with Sir Horace Wilson, referred to the dangers of leakage and rumours about informal inquiries which could lead to misunderstandings and ill-founded criticisms, Wilson replied: 'I do not at all mind the leakage giving rise to discussions on the subject; that may help in the building up of a body of informed opinion'.[4]

Timing is also important, both in edging the various elements towards consensus and in deciding when to introduce or activate reform proposals to achieve agreed objectives. Fred W. Riggs, in his studies of administrative reform in developing countries, has referred to this as the problem of dynamic balancing in administrative reform.[5] He has suggested that it is useful to think of all three branches of government

— legislature, executive and judiciary — as concurrently engaged in both political and administrative functions. It follows that a balance of power is essential between them in order to enhance the administrative capabilities of government as well as to safeguard its political responsiveness.

Commissions, committees and working parties played an important role in the administrative reform process in this period of British government. They have various purposes. Our study reveals the sheer variety of types and forms which such bodies have taken, ranging from well-publicised, formal, representative bodies to confidential, informal and small *ad hoc* working groups. Their purposes and their roles in government have been quite as varied as their constitutional forms. Sometimes they are a means of communicating ideas and stimulating the thought of interested parties; sometimes they help to create a consensus for action on a topic on which general public concern has been expressed, but for which no agreed solution has emerged; sometimes their function is, as Sir Geoffrey Vickers has shown,[6] to appreciate a situation and formulate recommendations for subsequent debate and government action. All of these purposes have been indicated in specific commissions and committees in the period of our study. The importance in the British context of such bodies rests in their ability to provide a sounding board for new ideas, and to act as a catalyst for reform — in particular providing a means of bridging the worlds of the officials and others. They cannot be viewed in isolation from other political forces. In general the smaller and more limited the type of inquiry, the smoother the implementation. The impact of the larger commissions by contrast is often more obscure. The Ridley, MacDonnell, Tomlin and Priestley investigations were scarcely radical or controversial bodies, but even their recommendations had by no means a clear passage. They provide endorsement for Harold Laski's reflection that 'on average, in our system, it takes nineteen years for the recommendations of a unanimous report of a Royal Commission to assume statutory form; and if the Commission is divided in its opinion, it takes, again on average, about thirty years for some of its recommendations to become statutes'.[7]

Realists, we are sometimes told, see bureaucracy as a conservative force in society and even idealists confidently say that bureaucracy should not modify the system, that modifications should be left to the electoral process, the executive and the legislature.[8] It is sometimes said that bureaucracies cannot reform themselves, and this is true in a number of respects, especially in the public sector. For one reason, bureaucracies tend by nature to be conservative. For another, the civil servant of a parliamentary democracy is the servant of the government, and it is the government that makes the most important decisions about the policies and values that control the decision-making of administrators. But this study makes it abundantly clear that the officials themselves have important roles to play. Outstandingly able men make their mark; the collective views of agencies or even the service as a whole is not a negligible factor in determining the nature and direction of reform. The important point to remember, however, is that ultimately it is the politicians who make the final decisions; they may decide to let the officials contribute more or less to policy-making but the term of office of politicians is limited. The British constitution is not based on a single document and there has never been a date from which all political and administrative principles were reconsidered in relation to a framework of principles; administrative structures and procedures are determined by a large number of factors and a complex of pragmatic decisions. A permanent and non-party political civil service, however, has a longer-term perspective conditioning its attitude to particular reform proposals and is therefore influenced, at least in part, by the significance of particular historical precedents. It also plays an important role in formulating the framework within which ministers make their decisions. Sir William Armstrong, referring to his service in the Treasury, has said

> We ... had a framework for the economy basically non-Keynesian. We set the questions which we asked ministers to decide arising out of that framework, so to that extent we had great power ... We were very ready to explain it to anybody who was interested, but most ministers were not interested, were just prepared to take the questions as we offered them, which came out of that framework without going back into the preconceptions of them.[9]

The sheer weight and persuasiveness of official advice to ministers, together with the framework in which it is set, does much to interweave the political and managerial elements of administrative reform.

The pattern of administrative reform in Britain since 1850 reflects the salient characteristics of the political system. Reforms in administration, like reforms in the broader political environment, were products of a flexible political system where the avenues to power, the means of influence and the methods of implementation were varied. The importance of this point was emphasised by Lord Simon when, in a House of

Lords debate he declared that 'it is easily assumed that in matters of public administration in this country we follow a formal protocol. There is nothing *très protocolaire* in our methods here. All the better ... Our constitutional machine is not nearly as rigid as some who have never had to work it ministerially may suppose.'[10] Formal procedures and constitutional arrangements may tell us little about the realities of power and only partially explain the process of decision-making. Radical innovations – in the sense of new departures which strike root and branch at existing practices – are comparatively rare. The prevailing pattern is for an institution or procedure to evolve and to acquire a new status and purpose. The development of the Cabinet' Office and the enhancement of the Treasury's position in the early part of this century are good examples of this phenomenon. Even when wholly new departures are made, with new machinery being set up, the tendency is for that machinery to be integrated into existing patterns of government, for example the Whitley machinery in the 1920s and the Ombudsman (Parliamentary Commissioner for Administration) in the 1960s. A high premium is accorded to gradualist incrementalism; the ways in which reform proposals are adopted also condition the expression and chances of implementation of future reform proposals. This has enabled administrative conservatism – like political conservatism – to play an unusually creative role in the process of reform in Britain. Such conservatism has rarely been the conservatism of reaction, but a conservatism prepared to accommodate change where necessary in order to conserve the virtues of a proven pattern of administration. As Professor David Corbett has said, 'Public services need to be creative as change agents, or at least some parts of them need to have that sort of capacity, the capacity to respond to, and even to generate system-modifying ideas and policy proposals.'[11] Thus conservatives like Sir George Cornewall Lewis played a major role in tightening up recruitment procedures in the 1850s and after, while rejecting the radical suggestions of the Northcote/Trevelyan Report; a similar reformist conservatism may be discerned in the cautious introduction of new methods of selection to the higher civil service in the latter part of our period. Hence, an area of special interest for the student of administrative reform in Britain is the interaction of pressures from outside with the concerns of those responsible for manning the administrative machine.

The Practice and the Study of Public Administration

The essentially empiricist inclination of leading practitioners of administration in British central government has acted as a two-edged weapon so far as their receptiveness to outside ideas has been concerned. On the one hand, as we have noted, it has fostered a high degree of flexibility and discouraged conservative dogmatism; but on the other hand it seems to have encouraged the practitioner to adopt a disdainful attitude towards outsiders. Academics concerned with the study of public administration, in particular, have generally been treated with scepticism by practitioners because their comments about central government administration have appeared superficial or lacking in originality. In the nineteenth century suspicion of such outsiders was less marked: the academic study of public administration barely existed at that time, and in any case the British civil service was less unified. In such circumstances it is impossible to make meaningful generalisations about the attitudes of civil servants. After 1919, however, the gulf became quite marked. So much so that in 1969 Sir William Armstrong, when Head of the Civil Service, could say that he did not know of any case of a teacher or student of public administration being asked to advise on a question of administration, of administrative processes or of administrative organisation in this country.[12]

It is unfortunate, however, that practitioners did not sufficiently appreciate the concern of students with the actualities of administrative practice. For the absence of a written constitution meant that the study of public administration in Britain developed from the study of government and politics, in contrast to many other European countries where it has been more related to the study of constitutional and administrative law. Similarly, the expertise of senior administrators lies primarily in the working of the system of government rather than in subjects like economics, accountancy or law, the reason for this being that ministers are less creatures of statute than of prerogative, so that the institutional and political environment has been one of the most important factors conditioning the relationship of officials to politicians.

Practitioners, and in particular leading Treasury officials, have tended to regard their work not just as an art, but an art peculiarly incapable of benefiting from any kind of professional study, an art which could be acquired by individuals who had achieved success in virtually any area of academic study (though in the past with preference for the more established traditional subjects taught at Oxford and Cambridge). It is small wonder if, as C.H. Sisson has put it, the British administrator travelling abroad is shocked to discover that many countries are administered by men who read books about public administration.[13]

Indeed, the prevailing attitude of practitioners towards academics and their work — especially comparative studies — far from being one of positive co-operation, has been that of unhelpful apathy tinged with apprehension. At its best the official response has been that of courtesy without respect: at its worst hostility bordering on arrogance.

Thus in the inter-war years significant American developments in public administration were viewed in the Treasury with cynicism and distaste, and official encouragement to the Institute of Public Administration seems to have been calculatedly modest (actual discouragement might have resulted in lack of control). The suggestion of the Tomlin Commission that 'outsiders' might be able to offer valuable advice seems to have been received by selectively deaf official ears. There is clear evidence during the Second World War that the study of public administration was associated in the minds of some officials with socialism, and it is known that Bridges, for example, was apprehensive about the possible theoretical nature of views about government administration from people like Harold Laski who could influence Herbert Morrison. This sensitivity in practice, especially in matters that might be viewed in a party context, is well illustrated[14] by the Treasury reaction to the Fabian Report on reform of the higher civil service, published in 1947. Professor W.A. Robson, Chairman of the Fabian Committee, wrote to Bridges on 25 November enclosing a copy of the report and inviting Bridges to lunch. In Bridges's minute to Padmore of 27 November he wrote: 'I met this man last summer when I went to lecture at Ashridge. He is fairly influential in left wing circles and it might be useful for me to go and talk to him — provided that you can tell me what I ought to say and can trust me to say it.' Padmore asked Winnifrith for comments and Winnifrith replied on 3 December that he thought Bridges would 'find it a fairly difficult interview to handle'. Bridges, having received several comments from his Treasury colleagues, then wrote to the Financial Secretary on 19 January 1948 with details of his brief for meeting Robson, seeking the Financial Secretary's authority for the meeting. He noted:

> ... the Fabian Society have drawn on the experience of many people who have served temporarily in Government offices, and much of their material really represents the lines of thought on which we are already and have been working for some time. For this reason, perhaps, there is nothing very startling in the Report. But the fact that the Fabian Society have clearly done their best to produce a practical and level-headed document is, I think, a good reason why

I should be reasonably forthcoming to them.

After the interview, on 9 February 1948, Bridges wrote in a minute:

> ... Mr Robson also volunteered that he thought it would be a very
> good thing if we (i.e. he and I) established a certain measure of
> informal contact on administrative questions which were being
> studied and pressed forward in the Civil Service. He thought that
> it would even be possible for certain subjects which were being
> studied in the Civil Service to be farmed out to some extent to a
> faculty of administrative studies. He gave as an instance the work
> of various types of public boards and non-departmental
> organisations.
> I said that I would welcome a measure of co-operation in this
> matter and I hoped that if he wanted to he would always come and
> see me and consult me informally. Though I did not put it to him
> in quite this way, I am sure it is worthwhile by means of these
> informal contacts to establish a degree of understanding with people
> in Professor Robson's position whose critical and constructive work
> is much more likely to be helpful to us if we take a little trouble to
> tell him what we are doing and to keep in touch with him.

This was interestingly followed up by a note from Padmore to Bridges
on 19 February 1948 in which he said that there had been a request
for the Chancellor 'to see Mr. Monck and one of two of his co-authors
of the Report together with "one or at most two" MPs'. He wrote:

> The idea of the Chancellor's being asked to waste his time in this
> way appals me. The Report itself is quite a respectable document
> and many of its ideas are in fact being put into practice. This is
> mainly because Mr Monck is an assiduous collector of other people's
> ideas and he and his collaborators were helped by people who had
> been in the Service in war-time and (quite informally) by many of
> us who are still in it ... Neither Mr Monck nor his co-authors are the
> kind of people who are to be expected to be allowed to waste the
> time of Ministers ...

This was a by no means untypical reaction in the post-1945 period.
It is, for example, closely paralleled by the way in which Treasury
officials handled Wing Commander Cooper in 1947, and diluted the
'outside' element in the Plowden Committee in 1959. One might also

point to the total silence which greeted Kelsall's study.

All bureaucracies perhaps tend to be defensive, and it would be wrong to construct here some kind of conspiracy theory. In Britain some quite fortuitous factors helped to widen the gulf. Public administration only developed slowly in British universities, and when it did become established the universities of Oxford and Cambridge, from which so many of the highest civil servants graduated, did not emerge as centres of excellence in it. Moreover, in contrast to many countries there is no tradition of academics coming 'inside' for periods in their careers. Very few academics have spent a period in Whitehall during their careers and hardly any civil servants have left Whitehall for a period of university teaching and research. This is largely a consequence of the British tradition of ministerial responsibility, which places a high premium upon the political neutrality of the service and the perman- ency of its career structure. However, the relatively small numbers of university teachers of the subject and the difficulty in arranging a really useful but relatively short secondment to a government depart- ment from a university presented additional difficulties. But the two world wars provided a number of significant exceptions to this pattern. Not only did they offer great opportunities for such teachers to gain practical insight, but war-time service also enabled a few individuals to acquire valuable contacts, acceptability and status on which they could later build. As a result, a very few selected academics like D.N. Chester (who acted as special adviser to the Estimates Committee in the mid-1960s) and W.J.M. Mackenzie (the only academic invited to meet the Morton Committee on training), both of whom have considerable reputations in the academic study of public administration, became in effect intermediaries between the practical and academic worlds. Furthermore, for some time after the Second World War there were sufficient experienced people available for needed 'outsiders' to be usually chosen from those who had some 'inside' experience.

Given the close war-time connections, it is perhaps somewhat surprising that academic students of government in the post-1945 period should not have yielded rather more illuminating accounts of the workings of central government administration in Britain. Practitioners themselves have pointed to the lack of practical relevance and the doubtful value of some research commissioned from academic specialists at public expense; and one of the reasons why public administration specialists in Britain do not enjoy as much esteem in academic circles as they do in other countries is the poor regard which central government practitioners hold for them. There seems to be something of a 'Catch-22' situation operating here. Younger academics (i.e. without war-time experience) have often felt denied the opportunities to make a real impact because they have encountered difficulties in gaining access to information to enable them to be better informed and make more useful comments. The Official Secrets Acts are often blamed for this situation. It is surely no coincidence that some of the most illuminating studies of actual decision-making in British central government have been produced either by overseas scholars — such as Gabriel Iglesias or Heclo and Wildavsky — or by administrative historians, who after 30 years have the run of the departmental files — albeit often erratically 'weeded' — in the Public Record Office. The difficulty, however, is more complex than this. The Official Secrets Acts and the difficulty of obtaining or relaying information only forms part of the problem. Perhaps they are symptoms of a more formidable barrier of communication. This is illustrated by some remarks of Sir William Armstrong. When he was Head of the Civil Service he noted that public administration research would be greatly facilitated if government departments could be less secretive;[15] but several years later, after leaving the civil service, he said he found it 'extremely difficult to discover what the government is up to'.[16] It seems as if the problem may be less one of information being concealed, than of outsiders simply being in ignorance of the existence of some information which might be available if requested and of the terms of reference in which government thinking is being conducted. Few outside the administrative system have sufficient awareness of the problems to be in a position to put forward constructive suggestions.

The barrier in large part stems from the working of ministerial responsibility and the simultaneous difficulty of separating policy-making, advice and administration. The application of administrative theories cannot be value-free or devoid of political implications, and some of the associated problems are well illustrated in the context of the debate on the machinery of government. As Evelyn Sharpe has written: 'The distribution of functions does not proceed on the basis of analysis and judgement — but on a basis of guesswork and personalities.'[17] Even the more theoretical debates are imbued with political value-judgements. The definition of 'efficiency' adopted by the Fabians at the turn of the century and the 'managerialist' school of thinkers in the 1960s, for example, reflects their respective ideological positions. All such debates and queries may give rise to sensitive issues, and sensitive issues and potential embarrassments are, in the minds of civil servants, to be avoided at all costs.

The period from 1850 to 1970 has seen the study of public administration advance from early beginnings to maturity. Nevertheless, its growth – certainly as far as central government is concerned – has been marked by pressures and difficulties that have on occasions separated students from practitioners in ways that have not happened in other countries. In contrast, such academic influences have been more evident in administrative reform in new or developing countries which have been more concerned with innovation than with adjusting structures and procedures already well established to somewhat less than radical societal changes. Indeed, there is evidence to suggest that the most important contributions to administrative reform from academic sources have been in guiding and influencing society and in aiding the development of consensus both on general attitudes and on particular issues.

The Intellectual Climate and its Influence

'Pragmatic', 'incremental' and 'gradual' are adjectives which are most commonly used to describe reforms in British government and administration. Administrative developments in British central government should not be seen in terms of the implementation of broad programmes based upon coherent philosophies. In Napoleonic France, Soviet Russia and in many Third World countries today administrative reform has stemmed from a desire, primarily motivated by political ideologies, to forge ahead with 'modernisation', by using the administrative system as an instrument for social and economic transformation. In Britain, on the other hand, administrative reform has been more a process of bringing the administrative system into line with other changing values and standards in society. In this exercise abstract ideas are not likely to be valued very highly, and many commentators have noted the lack of concern of British administrators with theoretical matters. Graham Wallas, for example, pointed out over 50 years ago the contrast between the French and the British tradition in this respect. In the former a high premium has always been placed upon the ability to think problems through from first principles using 'logical' analysis; the latter, on the other hand, has been characterised by a mistrust of 'abstract' principles and by a high regard for the ability to 'muddle through'.[18] The role of the senior official in Britain has generally been interpreted less as that of constructing and then implementing long-term programmes, than of adjusting to particular political and administrative pressures and of keeping the machine of government running smoothly. 'The brain of a great administrator', concluded Bagehot in 1856, 'is naturally occupied with the details of the day, the passing dust, the granules of that day's life; and his unforeseeing temperament turns away uninterested from reaching speculations, vague thought, and from extensive and far-off plans.'[19] Later generations of senior officials, when reflecting on the nature of their work, have generally endorsed this view, taking almost a perverse delight in disclaiming the values of abstract ideas. The official, writes C.H. Sisson for example, 'is a man who has been trained to a practical operation, not to an exposition of theory or a search for truth ... There is no need for the administrator to be a man of ideas. His distinguishing quality should be rather a certain freedom from ideas.'[20] This disregard for abstract ideas, which ironically is also shared by many British politicians, partly explains the relative lack of interest shown by practising administrators in any lessons which might be learnt from the academic analysis of government, which we have already noted.

It would, however, be rash to conclude from this that those responsible for initiating and implementing administrative reform in Britain had been uninfluenced by ideas, or that the intellectual climate has had no influence upon administrators. In the first place Britain during our period produced a large number of original thinkers and writers who had an active interest in politics or government: for example J.S. Mill, T.H. Green and the Oxford Idealists, the Webbs and the early Fabians, Laski, Keynes and Beveridge. It would be surprising if their ideas had had no influence, especially as so many higher civil servants would have encountered them and their ideas during their university education. Secondly, the British higher civil service has been renowned for the high intellectual calibre of its membership. Few other countries can intentionally have drawn their senior officials from so consistently an *academic* background. The MacDonnell Commission was in fact stating the accepted practice when it said 'we recommend the broad principle of gathering the natural fruits of the educational system of the country in its various stages at they mature'.[21] Although the academic backgrounds of so many senior officials appear to be so often from only a favoured few academic institutions, the content of their formal education was outstandingly non-specific. In most other countries they have been drawn from a wider variety of backgrounds: they may have more managerial experience and be more professionally conscious, but taken as a whole they are unlikely to have the same broad awareness of intellectual interests as their British counterparts.

There are, however, difficulties in assessing the influence of the intellectual climate. In the first place intellectual influences are not all of a piece. They range from broad schools of thought, like Utilitarianism, or early Fabianism, to more specialised thinking, like Keynesian economics, which may have indirect repercussions on administrative ideas, to the more general influences of education and socialisation. A second problem lies in the difficulty of measuring the impact of ideas or of the intellectual climate. In contrast to more specific political or administrative pressures which are usually clearly documented, intellectual influences for the most part permeate the discussion of reform. It is the ways of thought by which problems are approached, and the language in which discussion is couched that may be significant. For even the more coherent political philosophies of our period did not so much provide specific answers to particular problems of an administrative or political nature as help to create a climate of opinion which conditioned the attitudes and values in society and influenced the thinking of administrators. The more pervasive such influence is, the less tangible it becomes, and the more difficult to assess. Thirdly, it would be wrong to see the question in terms of 'ideas being implemented'. Equally important is the impact which administrative questions and problems in their turn have upon the development of ideas. The Haldane Report illustrates very well this two-way interaction. It owed much to the purely intellectual concerns of its chief authors: to Haldane's Hegelian interests, and to Beatrice Webb's ideas of social progress and socialism. However, the ideas of the Report equally sprang from the study of practical problems of administration which the members of the Committee were considering. The Reconstruction Papers left by Beatrice Webb, with their rich collection of letters, memoranda and successive drafts, show clearly the fertile interaction of general ideas and of specific problems. And the process did not end here. Even though the practical proposals of the Report had little effect, it crystallised ideas which were to permeate later administrative thinking: that Whitehall was a coherent set of government departments, that the Cabinet was a co-ordinating mechanism, and that efficiency could not be measured in quantitative terms alone.

The Haldane Report stands out as something unusual in the British context in so far as it was written largely in isolation from the hurly-burly of the political and administrative world. The Northcote/ Trevelyan and the Fulton Reports however, both of which were more closely connected to immediate political and administrative concerns, illustrate much the same sort of interaction. Trevelyan, while concerned initially with administrative problems, was strongly influenced by the ideas of his brother-in-law, Macaulay, and by Jowett and the strong lobby of those wishing to reform the University of Oxford. Gladstone, Northcote and Trevelyan mounted a strong educational lobby in favour of their Report. The headmasters of Harrow and Westminster both keenly championed the Report, as did Dr Richard Dawes, Dean of Hereford. Jowett felt convinced that 'the plan, if carried out, will do as much in its effect upon education as a direct grant of many hundreds of thousands a year'.[22] The Northcote/Trevelyan attack on patronage and its endorsement of meritocratic values appealed strongly to progressive, 'liberal' opinion: all those, for example, who were subsequently influenced by the writings of J.S. Mill. Mill, himself at the time an official in the India Office, described the scheme for competitive examination as 'one of those great public improvements the adoption of which would form an era in history. The effects which it is calculated to produce in raising the character both of public administration and of the people can scarcely be overestimated.'[23] These liberal sentiments were not sufficiently powerful in 1854-5 to overcome the doubts and hesitations of politicians like Russell and Palmerston, but over the next 50 years they became widely acceptable. Walter Bagehot, for example, changed his views significantly between 1862 and 1870.[24] Civil service reform here was marching hand in hand with social and intellectual developments in the world outside. Reform was at once a cause and a result of these developments. The Order in Council of 1855 undoubtedly stimulated educational developments – as Jowett and Gladstone had hoped – and these in turn gave a further stimulus to reform. By the end of the century so dominant were the liberal values upon which the Northcote/Trevelyan Report drew, that the Northcote/Trevelyan ideals received wide endorsement even though their application was fraught with practical difficulty.

The pattern of reform in the post-1945 period has similarly been much influenced by the prevailing intellectual climate. The spate of highly critical writings on the nature of British institutions which began to appear after 1960, influenced thought about the central administration. In particular the growing popularity of 'managerial' ideas in the 1960s helped to mould the vocabulary and the ways of thought in which matters of administrative reform were couched. The common feeling of the adherents of the managerial approach was that insufficient attention had been paid to the identification of problems in government, that a more important role should be assigned to specialists in central decision-making, and that useful lessons in the management of government might well be drawn from business, commercial and other administrative areas outside the civil service. The developments in both the recruitment of civil servants and their subsequent training owed much to the growing popularity of these ideas, especially during the 1960s, and the Fulton Report was influenced by these and in its turn helped further to popularise them. The Report, according to Lord Armstrong, was 'an ice breaker ... it was a catalyst and enabled all kinds of ideas to come through'.[25] The authors of the Fulton Report somewhat immodestly seem to have seen themselves as providing a Northcote/Trevelyan Report for the late twentieth century, a step towards reforming the civil service in line with the intellectual developments which they considered to be both desirable and progressive. Their difficulty lay in the fact that managerial views were a good deal less specific as regards political goals than liberal ideas of the 1850s. The managerialists of the 1960s were obsessed by techniques and failed to give sufficient emphasis to defining goals, to appreciating the meanings of concepts such as 'efficiency', and to assessing the practical constraints on public administration of the political environment.

If administrative reform in Britain has been subject to the influence of prevailing schools of thought, it has also been influenced by more limited ideas. A good example of this is the way in which the popularity of reforming the machinery of government waned and waxed in inverse proportion to the credibility of Keynesian economic ideas after 1945. The less the Keynesian ideas seemed capable of ensuring continued economic growth, the more politicians were tempted to experiment with 'structural' changes in government. Whitehall, moreover, is highly susceptible to changes in 'fashion'. Jock Bruce-Gardyne and Nigel Lawson in their studies of decision-making in the 1960s have pointed to the extraordinary rapidity with which the consensus of Whitehall opinion on questions such as floating exchange rates and entry to the EEC can change for no very apparent reason.[26] The same is true of administrative issues. The rise and subsequent fall in popularity of the 'giant' ministry is a case in point. Thinking on this subject seems closely to have mirrored the prevailing wisdom concerning the merits or otherwise of large businesses, although it has also been affected by practical experience: for example the amount and scope of business which one minister can handle in the House of Commons.

In contrast are the long-term changes in the personnel and structure of the civil service which over a period of a generation may bring about significant changes in attitudes to government. Three such shifts may be traced in our period. The first and most important was the replacement of the rather heterogeneous group of leading mid-Victorian administrators with an exclusively academic elite, drawn largely from Oxford, Cambridge and the Scottish universities, as a result of the reforms in recruitment after 1855 and 1870. Such an elite, trained predominantly in the liberal humanities, began to dominate the higher civil service from about 1890. The intellectual calibre of such recruits was higher than that of their predecessors, and it may not be coincidental that about the time when such recruits reached the very top positions the pace and character of most government departments began to change, with the official contributing more to policy-making. Moreover, the ideals of public service, preached by Jowett at Balliol, and the enthusiasms of the Oxford Idealists, percolated through the civil service. The second important shift followed from the first. It was the successful attempt by Warren Fisher and others to encourage a sense of *esprit de corps* in the higher civil service, by welding together an integrated 'Administrative Class' whose members would move around the Whitehall departments. This marked the development of the idea of the all-round, generalist administrator which was to hold sway unchallenged until the 1960s. The favoured approach was a form of 'collegiality' modelled closely on that of an Oxford or Cambridge college. Bridges in a lecture of 1950, for example, lamented the absence of 'those expressions of corporate life found in a College. We have neither hall nor chapel, neither combination room nor common room.'[27] It seems, however, unlikely that such formal institutions would have done much to strengthen the close bonds which had already been formed through informal channels. The Second World War proved only to be an interlude in the process of the formation of a degree of Whitehall exclusiveness, which has been marked by a gulf between insiders and outsiders. The third important shift in attitudes occurred at a lower level. This was the growth of trade union practices and attitudes among junior and middle-ranking civil servants during and after the First World War. This has affected far more than labour relations *per se*.

In the last resort, however, any attempt to isolate 'intellectual influences' from more general political considerations is futile. As C.H. Sisson has written, 'a good idea is no good unless it fits into the context of the time, has a place in the universe of discourse within which, by consensus, the division of public affairs is conducted'.[28] Of key importance are the 'intermediaries' who can move with ease from the intellectual *salon*, the university or the research institute to the government department, the minister's office or the party headquarters cross-fertilising the one with the other. Stafford Northcote, Lyon Playfair, the Webbs, Haldane, Laski, Keynes and Norman Hunt all fit into this category. As Lord Beveridge, one of the most successful of all these 'intermediaries', has stressed: 'Influence, reason and special knowledge have their chance, whoever the temporary owners of power may be. But they have this chance only if there is a channel of access to those who have power.'[29] No analysis of administrative reform therefore can be satisfactory if it omits consideration of the political element.

Political Pressures and Administrative Reform

Whilst administrative reform should not be seen as simply a political activity, in the area of public administration it necessarily involves political elements of various kinds. In so far as reform — in contrast to mere change — seeks to adjust the processes or structures of administration in accordance with the pressures of the social and political environment, it necessarily involves consideration of the political values of participants as well as their immediate political ambitions. There can be no 'ideal' or 'rational' method of administration, just as there is unlikely ever to be a neutral or agreed definition of 'efficiency'. Lord Bridges recognised this when he stressed that in public administration no clear line can be drawn 'between the objective study of facts and political considerations in a sense which implies the views of a Party politician'.[30] The course of administrative reform will be affected not only by the long-term ideological predilections of political leaders, but also by pressing short-term expediencies. As Sir John Hunt, Secretary to the Cabinet, declared before the English Sub-committee in 1977, 'the Civil Service is an instrument of Ministerial policies, and to some extent its structural organisation must reflect not only those policies, but also how a Prime Minister feels he can best deploy his Ministerial strength and the team he has got. So I think it is a political, as well as an organisational matter'.[31] Policy in other words necessarily involves politics, since, in the pithy words of Harold Wilson, 'policies without politics are of no more use than politics without policies'.[32] The political dimension to administrative reform, however, must necessarily be wide. It must include 'inside' politics as well as political pressures from 'outside' governmental circles. Moreover, any change or reform in the administrative system will contain various political pressures which will be closely intermeshed. Analysis of pressure from any particular source on its own may easily distort the overall picture. There is a danger of tearing apart a seamless garment: what matters is often the interconnection of the various threads. However, we will attempt here to examine the impact of pressures from five different directions: popular agitation in the country, Parliament, political parties, the ambitions of ministers, and the associations and unions within the civil service.

Popular agitation is not a factor that has loomed large in our study. The civil service and organisation of government are not in the public mind particularly interesting or exciting topics. They only affect the citizen indirectly and lack the glamour of many other political causes. The prevailing popular attitude has been one of apathy tempered by ignorance. There has been a general dislike of the 'red tape' in which public officials are popularly supposed to be entangled — Dickens's 'Circumlocution Office' has cast a powerful spell upon the popular imagination — but the civil servant has generally been the butt of good-humoured ribaldry rather than bitter invective.

The sole exception is to be found at the start of our period when the Administrative Reform Association helped to keep up the momentum of reform at the time of the Crimean War. The Association wanted to see the introduction of commercial methods and businessmen into administration, and its leaders used the public disquiet at the scandalous revelations of administrative bungling at the time of the Crimean War to launch a much broader political attack upon 'aristocratic government'.[33] It was partly to take the wind out of the sails of mounting criticism, which was being championed in Parliament by Layard and other spokesmen for the Association, that Palmerston's Cabinet introduced the Order in Council of 21 May which set up the Civil Service Commission. This was sufficient to appease most MPs and a critical motion on administrative matters in June only received the humiliatingly low support of 46 MPs.[34] Popular interest in the question soon waned as the military situation improved, and the Association quickly became a spent force.

Never again did popular agitation make such a direct mark upon administrative reform. An attempt at the time of the Boer War to form a similar association was stillborn.[35] The War Office was reformed but this was largely the result of the Esher Committee of 1903-4, an internal government inquiry. Subsequently popular feeling on administrative matters has occasionally been whipped up by the press, but it has been essentially passive in character. One of these occasions occurred towards the end of the First World War, when the press led a campaign against extravagance in government offices and excessive 'red tape'. One vocal outside critic was Sir Stephen Demetriadi, who had worked in the Ministry of Planning during the war, and who afterwards launched an energetic campaign for the introduction of more 'business' methods in administration.[36] Another occasion for public disquiet occurred in the late 1940s following the statements and activities of Sydney Stanley, as well as a series of governmental failures such as the groundnuts scheme and the fuel crisis of 1946-7.

Since the Crimean War, however, this periodic background unease has only had a significant effect when it has been channelled through Parliament. Trevelyan, for example, believed that his ideas only survived in the early years because of the 'large and important class of clergymen and retired officers and persons of the middle class of all sorts', who had an interest in bettering their sons' prospects through education, and who 'when the new system was in jeopardy ... wrote in shoals to their members, and that accounts for the majority' in the Commons. A secret ballot of MPs might have gone the other way.[37] But in the twentieth century MPs have acted more positively. It was parliamentary pressure which prompted the government to set up the Bradbury investigation into extravagance in government departments in 1918; and similarly during the Second World War, the Select Committee on National Expenditure was in part responsible for setting in motion important investigations into the machinery and organisation of government. Parliamentary feeling was an important factor in helping to set up the Lynskey Tribunal and the investigation into the Crichel Down affair in the post-war period. During the past 20 years parliamentary concern for administrative matters has undoubtedly greatly grown, as an increasing number of MPs have been recruited from those who previously have been professionally or academically interested in questions of management or who have been teachers in further or higher education. The investigation of the English subcommittee is the latest manifestation of this.

After the demise of the great agitational leagues of mid-Victorian times and the extension of the franchise, popular pressure for social and political reforms has usually been channelled through the political party. However, before 1939 the political parties seem in general to have displayed little interest in the civil service. In contrast to local government reform, the organisation of the central government did not

feature in the 'Newcastle Programme' of 1891 nor in any of the other
radical Liberal agitations or manifestos of the period. Nor were the
early leaders of the Labour Party any more interested in or concerned
with the question. Most Labour politicians in the inter-war years
confined their interest in the civil service to supporting the trade
unions' demands for higher pay and to questioning its social
composition. Between the wars, however, a few intellectuals loosely
connected with political parties, began to consider the question more
earnestly. On the Conservative side several, like Lord Hewart, became
concerned at the apparent growth of 'bureaucracy' (a phenomenon
previously believed to be confined to the Continent), while several
socialist thinkers gave thought to the possible relationship between a
socialist political programme and the machinery of government. The
Webbs in particular recognised first that new political and social goals
might well require new administrative machinery, and secondly that in
positive government the classic separation between policy-making and
administration might be much less evident. These concerns are clearly
to be found underlying the Haldane Report. In the new collectivist
age the administrative system might be the chief means of nurturing
social progress. The Webbs and their associates envisaged a new
pattern of political activity in which a key role in the policy-
formation process would come from the interaction of bureaucrats,
other experts and the leaders of professional organisations. Other
socialist thinkers, like G.D.H. Cole, Tawney and Laski, were
influenced by these ideas, even though their own perspectives were
rather different. The ideas were to permeate much later thinking in
Whitehall.

   After 1945 the political parties gave more thought to the question
than before, although it was less the main policy-making organisations in
the parties than small groups and associations within them that
produced the most constructive ideas and had the most influence. The
Liberal Party Committee on the Civil Service seems to have had some
influence in 1942. But the most important of these groups was the
Fabian Society. The Fabians had been concerned in the 1930s with the
social background of officials, and their ideas after the war helped to
create the consensus in favour of the Civil Service College. The Fabian
tract, *The Administrators*, was particularly influential in helping to
formulate many of the ideas and ways of thought which came to the
fore in the Fulton Report, and some members of the Fulton
Committee enjoyed close links with the Fabians. On an individual level
men such as Thomas Balogh, Peter Shore, Richard Crossman and, of

course, Harold Wilson, developed ideas which they had an opportunity to implement after 1964. The Labour Party's contribution to reform seems therefore to have been mainly an indirect one. Its influence in opposition has been considerable through the medium of reports, ideas and representations to official committees. In government on the other hand the Party's record has been less impressive, once its leaders find their time taken up with pressing matters of state. This has provoked the frustration of their supporters: for example John Garrett in January 1979 declared that 'it is as if Labour in office has now lost all stomach for administrative reform'.[38] The Conservative Party, however, between 1966 and 1970, under the enthusiastic direction of Edward Heath, embarked on what he saw as the most comprehensive analysis of the problems of the machinery of government ever undertaken by an opposition. The ideas and research generated then contributed to the 1970 White Paper on the Reorganisation of Central Government.[39]

If the sustained interest of political parties in administrative matters may be a relatively recent phenomenon, the same is not true of the interest of individual politicians. Again and again the episodes and developments which we have studied indicate the importance and encouragement of political leaders. Motives here have been varied. Occasionally the personal ambition of particular individuals gives a fillip to particular reforms. The setting up of the Ridley Commission and the Anderson Committee owed much to the political ambitions of Lord Randolph Churchill and Stafford Cripps, respectively; and the development of reconstruction work in 1916-17 not a little to the somewhat disingenuous scheming of Edwin Montagu. Matters, however, even in these instances, are rarely quite so simple. It is more common for politicians to push ahead with particular reforms because they fit in well with a broader political strategy or ideological commitment, although in the process they may reap what political advantage they can. An excellent example of this is the eagerness with which Harold Wilson seized upon certain ideas about civil service reform in 1963-4 which apparently fitted in with his concept of the 'white heat of the scientific revolution'. Undoubtedly the most striking instance of this, however, was the political concern of Gladstone and Northcote in 1854. Both, while eager for the removal of abuses, viewed the contemporary radical and iconoclastic attack on the aristocracy with alarm. Gladstone considered that 'one of the great recommendations' of the Northcote/Trevelyan Report 'would be its tendency to strengthen and multiply the ties between the higher classes and the

possession of administrative power' by opening up to the highly
educated classes a new career opportunity.[40] Even more attractive was
the prospect of the likely political benefits. Trevelyan envisaged the
civil service becoming 'the best school for Parliament' as talented
young clerks moved from civil service positions into politics. As the
'two parts of our Government would be alike raised to a higher
standard, they would also be reduced to harmony with each other'.[41]
The abolition of patronage, moreover, would help secure a more
elevated style of party politics and would help the advance towards a
free and liberal society. Civil service reform was thus a means of
bringing about political reform by the back door: 'This is *my*
contribution to the picnic of Parliamentary reform' declared Gladstone
to Sir James Graham in January 1854.[42] Not all of Gladstone's
colleagues shared his sentiments. However, in 1870, when he was
Prime Minister, he was able with Robert Lowe to push ahead with the
introduction of completely open competition despite the opposition
of some members of the Cabinet.

A prime minister enjoys particularly good opportunities to add impetus
to reform proposals. Other examples are the concern of Lloyd George
with reconstruction planning in the First World War and the sympathy
of Harold Wilson with the Fulton ideals. Here, however, it is necessary
to strike a cautionary note. Ministers, especially prime ministers, may
lack the resources of time and energy to push through a reform
proposal to a significant conclusion. Lloyd George could do little more
than set the reconstruction planning in process. Harold Wilson
experienced this difficulty directly. When questioned by the English
Committee, he admitted that the implementation of the Fulton Report
by 1969 'was tailing off a bit'. His Principal Private Secretary, Michael
Halls, warned him that 'the thing was losing steam' but 'with so many
urgent problems at that time, I was not able to give my mind to it
sufficiently ... the sheer rush and pace of Government at the present
time ... has prevented as much being done on this as I think should
be'.[43] The politician's realistic responsibility must be to set processes
in motion, to delegate and to depend upon subordinates or officials
for implementation. This, however, raises the vexed question as to the
extent to which even the minister may be becoming an 'outsider' with
regard to the government machine. Administrative reform is rarely a
painless process, and the closed world of Whitehall may tend to resist
the politician as a temporary bird of passage, or as an intruder. It
sometimes needs no more than a report from an official that there is
nothing new in a particular approach for all concerned virtually to

dismiss it — as, for example, seems to have been the case with the way
Wilson Smith commented on Attlee's letter of 9 January 1943 about
the Civil Service College: 'If I may say so with respect, there is nothing
very new in the four points raised by Mr. Attlee ... This is a matter
which has been engaging the closest attention of the Financial
Secretary and those associated with him in examining the problems of
the post-war Home Civil Service'.[44] The role of individuals, the
Treasury, and the procedures used by them are conditioned primarily
to avoid embarrassment, a key word in the civil service which, as
Anthony Sampson says, 'signalises the dreaded intrusion of the outside
world'.[45]

Another important political pressure has been that exerted by rank-
and-file civil servants themselves. Even at the time of the Northcote/
Trevelyan Report there was a simmering discontent over superannuation questions.[46] Trevelyan and Gladstone were convinced that any
concessions should be 'attended with real and substantial improvements
in the service',[47] and they hoped to develop a more generous system of
payments and superannuation as part of the new professional civil
service they envisaged. Not all of their successors were inclined to treat
discontent among public servants with such far-sightedness. Throughout
the late-nineteenth century an important pressure which contributed to
the consolidation of civil service structure came from disgruntled
employees who felt aggrieved at the anomalies of grading, of pay and
of promotion prospects. In 1874 it was the 'great dissatisfaction' among
the rank and file which led Northcote to appoint the Playfair
Commission. In the 1880s agitation from the growing number of
associations of clerks kept the issue alive, and in 1890 this agitation,
which spilled over into Parliament and the press, prompted the Order
in Council which reorganised the service. During this period the lobby
of aggrieved clerks found Parliament to be a potent instrument for
venting their frustrations. At a time when the franchise was limited,
civil servants formed a significant section of the electorate, especially
in constituencies where they were highly concentrated. It was pressure
from this quarter which was largely responsible for the setting up of
the MacDonnell Commission. The growth during this period of well-
organised staff associations was an important factor in encouraging
contemporaries to think in terms of a 'civil service' rather than the
'public establishments'.

During and immediately after the First World War, however, pressure
from this quarter took a new form. Some of the staff associations
adopted the attitudes of trade unions. They wanted an established

negotiating machinery, and some sort of say in the running of the service. The response of Austen Chamberlain, his cabinet colleagues and senior Treasury officials was to establish, after much hesitation, the Whitley machinery as a forum for negotiation and the settlement of grievances. Such a development was important because it not only condoned but actually encouraged the development of fully representative staff bodies throughout all ranks of the civil service, even in quarters like the First Division or among specialist professional employees where such bodies had hitherto been thought unnecessary. The consequence of this was that after this date no major innovation in the structure or methods of work of the civil service could be introduced without full consultation with the representatives of the employees of the service itself.

In the early years this led to some conflict of interpretation. On the one hand the unions envisaged the Whitley machinery and the subsequent Reorganisation Report as marking some sort of a contract between the staff representatives and the official management, and that 'the organisation and control of the Civil Service will henceforth be the joint task of representatives of the staffs and representatives of the State as employer'.[48] Ministers understandably rejected this on the grounds that ministerial responsibility would be impaired. On the other hand the Treasury leaders resisted pressures from some Conservatives to make an issue out of trade union activity in the 1920s. In 1923 H. Curtin, the civil service correspondent of the *Daily Telegraph*, started a campaign against 'paid Socialist agitators', who were not even civil servants, representing the Staff; he criticised the 'incomprehensible inaction' on the part of the Official leadership. Again in 1925 Sir Edwin Cadogan, one of the Conservative MPs sitting on the Official Side, wrote to the Chancellor, Winston Churchill, to protest at the 'apparent indifference' displayed by heads of departments at the activities 'of such firebrands as W.J. Brown' who harangued the Council with partisan speeches 'of the type you can hear on any Sunday you like in Hyde Park'. The Treasury leaders, however, viewed the matter phlegmatically since 'any heavy handed attempt to suppress such activities would be found more effective in increasing the trouble than the efforts of a few extremist leaders'. Any remedy might be 'more dangerous than the disease'.[49] Although the political activities of civil servants remained a delicate subject up till the 1950s, the Whitley machinery ensured that civil service grievances did not become linked with party politics — a development by no means inevitable. This in large part contributed to the civil service's ability to come through the General Strike of 1926 relatively unscathed. The unions were somewhat divided, but despite their membership of the TUC they avoided strike action. Official assurances were secured from the Treasury that during the strike no civil servant would be instructed to perform other than his normal duties, and civil servants were advised not to volunteer for additional work. Militants on both sides of the question were dissatisfied, but this compromise ensured that the service did not become embroiled in a difficult political situation.[50]

Since the Second World War the civil service unions have made a major, although unspectacular, contribution to the course of reform. The changed attitudes of the staff associations to the idea of a staff training college was an important factor in the consensus which made possible the creation of the Civil Service College. The views of the various associations on the grading and classification of the civil service constituted important evidence received by the Fulton Committee, although they did not of course speak with one voice on the question. The setting-up of the Priestley Commission, and, following its recommendations, the establishment of the Civil Service Pay Research Unit, were a direct response by the government to the growing complexities of issues of pay and promotion, the considerable dissatisfaction within the civil service and the conflicting views of the staff associations. Pressures from the staff associations may not always be a prime factor in initiating moves for reform, but they have played a considerable part in assisting the introduction of reform, shaping its form and guiding its implementation. In addition they possess a residual 'veto' power which may prevent ministers from pushing ahead with restructurings or reorganisations which might otherwise appear attractive. A recent example of this is the unwillingness of the Government in response to a recommendation of the English Committee 'to impose a unified grading structure on unwilling unions, or to pay a high price in terms of additional wage costs in order to secure their agreement'.[51]

Changes in the responsibilities of members of the government are not in themselves sufficient to constitute administrative reform if the changes do not have repercussions in the administrative system. Churchill's experiment with 'Overlords' in the 1950s, for example, failed to affect much more than responsibility for answering parliamentary questions. Nevertheless it is clear that no satisfactory account of administrative reform in public administration can neglect the political components in all their complexity.

The Impetus of Events

The evolution and development of institutions and processes of public
administration in a developed country like Britain can be more usefully
assessed within a time-scale of decades or half-centuries than in years or
months. Many of the themes which we have considered in this book
have consequently been viewed against a long time-span: for example
reforms in the recruitment of staff or in the grading or organisation of
the civil service. These have been reforms which have taken a long time
to be implemented or worked out. There are, however, inherent
dangers in this perspective, the chief being that hindsight can be a
hindrance as much as a benefit to the student of administrative history.
Certain developments may be made to appear far more inevitable than
historical reality warrants. The development of the Whitley machinery
is a case in point. There were several possible alternative ways in which
labour relations might have been handled, and many contemporaries
in 1918-9 must have regarded these as inherently more plausible
outcomes. Similarly in 1854-5, although there were powerful pressures
operating to open up the proposed examinations for the Indian Civil
Service to university graduates, there was a strong possibility that
Haileybury College might have been converted into a pre-entry training
college. Such an institution could have led to the development of a
specialised avenue of entry to the British civil service, with profound
repercussions for its later history. Moreover, the long-term perspective
in which such aspects of government are viewed encourages
administrative changes to be seen as major elements in trends or
movements such as 'the growth of collectivism', 'the emergence of
bureaucracy', 'the end of *laissez faire*', 'the advent of the welfare
state' or even 'the growth of government'. All may make excellent
sense in terms of academic analysis; but what must be remembered is
that particular participants in administrative decision-making at any
time were not so much concerned with such abstractions as with the
day-to-day handling of particular problems or pressures. The tyranny
of the 'in-tray' dominates the lives of ministers and officials alike.
Even those few who have the inclination to consider the long-term
perspectives rarely have the time or the energy left to fulfil their
interests. Furthermore, long-term perspectives may have a distorting
teleological effect; incidents or changes may be seen as contributing
to a broad historical movement as steps towards a foreordained goal.
A line of development may be traced out artifically from what is in
reality a tangled skein. The administrators involved in any particular
piece of decision-making will be subject to a great number of different

pressures and will carry with them a number of different and sometimes competing objectives. As a corrective to the distortions caused by the picture of administrators working systematically to implement particular goals, it will be useful to stress the extent to which they have to react to the particular pressures of the work around them. Our study reveals the important part which what may be termed 'the impetus of events' has had upon the course of administrative reform.

'The impetus of events', however, is a broad and rather loose term. We use it to include all those pressures from outside government which are neutral in a party-political sense, but which force those in government to adjust their practices: social scientists may refer to them as societal pressures of various sorts. These may range from some specific event, like a war or an economic crisis, to more general social changes. An example of the latter would be the pressures placed on the recruitment procedures in the civil service after the First World War. The infusion of temporary employees during the war, the return of ex-servicemen and the confusion of grading virtually forced a reorganisation scheme upon the civil service; the problem was so large and pressing that it demanded with some urgency a service-wide treatment. Indeed, one of the most striking features of the British civil service is the extent to which it has proved flexible in the face of external challenges. Lord Simey, in his reservation to the first chapter of the Fulton Report, made this point forcibly. He saw the creation of the administrative class over the years as due to 'events alone ... starting perhaps with Lloyd George's Insurance Act, followed by two World Wars and all the developments since'.[52] This interpretation is a salutary correction to the commonly-held view that in Britain the higher civil service of the twentieth century has been the 'creation', if not of the Northcote/Trevelyan Report, of the Northcote/Trevelyan 'philosophy'. We will examine briefly the impetus given to reform by four external forces: economic pressures, the impact of war, the changing social status of women and the growth of government.

The struggle between departments or services for the expenditure of limited public money, the handling of inflationary or deflationary pressures, and the raising of taxation are never far below the surface of any governmental activity. In this sense economic pressures upon government are the most 'political' of the 'events' we are examining here. They are channelled through such bodies as Parliament or political associations and are often linked to the broader policies of governments or even to the manoeuvrings of ambitious individual politicians: as was the case with Lord Randolph Churchill in the late

1880s. The constant pressure for economy in government has been a powerful force throughout our period. It has been at once a cause and a result of the Treasury's pre-eminent position in civil service affairs. Often this concern with economy has prevented the implementation of proposals for administrative reform. W.J. Brown in 1930, for example, judged that it was narrow financial considerations which had prevented what he considered to be the proper application of the Reorganisation Committee's Report.[53] A similar concern with short-term economy may have hindered the emergence of the systematic division of labour recommended by the Playfair Commission, and may have been partly responsible for the failure to develop O & M work before the Second World War.

On the other hand, a striking feature of our study is the extent to which economic pressures have frequently played a positive role in stimulating proposals for reform. On several occasions waves of pressure for economy in government have led to important investigations which in turn have stimulated bold new ideas. There seems almost to be a pattern emerging here. In the 1840s it was the pressure from Radicals and others in favour of cutting down sinecures and government patronage which led to the investigations of a parliamentary committee; this in turn gave the impetus to Trevelyan to start his systematic overhaul of government offices from which the idea emerged of achieving more efficient administration through the division of labour. Towards the end of the First World War the newspapers were full of denunciations of the extravagance of government departments, and this climate prompted MPs to bring the pressure to bear which resulted in the Bradbury Committee being set up; this in its turn set in train many of the important reforms of the period 1918-22 concerning the reorganisation of the service and the redefinition of Treasury control. After 1945 it was widespread public criticisms of the civil service on grounds of inefficiency which encouraged the further development of O & M work, and it was against the background of this agitation against waste that ministers continued to keep alive reforming ideas in the area of the machinery of government. Once again in 1957-8 the misgivings of a sub-committee of the Select Committee on Estimates led to the setting up of the Plowden Committee which formulated radical new ideas for the control of public expenditure; this, in turn, led to the reform of the Treasury in 1962 and the setting up of the PESC machinery, and encouraged the placing of more emphasis on the training of civil servants. Pressure for economy is not, of course, in itself sufficient to stimulate reform. Nothing creative in the field of administrative reform emerged from the cuts of the 1930s, and the Ridley Commission which resulted from economising pressure in the 1880s failed to produce any positive ideas. The right political and administrative intermediaries have to be in place to ensure the implementation of reform proposals: the Ridley story might have turned out differently had Randolph Churchill remained Chancellor of the Exchequer. However, the interesting lesson emerges that efforts to cut down the cost or extent of government activity have frequently stimulated proposals leading to administrative reform.

The impact of war has been more dramatic. The Crimean War, and to a lesser extent the Boer War, aroused a great deal of public discussion on the nature of administration as well as efforts to infuse an element of 'business' expertise into the civil service. The scandals unearthed at the time of the Crimean War ensured that some limited action was taken by Palmerston's government along the lines of the Northcote/ Trevelyan Report. However, it is the two world wars of this century that have had the greatest impact upon the administration of British central government. Their impact lay not so much – as in 1855 – in the political repercussions of the war as in the enormous demands which the mobilisation of men and resources placed upon the governmental machine. These wars not only caused upheaval in Whitehall for their duration but also were responsible for shaping the course of much later development. Virtually all of the reforms we have considered in the post-1945 period, for example, have roots which may be traced back to the Second World War. In many respects the period from 1945 to the mid-1960s can be interpreted in terms of working through or practical evolution of reforms which had been largely set in motion during the war years. The 'Method II' scheme for recruitment to the administrative class developed out of war-time selection procedures for the armed services. Reforms in the machinery of government and in the classification of staff after 1945 in fact owed much to the work of the Machinery of Government Committee and its associated committees. The train of events which led to the creation of the Civil Service College can be traced back to the ideas on training which were voiced in terms of maximising government efficiency during the Second World War. The First World War had repercussions almost as dramatic. It encouraged for the first time wholesale transfers of senior staff from one department to another which later became an accepted feature of the British higher civil service. At the centre, the Cabinet developed into a powerful co-ordinating organ of government, and from this time, too, can be traced important subsequent developments in the spheres of labour relations, establishments work and the machinery of government. Even when war did not directly cause change, it sometimes facilitated the implementation of ideas which had previously proved difficult to achieve: examples of this are the creation of the Ministry of Health in 1919, and the reforms in education and welfare during the 1940s. In this way it acted as a catalyst for reforms which received their original stimulus elsewhere.

The two world wars posed new problems to a well-established pattern of administration. The response to these challenges indicates the flexibility of British central government. The tendency was for established institutions or procedures to be adapted and even developed and transformed rather than for any fundamental alterations to be made to the basic structure of governmental institutions. Improvisation was the order of the day, with outside influence being grafted on to existing features of the administrative system rather than swamping it. For those affected by it the impact of war was unpredictable, confusing and pressing. Few could afford, like the members of the Haldane Committee, the luxury of analysing the broad meaning of the turmoil that was going on around them or assessing the likely course of future developments. Most had enough to do to meet the demands of the next day: to reconcile conflicting pressures or goals, to improvise where necessary in order to overcome an acute shortage of resources of money, manpower and time. Yet in combination these day-to-day pressures had a radical impact upon the administration of British central government.

The world wars illustrate very well the impact which a sudden and dramatic crisis can have upon the lives and work of administrators. Quite another kind of external pressure which has operated upon the civil service has been the impact of long-term, powerful social changes. One of these occurred in the educational system of the country. Throughout our period, recruitment procedures, and even the classification within the service, was influenced by various changes in the educational world. Another important influence was the emancipation of women. During the late nineteenth century the Post Office began to employ considerable numbers of women on work such as sorting and telegraphy for which they seemed particularly suited. By the 1890s many other departments had begun to employ a limited number of women as 'female typewriters', although they were often kept secluded from the male gaze in attics or basements. However, by the time of the First World War an increasing number of women had come to be employed on more responsible work, particularly as inspectors of one kind or another. Generally speaking women were found to work quite as well as men and had the advantage of being cheaper to employ. The quick turnover of personnel caused by their retirement on marriage, although inconvenient at the higher grades, was a positive asset at the lower levels. Accordingly the MacDonnell Commission devoted much of its time to considering whether women might be employed on broadly the same terms as men. The First World War saw not only a dramatic increase in the amount of female labour, but also the transfer of many of the more able women inspectors to ordinary administrative work. At the outbreak of war in 1914 there were only some 4,000 women employed in non-industrial posts in the entire civil service, four years later there were 180,000 of them.[54] After the war the Reorganisation Report of the National Whitley Council specifically recommended interchangeability of men and women within the civil service. For a few years special selection procedures were employed, but from 1925 women competed in the same examinations as men. The Tomlin Commission recommended a complete 'aggregation' of all civil service posts, i.e. a complete abolition of the segregated structure of separate male and female posts. However, it did not go so far as to recommend the abolition of the 'marriage bar' or equal pay. These were not granted until 1946 and 1955.[55]

These changes in the status of women in the civil service came about piecemeal and gradually. Governments were often put under pressure by outside lobbies, particularly from the House of Commons and various women's associations both inside and outside the service; but the civil service, although generally cautious and conservative on the question, was never so far at odds either with prevailing outside opinion on the question or with commercial practices as to prove susceptible to steam-rollering from without. In reading the copious evidence on the subject given before various committees and commissions of the period one is struck by the very undogmatic and flexible approach of administrators themselves on the issue. Opinions were often divided. Some permanent secretaries were conservative: others – including Warren Fisher – 'feminists'. But few were dogmatic one way or the other. Those who opposed extending the employment of women usually did so on practical grounds or because they did not want to move too far in advance of public opinion. Economic arguments were often important, and these could easily cut both ways. The civil service associations themselves were far from unanimous on the question, and even the women's associations held conflicting views in some instances, for example on the question of the 'marriage bar'. Changes often occurred as a response to developments – e.g. the growing use of typewriters, the impact of the two wars – before the rationale behind those changes had been discussed. Perhaps the most striking aspect of the changes before 1930 is the degree to which matters were settled on an *ad hoc* basis within individual departments, and the degree of flexibility which was contained within the general structure. The whole question was a complicated one with many ramifications over which a great deal of ink was spilt, but it is hard to resist the conclusion that the formal inquiries into the question merely followed a course which was already largely determined by changing social *mores* and expectations.

Another external stimulus to change was the growth of positive government during our period. This is a vast topic which is beyond the scope of this book, but it provided a backcloth to the history of administrative reform which should be constantly borne in mind. Incremental growth and steady adaptation rather than any 'revolution' in the administration of government was the chief characteristic of the period from 1850 to 1970,[56] but such incremental growth was only related in part, and then indirectly, to changes in the accepted role of the state in society. The continuous pressure placed upon administrators by the expansion of governmental activity undoubtedly provided an important environment for the stimulation of proposals for administrative reform and development. The growth of uniform standards of recruitment in the nineteenth century, the transfer of personnel across departments in the early twentieth century, the development of O & M work and the increased emphasis upon more systematic procedures for training after the Second World War can all be seen in some respect as responses to and consequences of the growth of government. An important role in the direction and co-ordination of these responses, however, was played by officials themselves.

The Direction of Administrative Reform

Our study has revealed the extent to which British central government has responded to political or ideological pressures from outside and also adapted itself to deal with the consequences of events over which it had no control. In these circumstances, however, it would be surprising if the civil service in general, and a small number of leading officials within it, did not play key roles in the direction and moderation of administrative reform. The reforms we have considered confirm that this was what actually happened. To speak in this context of the civil service as a single entity playing a specific and limited 'role', in accordance with some simple conception of the British constitution, is clearly misleading. For not only was the cast a large one, comprised of many talented individuals with widely differing interests, but the repertoire itself was also immensely varied. Each scenario indeed was unique. However, it is possible to distinguish three chief ways in which officials rather than politicians or outside specialists have played a part in the dynamics of administrative reform. The first concerns those instances where proposals for reform have originated or been stimulated from within the administration; the second is where outstanding individual officials have encouraged and guided administrative developments; and the third when officials, while implementing reforms originating from outside, have significantly modified or adapted their intended impact or effect. These three aspects are not mutually exclusive, neither can they be entirely separated from the broader political forces at play.

One persistent characteristic of administrative reform which our studies have revealed is the extent to which particular reforms have often been preceded by many years of patient spadework within the civil service. Sometimes seemingly radical proposals have originated or been first mooted within the civil service as a response to administrative difficulties within government departments. Northcote and Trevelyan's proposals for a division of labour, for example, originated not as an abstract principle but as a result of the investigations of Trevelyan and his Treasury colleagues into the inefficient conduct of business in government offices. Similarly the changes both in the recruitment procedures for civil servants and in the classification of the civil service after 1945 were in major part a response to administrative difficulties. The Fulton Committee's recommendations in these areas, although thought by some people outside the administrative system to be original solutions to problems of contemporary concern, had already been under consideration years before within the civil service itself. The gradual consolidation of civil service structure and organisation after 1870, on the other hand, is a good example of a series of incrementalist changes which amounted to a significant shift in the organisation of British central government without ever being debated in a wider 'political' context.

On other occasions developments within the administration have paved the way for the implementation of reform proposals which had earlier been regarded as unduly radical. The introduction of open competition in 1870 and the creation of the Civil Service College in the late 1960s are examples of this. In both instances the original ideas for reform had aroused fierce opposition from powerful forces within the public service. In time, however, the climate of opinion in the civil service changed, and experience of the workings of the Civil Service Commission and of the Centre for Administrative Studies rendered acceptable and even desirable what had previously been seen as dangerous and radical. In both instances, although the 'political' concerns of party leaders was of prime importance in initiating reform, the creation of a consensus in favour of further reform among officials was an important factor in ensuring a smooth implementation.

The atmosphere within the administrative system can therefore be important in determining the timing, pace, and even the direction of reform. However, our study clearly reveals that initiative from the bureaucracy on occasion takes a more positive form. At any period there have been able administrators who have played an important part in presiding over and guiding administrative developments already in train: George Hamilton and Reginald Welby, permanent heads of the Treasury in the latter half of the nineteenth century, may be taken as examples. But other public servants have played an altogether more creative part. In our period we can point to six individuals in particular who left a lasting mark upon the public service: Charles Trevelyan, Robert Morant, Warren Fisher, Edward Bridges, Alan Barlow and Percival Waterfield. All developed very clear ideas concerning the place of the civil servant in British government and society, and all of them cherished particular ideas for reform. Their achievements and their methods of work were as varied as their personalities, but all influenced their contemporaries or successors and made lasting contributions to the British civil service.

Charles Trevelyan was not only responsible for undertaking a radical overhaul of the Treasury and its subordinate departments, he also shaped the administrative thinking that was to dominate the next 50 years. His ideas of dividing labour into routine and intellectual categories, of ensuring promotion by merit, and of selecting the most able recruits by means of open competition, soon became the guiding principles of later reformers even though the practical application of these ideals was fraught with difficulty. He saw the need for a properly constituted civil service – an honourable profession in its own right – to replace the ramshackle assortment of public offices which had existed up to that time. An impulsive, incisive and intensely self-confident reformer he was perhaps more at home in the political and intellectual worlds than in the civil service, where many of his colleagues found him to be arrogant and over-dogmatic. Perhaps his major achievement was to put administrative reform firmly on the political agenda, by linking it with the aspirations of liberal reforming politicians and academics. Robert Morant was an equally forceful reformer with pronounced views on the desirability of social reforms. He also acquired the reputation of being a first-class intriguer who, it is said, would pursue a particular approach through tortuous and underground passages in order to attain some object of public service in which he had a passionate interest.[57] His greatest contribution was to ensure that the departments of state were capable of responding to the challenge of increased government intervention in the years after 1900. He believed that the Treasury needed to be drastically remodelled in spirit, attitude and tone in relation to the work of other offices. His influence on contemporaries was expressed both directly through his work on the Board of Education, in the establishment of the National Insurance commissions, and indirectly through the Haldane Report.

Warren Fisher was in effect the first formally recognised 'head of the civil service'. His concern was to restore the prestige of the Treasury, while adapting it to post-1919 conditions. His overriding aim was to integrate the higher civil service and to build up an *esprit de corps*. He viewed the Treasury as a general staff in relation to other departments, encouraging the development of establishments work there, and he and his associates were responsible for emphasising the advantages of an all-round generalist background for people filling top administrative posts. Edward Bridges, who had worked under Warren Fisher and had served as secretary to the Tomlin Royal Commission, in many respects developed and continued the work of Fisher, albeit in the more trying circumstances of the post-1945 period. A man possessed of great ability and personal charm, who 'thought nothing more important than human relations', one of his major abilities was to persuade depart-ments and officials to co-operate when there was neither formal provision nor legal sanction for such co-operation.[58] He saw clearly that no government after the Second World War could discharge its responsibilities unless it had a coherent economic policy and the framing of such a policy required the willing co-operation of several departments and its execution constant consultation between them.[59] His achievement was to maintain the traditions of the civil service which he had inherited, while encouraging sufficient flexibility to meet the new demands of government.

Barlow was another man of tremendous energy who played an

important part in the committee of officials which paralleled the Anderson Committee on the Machinery of Government; he also played a significant role in a number of committees concerned with the position of specialists in the civil service. However, his most outstanding work was probably as chairman of the committee appointed in 1945 to consider the policy which should govern the use and development of our scientific manpower resources over the next ten years. This committee made recommendations which led to the significant increase in the university population after the Second World War.[60] Of Percival Waterfield it has been said that no detail of any business in which he was concerned was too unimportant for his attention, yet he could take the large view, as was shown by the changes he introduced into the method of selecting candidates in the post-Second World War period:

> Having become convinced that the existing examination placed too much emphasis on academic attainments to the exclusion of other highly important qualities, he studied all the latest ideas about methods of selection in other fields, and especially the procedure adopted by the War Office for the selection of officers during the Second World War, and on this basis he evolved his scheme ... no one without a creative imagination and a power of initiative ... could have produced it.[61]

All six men can be described as creative reformers, rather than mere administrators. But their creativity often lay less in initiating change or producing their own original ideas than in making use of good ideas from wherever they happened to come and positively guiding developments that were already in progress. With the possible exception of Trevelyan, they did not attempt to force abstract reforming principles upon an unwilling civil service. Instead they took advantage of situations in which they found themselves. Warren Fisher, for example, furthered his idea of Treasury control by making use of the pressures for economy, the Whitley machinery and the popularity of establishments work.

What common qualities did these men possess which enabled them to make such an impact? First, they all possessed a remarkable capacity for sheer hard work, and a dedicated application to what they regarded as their duty. Macaulay described his brother-in-law, Trevelyan, as a man having 'no small talk'. His mind was 'full of schemes of moral and political improvement, and his zeal boils over in his talk. His topics, even in courtship, are steam navigation, the education of the natives, the equalization of the sugar duties, the substitution of the Roman for the Arabic alphabet in Oriental languages.'[62] Morant, too, was an idealist 'relentless in the pursuit of that which he believed in', 'a furious and indefatigable worker'. [63] Fisher at the height of his powers 'had personal qualities which few could emulate – a blazing energy, a ruthless determination and a complete absence of fear'.[64] Bridges was an extremely competent and tireless worker, a man of exceptional force, ability and personal charm.[65] Barlow and Waterfield were also dedicated workers who showed tireless energy in the pursuit of their work. Secondly, all six were men of high academic ability, which enabled them to get quickly to the heart of a question. They were, above all, generalists in the tradition so much criticised in the 1960s. Trevelyan was educated at Haileybury; Fisher, Morant and Waterfield at Winchester and Oxford; Barlow at Marlborough and Oxford; and Bridges at Eton and Oxford. They all had a catholic range of interests and also regarded the practice of administration as quite clearly an art, although one which had to be practised within the context of good organisation. The predominantly generalist tradition of the service in which these men shared, which did not recognise administration as a distinct profession with its own relevant qualifications and formal training programme, undoubtedly made the British civil service more sensitive and sympathetic to reform than the more professionally-conscious bureaucracies of other countries. All six men were particularly adept at recognising the political implications of reforms and showed a fine sensitivity to the political environment. Bridges, in particular, was an astute tactician in matters of administrative reform, a good judge of timing and outstandingly sensitive to political pressures. Fisher also responded to problems or situations in an instinctive manner; he 'preferred the intuitive to the scientific method'.[66] Morant and Trevelyan perhaps showed less finesse, but possessed valuable contacts in the political and educational establishments of the day: contacts which they did not hesitate to exploit ruthlessly when the occasion demanded. All in their various ways mediated between the ideological concerns of politics and the demands of administration. Few can doubt that higher civil servants constitute a professional group even if they sometimes prefer to deny it themselves. They may serve ministers and citizens brilliantly, loyally, and in the best interests of the country, but it is a form of service which goes beyond the mere carrying-out of orders.

It is no accident that all six of these outstanding reformers spent a major part of their careers in the Treasury, the department often regarded as the elite within an elite, and an institutional base of major significance in administrative reform. Our studies reveal the crucial importance of the role of the Treasury in the implementation of reform proposals. And this illustrates the third major way in which officials have influenced the pattern of administrative reform in Britain: the modification or adaptation of reform proposals which have originated outside the administration. One example of such a modification is the way in which the proposals for a division of labour in the civil service during the last quarter of the nineteenth century were continually frustrated by the overriding concern of the then heads of the Treasury for economies. Despite the clear recommendation of the Playfair Report in favour of a universal scheme for separate classes throughout the civil service, by the time the Ridley Commission investigated the situation in the next decade the confusion of grades and classes had grown even more marked. Similarly, the Treasury was able to shelve the recommendations of the Playfair, Ridley and MacDonnell Commissions in favour of the establishment of some kind of a co-ordinating committee of heads of departments who would assist the Treasury in implementing reform proposals. On the other hand, the Treasury was able to exercise a powerful influence in tightening up the standards of recruitment after 1854 and in bringing about some measure of uniformity in this area. This was brought about by its support for the Civil Service Commission and its enforcement of a requirement of the Superannuation Act of 1859 that recruits to the civil service had to have a certificate of fitness from the Commission if they were to qualify for pension rights. New institutions, tender saplings in the overgrown world of Whitehall, tend quickly to wither away, unless – like the Civil Service Commission of the 1850s and the Whitley machinery of the 1920s – they are carefully nurtured by the Treasury, and, one might add, pruned into a shape deemed suitable by the gardener. After 1919 the Treasury, which had come under severe attack from many quarters, was able to mould the direction which the new consultative machinery for labour relations was to take. The Whitley councils, which at first were seen in many quarters as representing an important check on the Treasury's authority, were soon used as a means of extending the effective influence of the department. In the late 1940s and 1950s the Treasury was able to steer very many of the developments in the machinery of government in the direction which its leaders favoured. During this time the Treasury acquired a reputation for aloofness, and niggardly and negative economising, and in other departments it was often seen as an obstructive force. In the process it kept itself aloof from contemporary developments in public administration elsewhere — either in terms of its practice or its study, as illustrated by its cautious and conservative approach to the publication of the New Whitehall series. There is no doubt that the Treasury has always attracted or transferred to itself some of the most able people in the civil service; Trevelyan, for example, saw the Treasury as 'really a supervising office' drawn from the best men in other offices and really monitoring the subordinate financial departments 'as a master manufacturer watches his machinery'.[67] But the resulting high quality of its staff, often exercising controlling functions, has enabled it to develop an unfortunate style of intellectual arrogance. These features have been highlighted because the Treasury has played a particular role in relation to reform proposals, since many of the committees set up to consider aspects of administrative reform have been Treasury departmental bodies or Royal Commissions which it serviced. This gave it control over the flow of information and knowledge about reform proposals together with what amounted to a watching brief over the scope and manner of research, even research commissioned by apparently independent committees. Consequently, in terms of the internal or 'closed politics' of Whitehall it is not surprising that on a number of occasions parliamentarians and commentators have noted that investigations by parliamentary committees have been not only not resented by departments but are often strongly supported and encouraged by them.

It is interesting to notice in the areas we have studied the processes and techniques used by various individuals, as well as by the Treasury as a department, to implement and guide administrative reform whilst maintaining their influence and position. There was, for example, the continual circulation of papers which ensured that issues and proposals were not forgotten — as with the circulation of the Northcote/ Trevelyan Report among heads of department for months after its publication. Another was the creation of investigatory and review bodies (from Royal Commissions through departmental committees to *ad hoc* working parties), which had the effect of maintaining reform stimulus within the system, especially when suitable external stimuli were absent — as with the series of bodies on both machinery of government and training in the civil service in the 1940s. These became especially important when on a particular topic or on allied matters the bodies proliferated in number, for then the interlocking membership of the committees became the key factor in maintaining momentum in a particular direction. This was a means by which Bridges, Barlow and Brook were able to play a prominent part in the period of the Second World War and immediately after it. Such developments illustrate the power of knowledge and the importance of controlling the flow of information, a factor which in our opinion is rarely given adequate attention in discussions of the role of the bureaucracy in the British system of government. This overall knowledge and appreciation of the situation has been seen on a number of occasions in advancing reform proposals. According to Helsby, in 1962 when Helsby and Armstrong became joint Permanent Secretaries in the Treasury, Helsby felt that Treasury officials had already decided in principle to set up the AP training centre and the problem was not whether it should be set up but how. When important officials are aware of the views of other actors in a given process this knowledge may affect the procedures adopted and consequently result in the acceptance or rejection of particular proposals. For example, in the early 1960s when Tomkins wrote his minute to Cairncross he already knew Cairncross's views and could word it so that he could be fairly certain that his minute would be well received. Similarly in dealings with the Cabinet concerning Waterfield's proposals for reform of the selection procedures and the creation of CISSB, Wilson Smith noted on 8 December 1944:

> The Chancellor will no doubt wish to consider whether it would be right to mention the proposal at this stage to any of his colleagues. The only view I have on that is that Mr Bevin must know of it at some stage and I should have thought now was the time. He will object violently to the psychiatrist unless he has changed his views in recent months.[68]

When the various parties involved in a question are in disagreement, the power which results from such knowledge is even more marked. It enabled the Treasury, when faced with the unwelcome suggestions on classification being considered by the Crookshank Committee in 1943, to steal a march on the committee by putting its own proposals before a series of meetings with Staff-Side representatives and with permanent secretaries.

To control the implementation of reform is therefore in very large part to control the future direction and nature of reform itself. And it is inevitable that those not intimately involved in the implementation of policies should often have viewed the process with concern. Successive committees of inquiry into the civil service in the twentieth century — of which the English Committee is the most recent — have for example drawn attention to the way in which the various recommendations of their predecessors frequently appear to have been shelved or at any rate emasculated. The explanation of this is in part straightforward enough, committees and commissions are somewhat static, bound in time and place, and by their very nature unable to adapt to ever-changing political, financial and administrative circumstances. Moreover their suggestions are not always in every respect practical and not infrequently conflict with the overriding political objectives of government. However, there still remain doubts. Dark suspicions are nursed in the minds of MPs and other politicians, to say nothing of the public at large, that the bureaucracy has on occasions overstepped its proper role, and, if not always hungry for power, has at least weaved a web of secrecy which has insulated its proceedings from external gaze. In short, debates on administrative reform have invariably given rise to debates on the proper relationship between the civil service and society itself.

The Civil Service and Society

Public administration is not an activity which takes place in a vacuum. It exists in all structured societies and within all forms of government; it is part of the complex system of interrelationships between people and public institutions in the modern world. Its nature and processes are conditioned by the society within which it exists and which in turn it affects. The numerous officials who are involved in public administration are themselves citizens: they react to and are influenced by the social and political environment to which they also contribute. Our study of aspects of administrative reform in Britain between the years 1850 and 1970 has provided ample illustration of this two-way interaction.

Much has been written about the place of the civil servant in British government. Some people have maintained that civil servants exist simply to execute the decisions of government and that when they do more, they are exceeding their proper functions. Indeed, this has often been stressed by leading civil servants who seek to emphasise that they do not themselves make decisions except on behalf of the ministers to who they are accountable and in accordance with the provisions of statutes. Others say that in modern Britain civil servants have too much real power and that contemporary British government is essentially a struggle between the executive (basically the Cabinet) and the bureaucracy (the civil service).[69] Some commentators have gone further and suggested that the civil service has acquired so much power that civil servants have become 'master servants'.[70] Our study suggests a situation more complex and more flexible than is indicated by any of these positions. Much depends on the particular issue at stake and the particular circumstances of each area of decision-making. The interest and strength of feeling in society, the nature and clarity of instructions from Parliament and ministers, and the level of commitment and interest from political leaders will all affect the outcome. It is quite obvious that in some areas of administrative reform there is little public concern or interest and very little direction from busy ministers engaged on more controversial issues, and if action is to be taken at all, the initiative has to come from civil servants themselves: the creation under Warren Fisher of a unified civil service and the organic growth of the Whitley machinery are two examples. Criticism in these areas that civil servants' conduct has bordered on the misuse of power is clearly misplaced. It has become accepted that in the face of what often amounts in Britain to overwhelming public apathy and ignorance about the system of government and its institutions,[71] officials have a responsibility not to wait until a major scandal or tribunal of inquiry focuses public attention on a topic upon which some action is overdue. Civil servants have long since ceased to be mere clerks carrying out the meticulous and precise administrative instructions of their political masters. The Northcote/Trevelyan Report was in advance of its time when it said that the government of the country could not be carried on without the aid of 'an efficient body of permanent officers, occupying a position duly subordinate to that of Ministers ... yet possessing sufficient independence, character, ability and experience to be able to advise, assist, and, to some extent, influence those who are from time to time set over them'.[72] Gradually, however, British society has been moving towards accepting this situation: a commission which inquired into the handling of the Dardanelles campaign in the First World War stated unequivocally that independence of mind and free expression of views were duties of officials as important as those of obedience.[73] In the British context what has come to be seen as especially important is the political sensitivity with which these initiatives are carried out. What is important is often not so much what is done as how it is done. Our study points to an inverse relationship between the political sensitivity of an issue in administrative reform and the degree of initiative displayed by the civil servants concerned with it.

The period 1850 to 1970 contains a large number of incidents which led to important inquiries on aspects of civil service administration, though we have not discussed them all in this book. Although such inquiries have not been primarily concerned with administrative reform, they have affected the attitudes of civil servants and politicians, which in turn has influenced the ways in which the system of public administration has been concerned with its own reform. They have also provoked degrees of public dissatisfaction with the civil service beyond the normal and expected level of newspaper cartoons and music-hall jokes. The occasional 'shot across the bows', whatever form it takes, is not lost on civil servants whose socialisation – especially in the absence of more formal and extended professional training – has made them acutely sensitive. Four examples will illustrate ways in which this has affected the civil service and helped to condition attitudes of mind which in turn have influenced the ways in which decisions are made as well as, sometimes, actual decisions in particular cases.

The first example concerns the controversy which led to the Donoughmore Report on Ministers' Powers (1932). This had been preceded by the publication of a series of articles by Sir Carleton Allen, subsequently republished as *Bureaucracy Triumphant*,[74] his book *Law in the Making*,[75] and a particularly ferocious volume by none other than the Lord Chief Justice of England, Lord Hewart, entitled *The New Despotism*.[76] These writers attacked 'bureaucracy' not on account of its red tape or inherent inefficiency but in terms of an unjustifiable increase in the power of officials. They singled out in particular the growth of delegated legislation and of 'administrative law'. In Hewart's view a sea-change was occurring. Although the facade of representative democracy and the rule of law were maintained, the liberty of the subject was in peril:

> an organised and diligent minority, equipped with convenient drafts, and employing after a fashion part of the machinery of representative institutions, is steadily increasing the range and power of departmental authority and withdrawing its operations more and more from the jurisdiction of the Courts.[77]

The threat to Parliament was as great as in the days of the Stuarts.

> The old despotism, which was defeated, offered Parliament a challenge. The new despotism, which is not yet defeated, gives

Parliament an anaesthetic. The strategy is different, but the goal is the same. It is to subordinate Parliament, to evade the Courts, and to render the will, or the caprice, of the Executive unfettered and supreme.[78]

Lord Hewart's book caused a great stir, and largely as a result, a special committee, presided over by Lord Donoughmore, was set up to review the situation and to make an inquiry into the powers exercised as a result of delegated legislation and judicial or quasi-judicial decision. Members of the Committee began their work by reading Lord Hewart's book and then went on to examine law officers, civil servants and constitutional experts. The Committee soon concluded that there could be no hard and fast line between administrative and judicial decisions, although in their Report they made a number of recommendations for improved procedures.[79] The Committee was particularly impressed by the evidence of Sir Maurice Gwyer, Procurator-General and Treasury Solicitor. Antagonism between the law and the administrator did not exist. The new situation was simply the direct result of an increase in social legislation: 'the more you are dealing with the details of people's lives, the more elasticity you must have'.[80] Parliament on its own lacked the time, the expertise and the facilities to perform all the functions it could wish. The real challenge was to ensure that Parliament and the public were kept informed about delegated legislation and to secure protection against undue use of departmental powers. Ministerial responsibility, Gwyer pointed out, was the traditional method of securing these checks, and any fundamental change would require the adoption of a new theory of government. Debates of this sort are never lost as far as impact on the British civil service is concerned. Their progress, irrespective of outcome, conditions the ways in which civil servants go about their day-to-day work and in particular affects the power relationships between civil servants and society to the point where a position of equilibrium is disturbed; and then re-established.

The second example concerns the role of intermediaries. Allegations were made that large sums of money had been, or were being, received by ministers or public officials in connection with the issue of licences in the period immediately after the Second World War. At that time there was a great deal of governmental control and regulation which had resulted in 'the quick growth of a stifling bureaucracy' and left the nation, according to some Conservatives, as 'the helpless victim of humourless, self-righteous civil servants who had to be begged for licences and permits'.[81] The allegations were largely the result of the statements and activities of Mr Sydney Stanley, a man who, it was said, 'will make any statement, whether true or untrue, if he thinks that it is to his advantage so to do'.[82] When the allegations became public a tribunal was created in 1948 under the Tribunals of Inquiry (Evidence) Act 1921, with Mr Justice Lynskey as chairman. The Tribunal found that Mr John Belcher, Parliamentary Secretary to the Board of Trade, accepted gifts from Stanley and allowed the relationship so established to influence his judgement. Other less dramatic improprieties were also revealed, but all the allegations concerning civil servants were found to have no factual basis. According to one journalist the Tribunal was the record of a love affair, recording 'the love which rakish Big Business bears for homely, respectable Miss Bureaucracy and the delicate feminine backslidings of that lady (such a nice girl) when wooed by wicked rich financiers with their expense accounts and private dining-rooms'.[83] Subsequently the Prime Minister set up a committee, known as the Committee on Intermediaries, with Sir Edwin Herbert as chairman, to inquire into the activities of 'contact men', who used their extensive range of contacts to secure concessions from government departments for others, in return for a handsome fee and whose existence emerged from the Report and from the evidence given to the Tribunal. Intermediaries are common in many countries, are not necessarily involved in irregular activities, and have been known in British government for a considerable time – particularly in the form of trade associations, trade unions and similar bodies. The Committee came to the conclusion that while risks were attached to this practice it was a necessary practice in the complex system of government in modern Britain. However, it noted that the more open the existing recognised channels were, the less opportunity there was for other forms of intermediary work. It recommended that departments should constantly overhaul their control systems, facilitate access by applicants to departments and communicate with people outside the civil service in terms they understood.[84] As Stanley Wade Barron has recorded,[85] several prosecutions after the Tribunal proved that bribery and attempted bribery of minor civil servants were not entirely unknown, but it can justifiably be argued that the attention given to such occasional prosecutions is evidence of its rarity, and inquiries of this sort (together with other factors like the fairly frequent posting of officials in positions where the exertion of influence on them may be attempted) have helped to keep the British civil service as remarkably free of corruption as it is. Furthermore, lessons from such an inquiry

quickly permeate the whole administrative system, reducing the likeli-
hood of further irregularities and influencing all activities of individual
civil servants, even of the most ordinary and routine nature. The
recommendations of the Committee on Intermediaries were clearly
designed to minimise the risks of abuse of the administrative system
and to ensure that at a time of constantly expanding governmental
activity both efficient administration and good public relations were
maintained.

From time to time allegations are made of disloyalty on the part of
civil servants. Sometimes it is suggested or implied that such 'disloyalty'
stems from their political allegiance. Linked with this question is the
debate on the extent to which civil servants should play a full and
active part in public life. These matters were the background to our
third example, the Masterman Committee on the Political Activities
of Civil Servants. In the late 1940s there were a number of suggestions
that civil servants were undermining the policies of the new Labour
Government. In 1947 wide publicity was given to a speech by Major
Ashley Bramall, MP, which referred to sabotage among officials,[86] and
in 1948 controversy circled around a leading article in the *Daily
Express*[87] concerning remarks reported to have been made in Kansas
City by Sir Godfrey Ince, Permanent Secretary to the Ministry of
Labour and National Service. Questions were asked in the House of
Commons about both matters and they were subsequently investigated
by senior officials within the civil service, but it was agreed that there
was no evidence to justify a public inquiry, though the incidents were
drawn to the attention of the Committee on the Political Activities of
Civil Servants. The Masterman Committee, however, was set up by the
Chancellor of the Exchequer in early 1948 primarily in response to
representation made by the Staff Side of the National Whitley Council
on political activities of civil servants. The Government made clear to
the Committee at the outset, that it was 'totally opposed to any radical
change in the non-political status of the Civil Service'.[88] The
Committee noted the general exhortation of long standing that 'civil
servants are expected to maintain at all times a reserve in political
matters and not put themselves forward prominently on one side or the
other';[89] they also noted that

> The Administrative civil servant voluntarily enters a profession in
> which his service to the public will take a non-political form ...
> The deliberate choice of a profession in which he knows that his
> service to the public will take this form gives a bent to the mind.

It is very unlikely that a civil servant formed by years of training
and exercise of administrative functions would hold clear-cut party
views ...[90]

The Committee presented firm conclusions in favour of maintaining the
political neutrality of the civil service. It supported the view that 'The
public interest demands the maintenance of political impartiality in
the Civil Service and of confidence in that impartiality as an essential
part of the structure of Government in this country,'[91] but it made
recommendations to divide civil servants into categories who were
either free to take part in political activities or whose political activities
were to be restricted. The Staff Side of the National Whitley Council,
which believed there should be no restriction on the political activities
of civil servants, opposed the Government's decision to accept the
recommendations and suggested an intermediate class between the two
proposed by the Committee; the Government subsequently agreed.
These rules still apply and not only reflect the agreed expectations of
politicians in central government but also have been willingly accepted
by civil servants. They constitute an important framework within which
civil servants work and seem to conform with general attitudes in
British society about the role of civil servants.

The fourth example, the major inquiry affecting the role of civil
servants and society in the 1950s, concerns the case of Crichel Down.
The case has been fully described and analysed[92] and the full details
do not concern us here. It arose from a decision to sell land compul-
sorily purchased by the Air Ministry at the beginning of the Second
World War and subsequently passed to the Ministry of Agriculture and
Fisheries. For the purposes of our present study it was important
because it drew attention to the procedures within government administration and raised questions about the relationship of civil servants to
the public. A departmental inquiry by Sir Andrew Clark, QC,
investigated the matter and, following the publication of his report,
the minister resigned. The report was clearly critical of some attitudes
present in the civil service. Although it found no trace of bribery,
corruption or personal dishonesty, it found that the Lands Service and
the Land Commission had become 'infatuated with the idea of creating
a new model farm'; inaccuracies in an official report which 'arose
solely from the passionate love of secrecy inherent in ... many minor
officials'; 'lack of liaison between officials'; 'some letters ... not drafted
as clearly or as tactfully as they might have been'; 'muddle and
inefficiency' in the Lands Service; in Crown Lands 'a lack of adequate

control over the activities of Crown Receivers'; and an 'attitude of
hostility' to the previous owner of the farm from civil servants for
which 'there was no excuse whatever'.[93] Mr Melford Stevenson, QC,
one of the lawyers appearing at the inquiry, asserted that, while officials
concerned in the case had no corrupt motive, 'they derive great
satisfaction from the exercise of personal power' and declared 'There
is a time when the public administrator can become, if not drunk, unfit
to be in charge of his personal power'.[94] After the Report was
published Sir Edward Bridges, Head of the Civil Service, took the
unusual step of writing to all civil servants telling them to 'read and
take to heart' the comments made by the internal committee of
officials who considered the future of the civil servants implicated in
the case. 'The interests of the private citizen are affected to a great
extent by the actions of Civil Servants', the Committee had written.
'They should constantly bear in mind that the citizen has a right to
expect ... that his personal feelings, no less than his rights as an
individual, will be sympathetically and fairly considered.' Sir Edward
Bridges ended his circular: 'It will do no harm if each one of us goes
over the ground with himself, and makes sure there is nothing
amiss.'[95] As a committee presided over by Sir Warren Fisher said on
an earlier occasion, 'The public expects from Civil Servants a standard
of integrity and conduct not only inflexible but fastidious ...'[96] The
Crichel Down case not only led to a situation of considerable political
significance in the 1950s, but it was also of considerable administrative
significance; its lessons affected the day-to-day decisions of a large
number of civil servants and it again drew attention to such perennial
unresolved questions as those concerning openness in government,
the power and attitudes of mind of civil servants and the effects on
them of the social and political environments in which they work.
Furthermore, it helped to prepare people's minds, so that the
recommendations in the Whyatt Report[97] in 1961 (which effectively
started the debate which led to the creation of the 'ombudsman') were
less alien than they might otherwise have seemed.

We could continue with more examples but space does not permit;
the issues raised tend to recur. Such specific cases or reports have been
particularly important in stimulating and focusing public attention on
areas of concern. They have in some instances had a lasting effect on
the civil service and conditioned the attitudes of mind of civil servants
as well as reflecting society's expectations. The issues are not how to
ensure perfect efficiency but how much efficiency and of what kind;
not how to implement some ideal system of representative democracy,

but how much democracy and for what purpose; not whether civil servants should exercise power and influence but how much power and influence and in what circumstances and subject to what controls. What is acceptable at one time may not be acceptable at another, and what is acceptable in one place may not be acceptable in another. This may be seen in the changes in the pattern of examinations for the selection of civil servants; it is difficult to conceive a better method than patronage at a time when no national examination system existed, but changes in the civil service selection procedures, whilst following changes in the educational system, in turn also had important effects on society. Similarly, allegations of bias in selection can only arise when other facets of society are sufficiently developed and when people are prepared to draw attention to processes they think need examination, with the expectation that in due course society will be convinced, express its opinions, and apply its will. Consequently, it is important for civil servants to be sufficiently integrated into society for them to appreciate what is acceptable, and how to adapt their methods and approaches appropriately to the practice of public administration.

The extent to which this integration and representativeness occurs and/or is desirable, and the manner in which it takes place, has stimulated a considerable debate. This has generally been associated with the concept of 'representative bureaucracy'. This concept gained popularity through the discussions and writings of a few American political scientists and British sociologists (including professors R.K. Kelsall and T.B. Bottomore) after the Second World War and following the publication of Donald Kingsley's book[98] with the same title. Questions about 'representative bureaucracy' seem to have been inspired by Harold Laski, who certainly guided and influenced Kingsley. In the 1930s Laski was lecturing and writing about the increasingly democratic character of the modern state in Western civilisation, raising questions about it, encouraging re-examination of 'the basis of our institutional habits if we are to find the formulae of a new world', and warning that those who are denied access to privilege seek to destroy privilege.[99] There is now a large literature on the topic but according to V. Subramanium[100] the basic argument of those advocating 'representative bureaucracy' is that bureaucrats carry their class attitudes and prejudices into their official life, and only when all classes (or castes) are properly represented in the civil service will their different needs and interests find due consideration. This, of course, goes much further than our concerns in this book, though it is certainly in line with pressures for change in the recruitment of British civil servants and in particular with the views of some of the MPs considering the efficiency and effectiveness of the British civil service in the 1970s.[101] Not merely administrative reform but the entire practice of central government administration is permeated by the respective attitudes of civil servants and society. It is hardly surprising that in 1944 the Foreign Office thought civil service selectors should ask themselves whether a candidate was 'a thoroughly representative British subject in his general outlook, morals, and manners'.[102] Although it is unclear to what extent the Foreign Office was at that time aware of what had been written by non-practitioners about representative bureaucracy, one of the most significant features of British central government is in fact the way civil servants are so professionally sensitive to the social and political environment which conditions their power and influence.

It may be said that a society gets the civil service it deserves; it may also be said that civil servants get the society they deserve. Whilst officials may in the last resort be servants, it is not always easy to serve without instructions or in circumstances where instructions must be stimulated or repeatedly called for. Nevertheless, this is not unknown in the British civil service, and in recent years some major developments in the administrative system have taken place in an atmosphere of little public concern or interest. This can also be seen in the way the content and style of British central government changed substantially in the 60 years before the First World War without any striking shift in even political leaders' conceptions of the role of the state in society. At the same time, it should not be beyond the bounds of reason to expect civil servants, who are chosen for their ability and personal qualities, to educate society. When Robert Lowe, in a political context discussing the Reform Act of 1867, in effect declared that 'We must educate our masters', he made a statement that need not be narrowly restricted to the role of Members of Parliament in the nineteenth century. It was only after the public mind had been educated to accept the principle of competition that the change in 1870 to open competition could be introduced. However, the opportunities for educating the public mind in this manner are inextricably concerned also with openness in government, a problem which in Britain has proved thorny in its own right. What ought or ought not to be done by civil servants in an educational role poses an ethical problem yet to be satisfactorily resolved.

Sydney Webb used frequently to declare that in Britain it was easy to change the form of an institution without changing its substance, or the substance without changing its form, but that attempts to change both form and substance were asking for trouble. Administrative reform in Britain since 1850 vindicates the truth of this remark; the usual pattern has been for old institutions and devices to be adapted to serve new purposes, or for new machinery, when set up, to operate in accordance with existing practices or to be modified by existing attitudes. This is scarcely surprising in an administrative system which operates in a political environment where formal codes are less important than unwritten conventions and understandings. As Nevil Johnson has pointed out, such a system 'may have a remarkable capacity to absorb and transform reform proposals, adapting them subtly to its perception of what is tolerable'. Hence an over-rationalist approach to administrative reform which views the question in terms of problems to be solved by setting up the 'right' machinery or by applying the 'correct' procedures is likely to be doomed to disappointment.[103] The case studies and facets of public administration which we have considered in this volume illustrate this, and prompt several general reflections about the nature of administrative reform in Britain. The first point which emerges is the importance of organic growth in British central administration. This gives central government administration in Britain a distinctive quality, both because of the importance of conventions and modes of behaviour acquired by officials through socialisation rather than through training or professional qualifications, and because few other countries (if any) have had such a long period of constitutional and political stability necessary for the development of such characteristics. As a consequence of this growth the gestation, formulation and implementation of administrative reform must be viewed in a long time-span. Many of the contemporary debates on such issues as the machinery of government, the co-ordination of government policy, the power of the Treasury, accountability in government, and the recruitment and classification of civil servants have very long roots indeed, although contemporaries are not always aware of the extent to which the path was trodden by their predecessors.

A second feature which emerges is the extent to which administrative reform has been linked with broader intellectual and political developments, and the degree to which the implementation of proposals for reform has been modified by economic and social conditions. In other words it would be futile to consider administrative reforms in isolation from more general political considerations; they are inter-dependent and often mutually stimulating. It is, therefore, not surprising that prevailing political tendencies and intellectual assumptions have permeated both the thinking behind administrative reform and the practical application of reforming ideas. No satisfactory account of reform during our period would ignore such important tendencies as the movement against aristocratic privilege and in favour of meritocratic values before 1914, or the egalitarian movement of the post-1945 world. These are not merely the 'background' against which administrative reform has taken place; together they constitute phenomena which infuse and permeate the process of reform. Thirdly, it follows that administrative reform in Britain has shared many of the characteristics of more general political reform, a conclusion which is amply borne out by our case studies. The pattern of administrative reform – flexible, multifaceted and pragmatic – illustrates no less than the various political reforms of the period the workings of British democracy: or, to express this another way, the nature of British democracy is illuminated by the way in which reforms have been secured in the institutions and processes of central government administration. The dynamics of administrative reform are found to contain many elements, and the pattern for each particular episode is unique.

Pressures come from various political quarters, from within the bureaucracy, and from societal values and influences, and are often brought into focus by the impact of events. But to disentangle the various forces, as we have to some extent attempted in this chapter, while illuminating for analytical purposes, is nonetheless to risk distorting the complexity of the process. Above all no general 'model' is possible: both because the different forces and pressures interact with each other in a fluid manner, and because administrative reform is continuous. Administrative reform should not be seen as a series of episodes; it is a process in which the implementation and working out of reform proposals are integral parts. Even the more specific of the case studies we have examined – the establishment of the Whitley Councils and the creation of the Civil Service College – illustrate this, although the point emerges even more clearly from the study of the broader reforms such as the changes in the recruitment and classification of the civil service. Administrative reform needs to be viewed from a variety of perspectives rather than in terms of a fixed framework, the elements of tactics and timing give it dimensions additional to those more easily recognisable and measurable. If tensions between different perspectives and factors often appear unresolved, this is a reflection of the tensions which often appear in the practice of public administration: tensions which in the retrospective analysis of specific reforms are seen to ebb and flow, and from time to time give way to consensus.

Notes

1. Jean Holmes, 'The Victorian Inquiry' p. 107, in R.F.I. Smith and Patrick Weller (eds.), *Public Service Inquiries in Australia* (University of Queensland Press, St Lucia, Queensland, 1978).
2. See Bernard Schaffer and Geoffrey Hawker 'The Rise and Fall of RCAGA', and Geoffrey Hawker, 'Inside the Coombs Inquiry' in Smith and Weller, *Public Service Inquiries in Australia*. See also Brian C. Smith, 'Reform and Change in British Political Central Administration', *Political Studies*, vol. 19 (1971), pp. 213-26.
3. Gerald Caiden, *Administrative Reform* (Aldine, Chicago, 1969); Gerald Caiden, 'Administrative Reform: A Prospectus', *International Review of Administrative Sciences*, vol. 44 (1972), pp. 106-20.
4. Waterfield to Ritson, 21 January 1942, PRO/T162/748/E45491/02/01/1.
5. Fred W. Riggs, 'Administrative Reform as a Problem of Dynamic Balancing', *Philippine Journal of Public Administration*, vol. 14 (1970), pp. 101-35.
6. Sir Geoffrey Vickers, *The Art of Judgment, A Study of Policy Making* (Chapman and Hall, London, 1965).
7. H.J. Laski, *Parliamentary Government in England* (Allen and Unwin, London, 1938), p. 117.
8. David Corbett, 'Putting it Together and Keeping it Together', in Smith and Weller, *Public Service Inquiries in Australia*.
9. *The Times*, 15 November 1976.
10. 125 H.L. Deb., 5s., cols. 239-40 (25 November 1942).
11. David Corbett, 'Putting it Together and Keeping it Together', in Smith and Weller, *Public Service Inquiries in Australia*.
12. Sir William Armstrong, 'The tasks of the Conference', *PAC Bulletin* no. 6 (May 1969), p. 2.
13. C.H. Sisson, *The Spirit of British Administration* (2nd edn., Faber, London, 1966), p. 28.
14. PRO/T162/969/E451965.
15. Alan Beith, 'Summary of Discussions', *PAC Bulletin* no. 6 (May 1969), p. 119.
16. *The Times*, 15 November 1976.
17. Sharpe to Barlow, 19 August 1947, PRO/T222/45/OM:355/01.
18. Graham Wallas, *The Art of Thought* (Cape, London, 1926), pp. 173-6.
19. Quoted Anthony Sampson, *The Anatomy of Britain* (Hodder and Stoughton, London, 1962), p. 242.
20. Sisson, *Spirit of British Administration*, p. 23.
21. MacDonnell, Royal Commission on the Civil Service, *Majority Fourth Report*, p. 29, *P.P.*, 1914 [Cd.7339], XVI.
22. Jowett to Dean Dawes, 5 February 1854, Gladstone Papers, Add. MSS. 44333, fo. 142.
23. *Papers on the Re-organisation of the Civil Service*, p. 92, *P.P.*, 1854-5 (1870), XX.

24. *The Economist*, vol. 10, 5 April 1862, pp. 369-70; ibid., vol. 28, 11 June 1870, pp. 724-5.

25. *Eleventh Report from the Expenditure Committee, The Civil Service* (English Committee), vol. II (Part II), H.C. 535-II (HMSO, London, 1977), q. 1499.

26. Jock Bruce-Gardyne and Nigel Lawson, *The Power Game: An Examination of Decision-Making in Government* (Macmillan, London, 1976).

27. Sir Edward Bridges, *Portrait of a Profession* (CUP, London, 1950), p. 32.

28. Sisson, *Spirit of British Administration*, p. ix.

29. Lord Beveridge, *Power and Influence: An Autobiography* (Hodder and Stoughton, London, 1953), p. 70.

30. Quoted H. Heclo & A. Wildavsky, *The Private Government of Public Money* (Macmillan, London, 1974), p. 39.

31. *Eleventh Report from the Expenditure Committee, The Civil Service*, vol. II (Part II), H.C. 535-II (HMSO, London, 1977), q. 1818.

32. Statement to Commonwealth Heads of Government Conference, Jamaica, May 1975, in H. Wilson *Governance of Britain* (Sphere Books, London, 1977), p. 246.

33. Olive Anderson, 'The Janus Face of mid-Nineteenth Century English Radicalism. The Administrative Reform Association of 1855', *Victorian Studies*, vol. 8 (1965), pp. 231-42; Olive Anderson, 'The Administrative Reform Association, 1855-1857', in Patricia Hollis (ed.), *Pressure from Without in Early Victorian England* (Arnold, London, 1974), pp. 262-88.

34. 138 H.C. Deb., 3s., cols. 2040-2111 (15 June 1855).

35. H.C.G. Matthew, *The Liberal Imperialists* (OUP, London, 1973), p. 257. An editorial and an article calling for the setting up of a 'Committee of Vigilance' appeared in the *Nineteenth Century*, vol. 48 (1900).

36. Sir S. Demetriadi, *A Reform for the Civil Service* (Cassell, London, 1921); Sir S. Demetriadi, *Inside a Government Office* (Cassell, London, 1921); see Rosamund M. Thomas, *The British Philosophy of Administration* (Longmans, London, 1978), p. 217.

37. Trevelyan, q. 3, Appendix F, Playfair Commission, *P.P.*, 1875 [C.1226], XXIII.

38. 960 H.C. Deb., 5s., col. 1425 (15 January 1979).

39. Edward Heath and Anthony Barker, 'Heath on Whitehall Reform', *Parliamentary Affairs*, vol. 31 (1978), pp. 363-90.

40. Gladstone to Russell, 20 January 1854, Gladstone Papers, Add. MSS. 44291, fos. 93-103.

41. Trevelyan to Delane, 2 February 1854, Gladstone Papers, Add. MSS. 44333, fo. 138.

42. Gladstone to Sir James Graham, Gladstone Papers, Add. MSS. 44163, fos. 109-10.

43. *Eleventh Report from the Expenditure Committee, The Civil Service*, vol. II (Part II), HC. 535-II (HMSO, London, 1977), q. 1931.

44. PRO/T162/806/47687/06.

45. Sampson, *The Anatomy of Britain*, p. 222.

46. See Maurice Wright, *Treasury Control of the Civil Service, 1854-1874* (OUP, London, 1969), pp. 306-9.

47. Gladstone to Russell, 20 January 1854, Gladstone Papers, Add. MSS. 44291, fos. 94-5.

48. *Red Tape*, August 1919, p. 125.

49. PRO/T162/97/E11532; *Daily Telegraph*, 11 and 12 September 1923, 3 and 4 October 1923.

50. B.V. Humphreys, *Clerical Unions in the Civil Service* (Blackwell and Mott, Oxford, 1958), pp. 176-81.

51. *Government Observations on the Eleventh Report from the Expenditure Committee, Session 1976-77* [Cmnd. 7117], (HMSO, London, 1978), p. 7, para 18.

52. Reservation to Chapter I by Lord Simey, para. 3, 'The Civil Service', vol. I, *Report of the Committee*, 1966-68, *P.P.*, 1968 [Cmnd. 3638].

53. W.J. Brown, Tomlin, *Evidence*, qs. 5075-108.

54. J. Donald Kingsley, *Representative Bureaucracy: An Interpretation of the British Civil Service* (Antioch Press, Yellow Springs, Ohio, 1944), p. 115.

55. H. Martingdale, *Women Servants of the State 1870-1938. A History of Women in the Civil Service* (Allen and Unwin, London, 1938); P. Walters, 'Women in the Administrative Class of the Civil Service', in PEP, *Women in Top Jobs* (Allen and Unwin, London, 1971), pp. 223-41.

56. G.K. Fry, *The Growth of Government* (Cass, London, 1979), pp. 4-5.

57. R.W. Harris, *Not so Humdrum* (Bodley Head, London, 1939), p. 152.

58. *The Times*, 29 August 1969.

59. See Bridges, *Portrait of a Profession*.

60. *The Times*, 29 February 1968.

61. Ibid., 4 June 1965.

62. Macaulay to Mrs Cropper, 7 December 1834, G.O. Trevelyan, *The Life and letters of Lord Macaulay* (2 vols., Longmans, London, 1876), vol. 1, p. 385.

63. *The Times*, 15 March 1920.

64. H.P. Hamilton, 'Sir Warren Fisher and the Public Service', *Public Administration*, vol. 29 (1951), p. 38.

65. *The Times*, 29 August 1969.

66. Ibid., 27 September 1948.

67. Trevelyan to Gladstone, 9 February 1854, Gladstone Papers, Add. MSS. 44333, fo. 158; Memorandum by Trevelyan, 2 April 1850, *P.P.*, 1854-55, XX (1870).

68. PRO/T162/932/45491/07/011.

69. Brian Sedgemore, *Eleventh Report from the Expenditure Committee, Session 1976-77, The Civil Service, Volume 1 – Report*, HC 535-1 (HMSO, London, 1977), p. lxxxix.

70. E.g. Joe Haines, *The Politics of Power* (Cape, London, 1977); Marcia Williams, *Inside Number 10* (Wiedenfeld and Nicolson, London, 1972).

71. See the evidence presented to the Kilbrandon Commission, *Royal Commission on the Constitution 1969-73, Vol. 1, Report*, Cmnd. 5460 (HMSO, London, 1963).

72. *Report on the Organisation of the Permanent Civil Service*, p. 3, *P.P.*, 1854 [1713], XXVII.

73. *First Report of the Dardanelles Commission*, Cd. 8490, (HMSO, London, 1917), para. 91.

74. Carleton Kemp Allen, *Bureaucracy Triumphant* (OUP, London, 1931).

75. Carleton Kemp Allen, *Law in the Making* (OUP, London, 1927).

76. Lord Hewart of Bury, *The New Despotism* (Ernest Benn, London, 1929).

77. Ibid., p. 12.

78. Ibid., p. 17.

79. *Committee on Ministers' Powers, Report*, Cmd. 4060 (HMSO, London, 1932).

80. Sir Maurice Gwyer, *Committee on Ministers' Powers, Minutes of Evidence* (HMSO, London, 1932), q. 126.

81. Stanley Wade Barron, *The Contact Man: The Story of Sidney Stanley and the Lynskey Tribunal* (Secker and Warburg, London, 1966), p. 11. See also George W. Keeton, *Trial by Tribunal* (Museum Press, London, 1960).

82. *Report of the Tribunal appointed to inquire into Allegations reflecting on the Official Conduct of Ministers of the Crown and other Public Servants*, Cmd. 7616 (HMSO, London, 1949), para. 335.

83. Cyril Connolly, *Horizon*, January 1949, quoted in Barron, *Contact Man*, p. 234.

84. *Report of the Committee on Intermediaries*, Cmd. 7904 (HMSO, London, 1950).

85. Barron, *Contact Man*, p. 240.

86. *Daily Mail*, 15 October 1947; PRO/T162/969/E52014.

87. *Daily Express*, 7 June 1948.

88. *Report of the Committee on the Political Activities of Civil Servants*, Cmd. 7718 (HMSO, London, 1949), para. 2.

89. Ibid., para. 16.

90. Ibid., para. 39.

91. Ibid., para. 37.

92. R. Douglas Brown, *The Battle of Crichel Down* (Bodley Head, London, 1955); D.N. Chester, 'The Crichel Down Case', *Public Administration*, vol. 32 (1954), pp. 389-401.

93. *Public Inquiry ordered by the Minister of Agriculture into the Disposal of Land at Crichel Down*, Cmd. 9176 (HMSO, London, 1954), paras. 32, 27, 31.

94. Quoted by R. Douglas Brown, *The Battle of Crichel Down*, p. 102.

95. Ibid., p. 176.

96. PRO/T162/907/E9913/014.

97. Report by Justice, *The Citizen and the Administration* (Stevens, London, 1976).

98. Kingsley, *Representative Bureaucracy*.

99. H.J. Laski, *Democracy in Crisis* (Allen and Unwin, London, 1933), pp. 30 and 51.

100. V. Subramanium, 'Representative Bureaucracy: A Reassessment', *American Political Science Review*, vol. 61 (1967), pp. 1010-19.

101. *Eleventh Report from the Expenditure Committee, Session 1976-77, The Civil Service*.

102. Letter from David Scott, 5 December 1944, PRO/T162/932/45491/07/011.

103. Nevil Johnson, 'Administrative Reform in Britain', in Arne F. Leemans (ed.), *The Management of Change in Government* (Nijhoff, The Hague, 1976), pp. 294-6.

INDEX